are All those Kids Yours?

are All those Kids Yours?

Fostering, Adoption, Teenagers ... a memoir

jonquil graham

Copyediting by Renell Judais, Proof Perfect Ltd NZ
Illustrations by John Helle-Nielsen
Cover design by Suzanne North, The Copy Press

Published 2019
by Jonquil Graham

ISBN 978-0-473-49371-4 (Paperback)
ISBN 978-0-473-49396-7 (Epub)
ISBN 978-0-473-49397-4 (Kindle)

© Copyright 2019
All rights reserved.

Except for the purpose of fair reviewing, no part of this publication may be reproduced or transmitted in any form or by any means, electronic or mechanical, including photocopying, recording or any information storage and retrieval system, without prior written permission from the publisher.

Printed by The Copy Press, Nelson, New Zealand. www.copypress.co.nz

To four fabulous women who have been kind, supportive, wise and encouraging over the years: Joanna Rifaat (my English cousin in the UK), Sharon Doss (my special American pen pal), Pidge (Christine James, my Australian schoolfriend), Megan Simmonds (my New Zealand pen pal).

A few of the children, and Bryan in the background

Contents

	Prologue	ix
Chapter One	Bonding with Mother	1
Chapter Two	Newlyweds	11
Chapter Three	Creating a family	16
Chapter Four	A priceless gift	24
Chapter Five	When I was a teenager	33
Chapter Six	Food for thought	40
Chapter Seven	We have teens in the house	51
Chapter Eight	The babysitter	62
Chapter Nine	Puzzling behaviour	72
Chapter Ten	Family life	84
Chapter Eleven	The orchard	96

Chapter Twelve	Ground control	106
Chapter Thirteen	Shopping	117
Chapter Fourteen	Pets	128
Chapter Fifteen	Gifts	139
Chapter Sixteen	Other people's kids	151
Chapter Seventeen	Muddling along	161
Chapter Eighteen	Book launch	172
Chapter Nineteen	Renovations	182
Chapter Twenty	Occasions	192
Chapter Twenty-One	Holidays	203
Chapter Twenty-Two	Tragedy	213
Chapter Twenty-Three	Natasha	224
Chapter Twenty-Four	Losing Natasha	235
Chapter Twenty-Five	A hovering spirit	244
Chapter Twenty-Six	Return to Romania	254
	Epilogue	267

Prologue

The story of how we parented so many foster and adopted children is told in my first book *How Many Planes to Get Me? Nine children adopted into a NZ family* (2006). After its initial success, readers said, "You must do a follow up. What happened after that?"

The following chapters are a glimpse of how we coped with raising our growing teenage kids. The content is meant to amuse the reader, not serve as material for judging us. We did what we did because every child born should feel loved and wanted, and we took on some kids who were challenging.

I have trawled through my diaries, researching where a child may have strayed, the influences they experienced, the input they received from other people, how the child adapted and behaved, the things they said, and how we coped.

Reflecting on it all, we did our best with the resources we had. Hindsight is a wonderful thing, but times change. Society changes. New devices are invented, and your kid is embarking on a world that is different to the one you grew up in. The anecdotes I tell intentionally mix-up those about our foster children and our adopted children because we have an ongoing relationship with all of them. We treasure them, so this is not an exposé. And don't take some remarks too seriously either. Parents need a boost while raising teens, and if anything offends you, then it is probably just a tongue-in-cheek statement.

Imagine you and I are chatting over a cup of tea, perhaps a glass of wine, even a nice meal. I'd like to share some funny, sad, happy and enlightening times.

Would we do it all over again? Judge for yourself.

Chapter One
Bonding with Mother

I never yearned for a career, a bank account full of money or a fancy house, just a nice man – not too old, not too bald and not too bossy. My dream man would be compassionate, have a sense of humour, a refined voice, and not squander his pay shouting his mates at the pub. And he must like children, especially abandoned babies. And as far as their colour was concerned, I would be fine with black or brown babies as well.

"Don't know if such a man exists in Australia," said Mum, glancing at the clock. "And what do you mean about adopting other people's children? Where on earth did you get that idea?"

Across Australian households, six o'clock was the magic hour when 'decent' people, who'd stared longingly at the sherry decanter, could imbibe without guilt.

Dad said he needed a liquid reward after his godawful day at the office and having to give up his seat for a woman, laden with David Jones shopping bags, on the crowded double-decker Sydney bus. Mum said she had a thankless job too. Three teenagers – me ("but you're alright, darling"), one son booted out of the Navy, and another daughter who scowled because they wouldn't buy her a horse.

"Kids drive you to drink," said Mum. "You need something to look forward to at the end of the day. God knows parents deserve their medicine once they have teens in the house."

Cocktail hour was common in Australian households. Back in the '50s and '60s, housewives donned a frock, unleashed curlers from their heads, slapped on crimson lipstick, pinched their cheeks for colour, and greeted their husband with fake joy. Mothers warned, "Your father's here. Quick! Tell your friends to go home. He might be in a mood." For wives the biggest sin was to talk about your ghastly day with the ghastly teenagers before the breadwinner hung up his felt hat and ripped off his tie.

"Why did we have so many blasted kids?" was a common masculine sigh echoing around Sydney suburbia.

"Search me," wives replied, gingerly adding, "but I think you had a hand in it, didn't you?"

In the '50s and '60s, despite internal bickering, most households were stable. Divorce was frowned upon, and there was no Domestic Purposes Benefit (DPB) at the time. Grandparents often lived in the country, where children spent occasional school holidays, so they weren't always on tap to babysit.

The exceptions were the migrant families who holed up in semi-squalor above their greengrocer shops, with all members contributing to their livelihood. Grandmothers cared for copper-coloured toddlers with gold studs in their tiny ears and caterpillar nasal discharges, while the older siblings helped their parents in their fruit and vegetable stores or fish 'n' chip shops. Pungent whiffs of cooking oil oozed out of their forlorn dwellings, but the migrant families appeared happy and united. It was an enigma to those who lived more affluently further up the road. In those days, having the latest household appliance gave you status, and your street defined your social standing.

Our family lived on the main road, Pittwater Road, opposite the Collaroy Salvation Army premises. Mum said to be polite to the war vets who had been gassed in the First World War, but to keep our distance as some had mental issues. One old veteran called Willie spent his days sitting on the bus-stop seat writing down bus numbers as the double-decker buses lumbered past.

Wealthier families lived on the hill and sent their kids to private schools. Mum said our family had standards and that we were as good as they were, probably better, as Dad could trace his genes back to William the Conqueror – almost. Could they? She said money didn't make you a better person. Some might have won a fortune in the lottery, but their voices and accents let them down. You could sniff them out a mile away. If they said 'haitch' for an H, they were Catholic. Nothing wrong with that, according to Mum. but you can't go past being a good Anglican for the local minister had a large flock, and besides, you never know when you'd need him for a decent burial. The church minister's daughter might be a widgie as well, but she was only a teen. Mum said she had hormones and her dad was the pillar of society.

My British-born father was employed as a cost accountant with the Vestey firm that had meat and shipping works around the world. During a stint in Argentina, where he learnt to speak Spanish, World War Two broke out, and he was ordered back to London. On the ship he met my mother from the other end of the world – New Zealand. Engaged to a dashing naval officer, she was travelling to England to meet his parents. But she changed her mind and married Dad instead.

"It was wartime, darling," she explained. "People did mad things then."

They were opposites in many ways. She was a social butterfly, whereas he was short, steady and reliable. Mum was initially thrilled when Dad was posted to sunny Australia after World War Two. His contract was renewable every five years, meaning free sea voyages between Australia and England on cargo or passenger ships for him and his family. She didn't expect to spend the next twenty years living "in exile" with a ratty husband and three children in quick succession. She wept every time Dad renewed his contract at the London office. After the firm offered classier ships with interesting ports of call to lure them back to Sydney, Mum sighed and looked forward to the next voyage.

After a long day at the office, my father looked forward to peace and quiet at home. "Otherwise," he said, "a chap can't think and could end up in the loony bin."

Nightly, he was greeted by meaty odours and vegetables bubbling prematurely in the kitchenette, a Mantovani LP on the new walnut veneer radiogram, and a wife waving a fly swot. Sticky fly-ridden papers dangled from the ceiling like art nouveau. When a blowfly flew mindlessly into it, its demise aided by squirting a dab of Mortein Plus from a pump-action spray can, Mum gave a smile of satisfaction. She was against procreation.

"And did our daughter say anything amusing today?" Dad would ask, once out of his city suit and planted in *his* chair, puffing on his pipe, forming oval grey rings in the air. Followed by, "Pour us a drink, Dot." Dad often asked about what I had said as I was prone to malapropisms.

Mum said she couldn't think of any today "because your daughter has things on her mind, like the opposite sex." And added, "She might need some parental advice."

Dad rattled the sports page of *The Sydney Morning Herald*, and said, "Hmm."

If girls weren't married by the time they were twenty-one, there were options like boarding a P&O liner and landing on your rellies in the Mother Country (England), and then going feral on the Continent. It was called having an OE (overseas experience), and once you got that out of your system, your future husband had most likely already served a few years learning his trade or completing his stint in the army, and was, therefore, more receptive to walking down the aisle.

Some guys did the hippy trail across Asia, while others sought comfort with fellow Aussies in Earl's Court and got jobs at London pubs. When they became disenchanted and missed their home comforts, they booked a cheap passage back to Australia or New Zealand on a Greek or Italian liner and holed up at the bar knocking back the duty-free drinks. Once back in 'Godzone', it was time to find a compatible *sheila* (girl) who was easy on the eyes and think about settling down. Jobs were plentiful in the '60s and buying a house was within grasp for most couples.

When a teenage girl at my workplace flashed her tiny diamond ring (and a couple of neck hickeys), the click-clacking of typewriters ceased. We office girls wanted the low-down. Apparently, she became engaged to a policeman over the weekend.

Not much older than her, I thought. *Crikey dick* (Australian expression), *how'd she land him? I'm more attractive than her. She's mousy, has sinus problems and smothers her facial eruptions with heavy pancake makeup.* I stopped being envious when I thought about her nuptials. Would she get arrested in bed if they had a 'domestic'? No! I'd never wed a cop.

Marrying a fitter and turner was also out because it sounded rude. Nor a printer because they were prone to dermatitis with all that ink, and who wants rough hands wandering over your nubile body? Definitely not a night-cart man either, even if he doused himself in Lifebuoy soap after hauling toilet cans for a living. Too embarrassing. Wedding an electrician had its drawbacks as well. He could electrocute himself prematurely and leave me, a young widow, raising grizzly brats on a widow's benefit. And what man would look at you then? Lawyers were out of my league because we didn't live in the right suburb. Besides, given their smartness, they could mess with your brains or fiddle the accounts, so you were probably better off with an honest dunny man. Doctors were unobtainable unless your parents were affluent, for the rich are attracted to their own kind. Then too, that intimate profession included poking ladies' privates, which could potentially leave him dissatisfied with his sleep-deprived wife who was suckling a newborn and not giving him nookies. In a worst-case scenario, a perky nurse (the little slapper!) was also a nocturnal threat during evening shifts.

Creative, drug-inspired musicians were a 'no', as were butchers with bulging biceps who could become axe-happy. Plumbers might reek of raw sewage, and bakers were spotty and poorly paid. That left accountants (like my dad) – boring – and teachers (but only if they didn't lecture you).

And not anyone called Smith or Jones (too common), or who had a name with a 'cock' in it unless it was double-barrelled, and the 'cock' was pronounced with a French accent. "My husband is an architect," had a nice ring to it but that likelihood was as dim as my hedonistic brother giving up surfing. Such families lived in Snobsville, suburbs away from us.

We took Sunday drives around those rose-draped areas, peering at sunken gardens, swimming pools and fancy houses perched on hills. Mum liked to dream, but Dad's erratic driving put everyone on edge. He'd swear in Spanish at other drivers who were in view.

"Nearly cut that sewer's water off," he'd bark if a driver came too close. After such outings, Mum said she needed her poison (sherry) at night because her nerves were in tatters.

"Is your daughter being fussy?" wondered Dad when it came to my future. "You can't expect perfection. Tell her: you live, you eat, you die."

"Tell her yourself. She's your daughter too. And don't give her a complex. She's sensitive."

"Yes, Dad," I said. "Don't hurt my feelings. I could die of a coronary conclusion."

"She's done it again," guffawed Dad. "Another malaprop. She's good for a laugh."

By the time I was twenty, I fretted I was going to be an old maid despite several marriage offers. "What about that chap who came to dinner the other night? He's a man's man. Could talk about cricket. Seemed a good bloke for an Australian. Can't do much better than that."

I rolled my eyes.

"He did seem besotted with you, darling," Mum added. "Do you think you could make sweet music with him?"

"Jeepers, Ma! Are you trying to get rid of me? Am I restricting your – you know – love life?"

"Don't be silly," blushed Mum. "Well past that. Oh, look at your father. He's trying to tell us something."

"Woman!" My father clapped his hands jovially. An empty crystal glass balanced precariously on his bald pate. "Give us a top up, ole girl. Splendid wife. Salt of the earth."

Mum tottered over, giggling girlishly, replenishing the glass.

"Don't do that when I bring someone home," I hissed. "I don't want them thinking I come from a madhouse."

"You'll find someone just right for you," soothed Mum. "Your turn will come."

"How do you know?"

"Your hair," Mum said. "It's your best asset." She, too, once had my blonde hair, but now it was a dun colour with aggressive grey roots and prone to dandruff. Mum was a beauty in her time – alluring and demure with a pageboy hairstyle. She came from a large happy family in Nelson, New Zealand, where her doctor father was loved and respected. Good pedigree, crème de la crème. Made the society pages in the *Nelson Mail*.

"The trouble with women," my father offered, peering at the cricket results, "is they don't know what men want."

I knew what men wanted, but they weren't going to penetrate my temple. Nice girls were *saving* themselves for Mr Right. Other girls had more fun until they were dumped, and their boyfriends sought greener pastures. What did Dad mean?

"Women can't go wrong if they wear a smart black dress and keep their mouths shut. Their voices let them down. Who wants to hear a woman go blah blah blah! No mystery in that."

"Shut your trap, Fairley," snapped Mum. He roared with laughter. He loved it when his feisty wife became slightly vulgar. It put him in a good mood. "Don't take any notice. He's the last person who should be giving advice."

"Gee, your husband's old-fashioned," I snarled. This was the '60s, for heaven's sake: miniskirts, rock 'n' roll, Women's Lib, Ban the Bomb, anti-Vietnam War marches. "Why did you marry him, Ma? He's such a fuddy-duddy."

"God knows. Oh, he wants a final top-up before I start serving dins," she said lightly, noticing the empty glass balancing rockily on Dad's head once more. "He doesn't understand women. Lost his father at the age of two; got spoilt by his sisters."

"Not taking your advice, Dad. Not going to be a slave to any man. You don't dig our generation."

Dad grunted and hoped dinner was steak and kidney pie, his favourite, and an apple tart for pudding. Very English. Mum said she was serving the tongue, which he'd bought back from that trip to Queensland working for Lord Vestey's firm, for dinner. If he wanted fancy meals, he'd better give her more allowance.

Cocktail hours were lively with Mum. Her brain was fertile at booze hour. Sometimes she wept over my brother's lamentable behaviour. He'd dashed her hopes of following in his uncles' footsteps, with their brilliant naval careers. He'd become a charismatic beach bum addicted to surfing, working in surfboard factories, garages, even a morgue, making shady deals and littering the back lawn with his latest acquisitions – old ambulances, a bread van, wrecked cars, and his mates. Mum didn't know how to make him *normal*. He said, "Ma, life is to be lived. Those beautiful waves. I could die tomorrow and not have enjoyed myself."

Dad cried, "Jesus wept. The boy needs to be shoved into the army and get a haircut – short back and sides. That would straighten him out."

Mum thought the answer was us moving to another country. "How about England? Then the children could have trips to the continent and get a bit of culture."

Ship travel was culturally enriching. Passengers boarding the gangplank in ports at Sri Lanka, India and Aden gossiped about their bargains and the deals they made with taxi drivers. But it was the begging urchins, the maimed, and the bedraggled homeless families washing under fire hydrants that haunted me. When a skinny woman in a sari thrust a baby at us, Mum said she'd had her fair share of raising kids and that I should not to be miserable about other people's plights. "You can't save the world," she would say.

I liked it when Mum talked about my future.

"Mum, I think my destiny is to marry a bald curate and look after black babies in Africa. It makes me rather sad, though – not the babies – but the preaching. I don't think I have it in me."

Mum looked stricken. She could be flighty, even outrageous, but she was supportive and kind. Many families went to church, not because of their convictions, but because it was the right thing to do, especially so in sending offspring to Sunday school. It was an excuse for parents to do the mattress-mambo without interruption unless, of course, your neighbour banged on the door to borrow a cup of sugar. All over the neighbourhood, re-energised dads cheerfully pulled the cords on their Victa lawnmowers while their apron-clad spouses planted fatty Sunday roasts in the ovens, awaiting the arrival of their infants clutching pictures of Baby Jesus to colour in and scripture verses to learn.

Mum's advice was to bide my time.

"Go travel the world because once you're saddled with kids, you're never free; your life changes." And, when it came to looking for a life partner, she warned, "Don't marry a man you could live with. Marry a man you can't live without."

"What if I can't find anyone suitable in Australia?"

"Don't worry, darling. When your father and I retire to New Zealand, we'll have lots of cocktail parties. I have oodles of friends with eligible sons."

After bussing across Asia and hitchhiking around Europe, I ended up in New Zealand. I didn't fancy my mother's friends' sons. I found the perfect man all by myself.

Chapter Two

Newlyweds

I met my future husband at the front door of the home we now own. It's a two-storey historic house in Golden Bay in Upper Takaka, north-west of Nelson on the South Island. It was once a boarding house. Set on ten acres of farmland, it was built around 1890, possibly earlier, by a goldminer called Samuel Carson who raised a large family. It has a steep staircase, five bedrooms and the remnants of a ghost. The house has witnessed births and deaths and the thundering feet of children throughout the century. It has a vast back garden with a magnificent walnut tree – perfect for climbing – and out front is a magnolia tree with a heritage plaque on it.

"I've always loved that house," said my mother, all those fateful years ago as we passed over the Takaka Hill from their upmarket home in Nelson. My now retired parents were on their way to spend a weekend hacking gorse on a large block of land they bought by the sea at Onekaka, where they intended building their dream home. "I'd love to get some cuttings there. Wonder if the owners would mind? You go in, darling. Be brave."

I gingerly knocked on the door of the tired-looking dwelling with its wobbly verandah. A tall, smiling man appeared.

"Where are my rose cuttings?" Mum asked after I hopped back

in the car. I said, oops, I'd forgotten, but that I'd just met the man I wanted to marry.

Cocktail hour in my parent's clifftop home overlooking Nelson harbour was the highlight of the day. Mum was happy to be back in New Zealand, catching up with her siblings and well-to-do old schoolfriends. Guests never minded if the vol-au-vents were slightly burnt or if Dad rattled the Austrian cowbell signalling it was time to leave. "Haven't you bastards got a home to go to?" he hinted. Mum's friends thought he was quaint for an Englishman.

They chuckled when they heard about his gaffe at a posh wedding. Introduced to a be-sequinned and dolled-up widow in her seventies, he enquired about her surname. "Hoare," she replied.

Nearby guests froze with embarrassment when he leaned across the table and whispered loudly, "Is that spelt with a W or an H, madam?"

"No, he hasn't proposed yet," I'd sigh at cocktail hour, referring to the man who'd snagged my heart when he'd opened the door of the old historic house in Golden Bay.

"What's his name again?" teased Dad, puffing on his pipe.

"Bryan, with a Y."

Mum and I weren't too keen on the name but agreed the Y made it classier. My chirpy godmother, Aunt Enga, a writer and artist, often trotted up the hill for meals. She diplomatically said the name had a certain *je ne sais quoi*. We didn't know what it meant, and after a couple of drinks, she didn't either. We had merry evenings talking about my dilemma while Dad occasionally clapped his hands to remind Mum and her sister there was an empty sherry glass balancing on his pate, balder than ever.

Bryan lived ninety minutes away and, since he didn't have transport, I had to visit him, sometimes at my peril. The narrow, winding Takaka Hill road was treacherous in winter when enormous trucks with blinding lights bore down on my 250 cc Daihatsu in thick fog, taking up most of the road. Driving rain and heavy dumps of snow also led to road closures. "It's not worth going in this weather," warned Mum. "No man is worth risking your life for." I envisaged a rival comely wench randomly knocking on his door, like me, and dabbling with his heartstrings. I *had* to go.

Now that Bryan was back from his stint in Antarctica as a geologist, and had already done the big OE, what was the hold up? Mum said the way to a man's heart is through his stomach and suggested taking him a tender piece of sirloin and a bottle of red. Another well-meaning myopic aunt/godmother, a glass of gin in one hand and a couple of inches of cigarette ash dangling from the other, pored over Mum's best porcelain cup where, apparently, my future could be read in the tea leaves. I could see why Mum was happy to be back with family.

It was a worry, though, when Mum became imaginative.

"He might have a terrible illness he doesn't want to tell you about, darling," she pondered. "Or a wife hidden in another country. It is odd, though, isn't it! He looks normal. We'll have another cocktail party next week. I know a few lawyers and doctors with nice sons."

When some cheeky guy asked Dad, "Has he slipped a length into her yet?" (Dad forgave him because he was English and Poms are eccentric) and my father taunted me, "You'll never catch that fish," I became emboldened.

Fed up with uncertainty and listening to the Carpenters bleat their hit 'Solitaire', I made a deal with God. "You know I'm a nice person. I've never been nasty to my parents and I am quite kind. Let me have this man and if I don't have kids, it doesn't matter." Turns out it did matter, but I was ready to bargain.

The following weekend I proposed, and Bryan-with-a-Y said, "Yes."

"By Jove," said Dad, puffing on his pipe. "When our daughter wants something, she is single-minded and won't be swayed. Slow at first but she starts streaking ahead."

"I'm not a ruddy racehorse, Dad."

"Yes," sided Mother. "She's nearly a married woman. Let's get the wedding underway before he changes his mind."

It was a perfect wedding. Mum was in her element and invited all her friends who gave us pottery, fondue sets, clocks, tablecloths and coloured sheets. One of her friends, recovering from electroshock therapy, offered us her double bed. She was living with a pig farmer and it was surplus to requirements. "Had a wonderful time in that bed," she said wistfully. "My twins were conceived in it." It sounded like a good omen.

Thrilled about my new status, Mum gushed, "This is my daughter – she's married," to acquaintances, and I proudly flashed my little gold band even though I did have to buy it myself. She thought Bryan was good 'husband material' and stopped warning me, "For God's sake don't have kids, they'll ruin your life."

Our house at Upper Takaka

Back then, in the late '70s, we were living a conventional life in a hippy setting. City friends found our lifestyle fascinating. How could we be happy in a rundown house with a bad-tempered goat, sheep that got the staggers, and visitors with hairy armpits who were popping out bronzed mammary glands to suckle chubby toddlers old enough to be learning the alphabet? It was a far cry from being a city girl working for a law firm.

Our garden was overrun with oxalis. There was an outside dunny, and the water pipes froze in winter even when we lagged them with rags, sometimes using old ladies' jumpers. On the plus side, the coal range warmed the kitchen when it wasn't belching out smoke, and it was useful for cooking if there was a power cut. The oven part never worked, but it was a warm place to pop in orphaned lambs or hide Christmas presents. Fermented hops bubbled happily in plastic drums, and newly cut flowers added a touch of class to the fifty-cent dining table, which was once a ping-pong table. Well, half of it anyway. Perhaps we weren't conventional!

To complete our happiness, we hoped for the patter of tiny feet.

Chapter Three

Creating a family

Our family began unexpectedly. Most people get a toaster, linen or cutlery as a wedding gift. We were given a three-year-old child on our honeymoon. Krissie was my Australian niece, my brother's daughter, who had been flown 'across the ditch' while her parents were embroiled in a custody battle. My mother was caring for her, but it was causing friction in my parents' home. "Your father can't think beautiful thoughts and rewrite his will in peace," she confessed. "He's allergic to children."

We readily agreed to have her, expecting it would be a short-term arrangement. She was a middle child and, judging by her behaviour, had missed out on vital bonding. Tiny, blonde and extremely active, there was something not quite right about this vulnerable little girl who needed firm, loving boundaries. She had screaming tantrums, was a bed-wetter, and ran around the house until she was exhausted. We were mystified. I could calm Krissie down by wrapping her in a velvety blanket, rocking her on my knee, mindlessly humming, and engaging her in a fairy-tale book. When I took her to play group, the teachers looked at me as if I was the cause of her odd behaviour. She would climb into a play bassinette and suck her thumb. I was inexperienced; I didn't know why she did that. I couldn't give them an explanation for her behaviour except to say we had taken her on and were doing our best as new parents.

I quit work to mother this little girl.

While she was a handful, we talked about adoption and fostering, unaware at the time that we weren't able to have our own children. Bryan's sister and her husband had adopted a little boy, and they were perfectly happy with him. I loved Bryan even more when he agreed another child in the family would be fun, and that it might settle Krissie. Like me, he wasn't overly fussed about the importance of having a biological child. We'd both seen enough of the world on our separate travels and the miserable conditions some kids had to endure. We were happy to parent any child who needed a family.

Some evenings were blissful when Krissie was a tot.

When strains of 'Scottish Fantasia' or 'Theme from Elvira Madigan', playing on the stereo, wafted from the dark, shabby lounge and flooded across the tatty linoleum hallway, the three of us sat on the sun-trapped back porch on sawn-off logs and soaked in the evening ambience. "Look at the swallows," said Bryan, rolling a ciggie and clamping it to his teeth while making notes in his diary, which recorded the weather, how many lambs had been docked, what he'd plant, the state of the compost, and other things of interest to men. Krissie rested her little blonde head against my arm as we laughed at cunning wekas (wood hens) scuttling towards the garden against a backdrop of towering blue hills partly obscured by poplar trees.

"Reckon those rhodos need a tidy up," Bryan would say, peering critically at the bush, and write it down on his 'to do' list, or "Check the block over the creek and get those trees milled for posts." He initially planned to grow grapes, but we ended up growing kiwifruit instead.

Krissie, our first child, laid the foundation for what we might encounter once we began fostering and adopting. The foster children who came along were slightly easier to manage, but we still had some bumpy rides. They all came from broken homes and it reflected in their behaviour.

During the ten years we had Krissie, her dad visited yearly from Australia, bringing his other children along. We had her younger sister stay with us for a year, while my parents had the older two, putting them into boarding school at Nelson College. These two wanted to stay with us as well, but my brother took them home. He thought Krissie was better off living with us. At the time, it wasn't possible for her to be with her mother.

The problem was that when my brother visited Krissie, he lavished attention on her and spoilt her with treats, which was understandable. But he was a 'good-time' father, enjoying the fun but not keen on the responsibility. When Krissie was thirteen, she wanted to be with her birth family. It was the usual teenage stuff – "You're not my real parents. I don't have to do what you say." In the end he agreed to take her, but when he broke his neck in a diving accident, she and her siblings stayed with friends and, sometimes, their mother. Still, it was a happy outcome. Krissie kept in touch with us, calling us Mama and Papa Bear, and grew close to her sisters.

Krissie has her own family now. She is calm and serene, quite unlike the little girl we nurtured. We see her and her siblings as often as we can. It was Krissie who gave us hope, allowing us to believe that fostered children can absorb the worth of a loving family and a structured life. It can be healing. And for that we are grateful to have had the experience of raising Krissie.

We fostered mainly sibling groups because they were offered to us. After all, we had a large old house in the country and plenty of space, with trees and paddocks and a creek. Most of our foster children were aged between three and fifteen.

When fostering, there is a honeymoon period. We were keen to provide a pleasant home for the child. The children you already have are excited about the new arrival and everyone is in a party mood. The euphoria only lasts a few days. Some children become obnoxious and test you, playing out their frustration and grief at being removed from their dysfunctional family. The children in our family never resented another foster child. The new kid was a source of fascination to them.

Depending on the age of the new child who had arrived, our own children were co-operative in sorting out toys and making up a bed. I didn't tell them the reasons for a child staying with us temporarily. My job was to make the child feel safe and wanted. We didn't quiz the new arrival either. Social Welfare provided some background information to help us understand the child's needs. One child, for instance, wished to change his name, so we went along with that until he decided his own name was okay again. This alarmed Social Welfare, but not his teacher, and today he is a well-adjusted, successful young man who calls in periodically and has invited us to two of his weddings. He is like another son to us.

It is heartbreaking when estranged parents promise to visit and then don't turn up. The child stands excitedly at the front gate peering at the traffic, only to be let down again. We'd make up lame excuses for the parents' shabby behaviour, and reward the child with a treat or some distraction – whether it's popcorn and staying up a bit later, toasting marshmallows over a bonfire, playing spotlight (and using up our batteries), or putting on an impromptu concert for the whole family. I can't remember a foster child going to bed sobbing, since we found the best way to get a bruised and tired child to sleep was through music. Bryan rigged up a music system upstairs, and every night a child selected a classical CD to play, so beautiful music wafted into their bedrooms. They never had problems sleeping while getting their fill of Bach, Brahms, Mozart and Chopin.

Once we had a family of four siblings, all of whom refused to go to bed at the normal time. It affected the other children. I suggested they do races running up the back lawn while Bryan held a stopwatch and timed them. They loved it and soon were all tired and glad to go to bed, filled with thoughts of being successful athletes. It was our way of changing irritable, negative behaviour into a positive without causing friction. You need to be inventive. I knew taking on other people's kids wasn't going to be easy, so I'd be adaptable, but not a pushover.

Teenagers were much harder to foster. When we learned their interests, we'd engage them in activities they liked. Our circle of friends widened. If they had attended a particular church previously, then we'd go too. It was to provide them some continuity with their past life.

One of our foster teen-daughters was so nasty and offensive, I was on the verge of giving up. Bryan reminded me that, for now, it was in her best interest to be with us, so could I change my attitude towards her?

How?

"Darls," he said, "treat each new day like a book. Turn the page over and start afresh. Don't dwell on past negative behaviour. The kid has moved on and you can too." I found this particularly helpful advice. Also, I was grateful he was supportive and that he felt the child's needs were vital in this case, compared to me being upset by a temporary blow-up.

When we were offered a Fijian toddler as an adoption, a boy whom another couple also wanted to adopt, Bryan said our first commitment should be to the children already in our care. He said our foster children were our priority until their family situations improved. I was a bit upset, but later we were offered a Rarotongan baby to adopt.

To foster or adopt you have to be on the same page as a couple. For instance, a seven-year-old came into our care when his adoption fell through. Of the two adoptive parents, the lad preferred the new father-to-be who did boy-things with him and gave him space, while the protective mother-to-be wanted to nurture him. The boy didn't want to be close to anyone, and he felt smothered. The conflict caused marital disharmony for the couple involved in the adoption. When we saw a notice in the paper advertising for prospective foster parents, we rang up Social Welfare. The boy sounded lost. "We'll have him," I said gaily. "He should fit in with our kids." And he did.

Foster children always have feelings of loyalty towards their birth parents, however damaging their past. We knew that. People would remark, "How can you do it? Don't you get too attached to the child and not want to give him back? I could never do what you do."

Sometimes it felt like a blessed relief (a term usually applied to those burying their loved ones) when a child returned to their birth parents, but mostly we felt a sense of temporary loss, one less kid at the table. Interference from the birth family, for example, and their quizzing of the child during brief home visits about how much they were getting from the foster parents, got one of the children in our care all worked up. "You-sa mean. You-sa spose to give us what we want. Youse get paid for it," the child said.

I gritted my teeth. I could see the other kids' little eyes goggle in surprise. I said, "That's because you're special – but not that special. Everyone is special in our family." When they looked confused, Bryan explained the way things worked here. By then he'd been a teacher and was good at boring sermons. "If you want something in life, you earn it. My job and Mumma's job," he said, putting an arm around my shoulder, "is to prepare you for the real world."

"Yes," I agreed. "I wanted Daddy so much I worked hard at getting him. I was nice and pleasant and …"

The oldest kid interrupted, "Mum, there are younger kids in this family. Think about it. This better not be a sex talk. We know everything."

"Do you?" I was amused, confused and interested.

All the kids nodded.

"Crikey dick," I gasped, reverting to my childhood Aussie expression. When I was a teenager, I never uttered words like *sex*. I'd attended an expensive private school, and it made the old spinster biology teacher blush simply touching on the subject of procreation. We pupils froze in embarrassment, more for her sake than ours, when she gave a two sentence facts-of-life talk ending with "You are the mothers of the future generation. Act with decorum." Mum was annoyed at the expense of the dreary, compulsory biology textbook which she couldn't understand either. It seemed even plants had a sex life, according to the graphic line-drawings of shrubs. Uttering words like 'pistils' and 'stamens' was dodgy for well-bred, young Anglican pupils. So, when my small charges seemed knowledgeable about perfectly ordinary words that used to embarrass me when I was older than they were, what was going on in their little brains? The boys and girls in our family had separate bedrooms of course. We were used to Social Welfare inspections.

Some comments amused and floored us.

One of our foster daughters, confused by the array of rainbow-coloured children in our family, asked point blank, "Did youse and Dad have sex to get all your kids?" I shook my head. And before I could explain the meaning of adoption, she triumphantly announced to the other children, "So that means Mum is a virgin. She never had youse. Remember at church they talked about the Virgin Mary?" And she beamed, while the smaller kids looked puzzled. Hubby and I exchanged a tiny smile at our elevated status.

"No, that's not right," said an older child. "You can have sex for fun, you know."

"Um, what have you been learning in home science?" I asked, changing the subject. "Dad and I don't know about sex very much because we're too busy growing kiwifruit and trying to encourage you kids to save and not waste your pocket money on gut rot."

"How old are you and Dad?" one of the children asked.

"Mum and Dad must be getting that old-age disease," one child thought out loud when I hesitated. I crossed my fingers and said I was a very old twenty-one-year-old, going on a hundred, and because all the kids struggled with maths, they marvelled. My mother said it was bad manners to reveal your age, religion, politics, or how much you had in the bank. Only common people do that, and Bryan agreed, not because it was common, but because it was our private business.

We realised fostering was not the same as having a 'permanent' child, whether your own or adopted. With fostering, one has to be mentally prepared and flexible as it's not about you and your needs, but rather about what is best for the child. Sometimes you may disagree that going back to their birth family is best for the child, but you are simply a cog in a big administrative wheel. At first, we had social workers popping in unexpectedly. We welcomed them and never felt any undercurrent of doubt about our suitability as foster parents. They even put in a good word for us about adopting. The social workers were happy to see the kids in our care thriving even though the house may not have been pristine because of all the little feet running in and out. In fact, one social worker gave us a backhanded compliment: "I see housework is not your priority." And then she made a big tick recommending us as adoptive parents.

So how did that happen?

Chapter Four

A priceless gift

The stinging words cut deeper than a knife wound. "Your chances of ever having a child are practically nil," said the surgeon, and he briskly walked away to attend to other patients.

I buried my head in the hospital pillow and wept at the futility of it all. Ever since I got married, I longed to be a mother and now my hopes were dashed. I cried for my lost dreams of seeing a child of our love – pink and crinkled, helpless but sturdy – enter a world we created. A tiny miracle. I longed to cuddle and nurture and sprinkle talcum powder on our baby's chubby body and gaze into unfocussed eyes and wipe curdled milk from rosebuds lips. I'd gladly get up at night and rock my baby, sing lullabies and imagine the future while stars twinkled promises. I'd do anything for that baby, anything. Now the future looked bleak and empty.

"We could adopt," said Bryan, and I leapt onto his lap and smothered him with kisses.

"You mean it?"

"Of course," he said, and my hopes soared with unbridled love as I imagined cradling a newborn. Together we embarked on a challenging journey, full of hope.

The social worker dealing with adoptions said babies were as rare as hen's teeth, but by this time we'd already filled in applications, written essays, gotten police clearance, and obtained written references from friends. "We may not have made this baby ourselves," I reminded my husband, "but it will be so wanted. We've had to prove ourselves over and over again to people we don't even know."

"Yes," he agreed. "Most people create their own child without any fuss or interference."

"Ours will be doubly-loved," I assured him. "I understand why some mothers are unable to keep their baby. But it doesn't have to be tragic. We shall love our baby forever."

As the months passed, our hopes rose and fell like the seasons. Land, a house, money – none of these buy a child. Wealth might buy some happiness, but it doesn't buy completeness. Mum invited me to a function in Nelson at which locally made arts and crafts were auctioned to raise money for the Suter Art Gallery. I bought a christening gown, frivolously designed and complicated, like my life, a spiderweb of unfulfilled yearning.

Another year passed. Where was our baby? Were birth mothers overlooking us in favour of other couples? What made them more special than us? I wish I knew the answer. I bought tiny singlets and cute baby clothes and lovingly knitted cardigans while the TV flickered ads of happy families. I had my niece, of course, but it didn't feel permanent, like the children we fostered.

"Get a dog," suggested well-meaning people. And Mum added to the sting: "You don't know what you're getting into adopting someone else's child." My mother-in-law worried about 'bad blood'. She lived near a racecourse and knew about the bloodlines of horses.

"They don't understand," said my brain.

If newlyweds weren't pregnant within a year, then there were snide remarks and subtle comments accompanied by unwanted advice. "My man's rampant. It's a wonder we didn't have triplets," was one comment I received.

"Triplets!" my brain cried. Just one teeny little baby and I would be happy for the rest of my life. Even then, having my own biological child wasn't important. I didn't think Bryan and I would create a child more special than any other child. I thought every child created was special.

Some young women who lived in our village shook their heads when I mentioned adoption. "I'd be up for it, but me hubby wouldn't. If we can't have our own kids, then he doesn't want any."

How extraordinary, I thought. They were young and trying to avoid another pregnancy. I was slightly older and tried to shake off the unfairness of life. "Please God," I cried. "You've given me the man of my dreams and he is happy for any child to be in our family. I will continue to foster, but just one permanent little baby. Can you make us a family?"

There's a fine line between keenness and desperation, and I was hovering in-between. Bryan was more relaxed; he balanced hopes and dreams with reality. I knew he'd be an amazing father – considerate, non-judgmental, caring.

While we were fostering, the magic phone call came. We were on a party line and you could hear the telephone click when nosy neighbours picked up on the ring tone even though the call wasn't for them. We were chosen to adopt a newborn baby girl. I hyperventilated. *Thank you, beautiful birth mother; thank you, social workers; and thank you, God.* "We're going to adopt a baby girl," I cried to my mother when she and Dad drew up outside our gate on their way back to Nelson after a busy weekend working on their lifestyle block in Golden Bay.

"Can't you ask Social Welfare for a boy?" she said.

I was aghast.

"No, Mum. Adoption doesn't work like that. We are grateful to be chosen, boy or girl." I wanted her to be excited and happy. She was, but cautiously so. Those who struggle with infertility know about this gratitude. Those who easily fall pregnant don't understand the disappointment, the heartache, the longing and desire to cherish a child that the infertile experience. Some learn to live with it and get on with their careers, but for others it's a deep sense of loss and sadness.

My husband of almost two years was elated too. As we drove over the winding Takaka Hill pass to go and talk to the Nelson social worker about the infant, we discussed names for our child. However, the little girl turned out to be a baby boy. "We did offer you a girl," said the motherly social worker, "but a baby boy has just been born and he is a perfect fit for your family. Would you consider this change to the adoption?"

Of course! We felt privileged to be selected by the birth mother.

Some families turn down the offer of a newborn because they're wary about the baby's background. Adoptive parents are asked preliminary questions, such as "Would you accept a child born of rape or incest, a baby whose mother had been drinking (foetal alcohol syndrome) or who had been on crack? Would you be prepared for open adoption where the birth mother and family could be in and out of your lives? Would you accept a child of mixed race, and if so, how tolerant are you of the racial mix? We had ticked 'yes' to all the boxes except the one about severe disability, simply because we lived in the country, a long way from hospitals. Living at the bottom of Takaka Hill means travelling over a long, winding mountainous pass to get to Nelson, and if I haven't spewed along (call it 'christened') every winding corner, then our kids have.

Most adoptive families on the waiting list want a baby because there's a good chance they'll bond more effectively, putting their 'imprint' onto that tiny being. The babies we adopted from birth had a slightly better success rate in terms of being happy adults, but it depended on choices they made as adults too.

Older children whom you adopt or foster, have suffered some degree of trauma in being taken from their birth families. Many adoptive families don't fully understand that at first. We, like all families who adopt and foster, were keen to love and bond with the new child, not realising that when the new addition slipped into our family, the child was on high alert. We ignored the warning signs of manipulation because we wanted the child to feel happy in our family. Your maternal instinct is to gloss over the past hurt and give the child a brand new, fresh start. Then little irritating behaviours happen, and you think, "Whoa! Where did that come from?" You don't want the child's disturbing behaviour being inflicted on the other kids in your care. How did the new kid learn to swear like that? Why is that kid rubbing its privates? Why is the kid grovelling under the table for food? Why, why, why? Red alert. But you don't want to give up. The social workers sought you out as parents who can cope with any situation. After all, we were away from the complexities of city living, away from their interfering rellies, and our back garden was a vast playground where the children often put up makeshift tents on the other bank of the creek and looked for dinosaur remains (which were sheep bones and deer antlers).

As the years rolled by, our family of two increased until we had adopted nine children, with more than double that number being fostered by us as well. Some of our friends also fostered many children but that was over days, not years, for we often had long-term children and sibling groups. Sometimes, we were emergency parents. Could we have a teenager for a few days? was a frequent request, but one which always stretched to weeks because placements for older kids were hard to find. We never turned anyone down. It was a challenge, but we thought more about the kid's plight and Social Welfare's desperation to find a safe haven for the child, than our own comfort. We could manage.

Our house with original shingled roof

When the phone rang and we were asked to take a child into care, I involved the children. They wanted to know if it was a boy or girl, how old the child was, and whether that child could sleep in their room. They were excited and they all wanted that new kid. None of them moaned, "I don't want any more kids in the family." Never. It simply didn't happen. The new kid was like a Christmas present – an unknown surprise who could become a mighty great challenge. Sometimes, I'd have to remind the newcomer, "Sweetheart, can you not swear in front of the kids," or "We know it's hard for you being separated from your family, so let's pretend you're on holiday here and let's do fun things. What do you like doing?"

"Let's have a concert," I'd cry. I had a big box of dressing-up clothes with funny hats and handbags. "Shall I start it off?" We'd draw the large drapes separating the lounge and kitchen and used them as stage curtains. The kids were in stitches when I did out of tune renditions of my '60s music, which got the ball rolling. Several of our children played the violin and needed practice for an upcoming concert, while others sang nursery rhymes with cute lisps that made the songs unrecognisable. If the evening went well, you hoped the happiness would spill over to the next day. It was a shock when something set a kid off, as if they'd forgotten the euphoria of the previous night. But that's how it is in real life, so we took life one day at a time and faced the challenges. Most were fleeting, but you always wondered about trigger points in a child's memory that could set them off. Even those parents who have their own biological child can be flummoxed by their kid's reactions or choices in life.

Of course, noisy bickering among the children occurred, as happens in all families. Bryan had a good rule: The first one to stop is the winner. He and I rarely disagreed and certainly never argued in front of the children. My father had post-war blow-ups that caused tension when I was a teen. "Never marry a short man," my mother warned. "They use their voices to make up for their height." Bryan was tall, even-tempered. I'd hit the jackpot. There was no point in destabilising the home just to score points.

What then was the best part of fostering compared to adopting?

When fostering, you could've been in for the long haul, but you could rely on social workers to encourage you to continue if you were stressed. They didn't want to see the placement break down. In a way, they rescued you, soothed you and promised to visit to sort out problems. They were our friends; they were grateful we had their troubled kids in our care, just as we were grateful to be allowed to parent those children. But when the relationship soured and you had to deal with juvenile behaviour you didn't understand, then you had access to the

Big Backup. An aunty-someone would take them because they were family, but she couldn't have done so earlier because she had drama in her life. Then you felt guilty, and that aunty might be family, but hey, her partner was a rough-looking tattooed dude who had turned his life around. So, was the kid better off with you, a temporary, foster mum (a stranger really), or back with the family the child wanted to be with? We knew that our foster children would gravitate back to their family, and it was our wish that they did so, but we hoped their family would sort out their problems and put their children's needs before their own.

"Nah. I don't reckon my parents are normal. They're not divorced and they love each other."

Chapter Five
When I was a teenager

When I was a teenager in the '60s, life was simpler than when we raised ours in the '90s and the new millennium. No credit cards, cell phones, Internet or plastic junk, and computers were in their infancy. School-leavers either went to university, learnt shorthand and typing or a trade, or they worked in shops. Some left school at fifteen and jobs were plentiful. Life held hope and opportunity.

During World War Two, our parents had experienced deprivation as well as heartache when family members died, and they had to adjust and make do. Men never revealed their feelings, although some sought comfort at the local RSL (Returned and Services' League of Australia) and staggered home from excessive alcohol relief. The camaraderie there was more relaxing than wives wanting to talk about problems at home (teenagers, needing the latest appliance, neighbour gossip). Women baked, took care of the kids, and pandered to their husbands. Their job was to keep the household running smoothly while he brought in the wage. It helped oil the wheels of living.

There weren't 'helicopter parents' about because children were sent outside to play and amuse themselves. My siblings and I found snails in the garden, named them, and soon had them running races up the garage wall. We put dolls' frocks on our kittens and took them for a walk in a pram to the shops to do 'the messages' for Mum. As teenagers, we were expected to help with household duties before being set free. If teens wanted pocket money, they earned it by babysitting, doing chores, running errands, roaming the golf course for lost balls (and selling them back to the caddies) or delivering papers.

When young males were conscripted to fight in Vietnam, they were generally unenlightened. Big Brother America and the Australians were mates, weren't they? It was a shock for lads to be balloted to fight overseas in a country that they'd never studied in geography class. The underlying warning was – if you weren't onside with Big Brother, then don't expect them to help you when the Yellow Peril or the Communists invade. It was a niggling worry. We were an isolated continent, so who'd invade us? But when in World War Two a Japanese submarine came into Sydney Harbour and Darwin was bombed as well, Australia was as vulnerable as any other country.

As to serving in the Vietnam War, my brother took off up the coast and went surfing until his knees bulged, and he was subsequently declared medically unfit for duty.

"I'm not going to lose my life fighting in a country I've never heard about and slaughter beautiful women and children," he responded when tracked down. Non-compliant youths were arrested for stating they were conscientious objectors or for resisting conscription on religious grounds. It was a difficult time in households because fathers who'd been through the previous war never envisioned their sons would follow in their footsteps a couple of decades later.

The joy of being a young teen in the '60s, expressing freedom and love for mankind through music, was turning. Now the gentle tide of safe rebellion against parents' restrictions was checked by reality. You do what is right for your country and conform. Don't be a coward. Show respect for your leaders. Dads who feared losing their sons didn't want them to be labelled as sissies. Mothers were anxious and upset, especially if they had lost male members of their family in the previous war. Australia was divided about sending troops. It was a terrible war with no winners.

My mother had an inkling about where my brother had disappeared to, but she didn't let on to Dad. She was not going to ruin the cocktail hour being lectured about my brother's disrespect towards authority and his streak of non-conformity. As it turned out, there were a lot of casualties in Vietnam, and Aussies and Kiwis alike felt soured about losing the youth of their nations. Bob Dylan sang protest songs; he understood.

Parents in the '60s were resourceful when it came to economic savings. They grew a garden and pickled and bottled available fruit and vegetables. They queued up at post offices to deposit their savings from the work they did, and wives banked their housekeeping money. The bank was your friend. They gave children green, tin money boxes into which coins were inserted, and the teller unlocked the box when it was full, praising the little saver. We were told to save for a rainy day, for you don't know what is going to happen in the future.

People knew the names of everyone on their street, and if you strayed, your parents heard about it. It was like a neighbourhood watch scheme. We called them nosy parkers but it was well meaning. Neighbours saw your kids grow from building go-carts, selling glass bottles and papers to retail outlets, and mowing lawns with a hand mower, to being long-haired teens who spent some of their earnings on the latest pop record.

Parents never indulged their child in the latest music as they thought rock 'n' roll was a fad and trashy, and that it would turn their darlings into juvenile delinquents. Admittedly, some of the lyrics were rebellious, but they were mostly syrupy and angst-ridden. Pop stars sang about being misunderstood by parents, who were nicknamed 'the olds', 'oldies' or 'fossils'. Singers like Elvis Presley, Gene Pitney and Roy

Orbison related to our feelings. Jerry Lee Lewis, Chubby Checker and Fats Domino songs were fun to dance to. Their hits have stood the test of time. We never thought that once our parents had been our age.

"Bunkum," said Dad. "Filth. What has the world come to? Turn off that rubbish on the radio."

The Rolling Stones didn't help with 'Can't get no Satisfaction' and the thrilling sounds of the Beach Boys added to the fuel. Dad thought bands like these contributed to my brother becoming a beach bum, sending the wrong message about working hard and saving.

Those of us who hitchhiked around Europe found music a way to relate to one another and the cultures we encountered, even if we could not speak the same language. It was universal. It was all flower power and love, and everyone across the globe was our friend. We didn't know about hate crimes or violence. The shooting of JF Kennedy was a big wake-up call. It shocked the world.

My generation mostly transitioned from being pleasure-seeking teens to doing what our parents did – we got engaged, looked for an affordable house to buy, got married and raised a family. And they named their offspring Melissa, Melanie, Stephanie, Michael, Jason and Paul, as opposed to the names of their classmates – Jennifer, Christine, Deirdre, Pamela, Jeanette, Susan, Barry, Robert, Peter and John. By the early '70s, young parents became more imaginative and the names they chose for their offspring depended on their lifestyles. Some were influenced by psychedelic names like Ziggy, or earthy names like River – if they were living in a commune. Others were influenced by TV dramas popular at the time, like *Poldark*, where the name Demelza rose in the charts.

For youngsters to understand why we parented the way we did in the '90s and beyond, they need to understand that it goes back to our growing up experiences. You learn from your parents, remembering their pithy sayings, and you either conform or rebel. Rebelling against your parents was not life threatening then. It involved just silly fusses such as youths growing their hair long, and dads waiting up for their daughters to be returned home before midnight and then turning on the porch lights just when her date was planting a goodnight smooch beside his beat-up jalopy.

American movies and songs had an enormous influence on baby boomers. It was fun and exciting to be young and embrace music and fashions. Mothers bought McCall magazines or purchased Burda patterns to make our frocks for an upcoming ball. Many '60s teens could knit and sew, and if they couldn't afford a dress they saw in the shops, they'd put it on lay-by, paying it off weekly. As a teen, I once experienced an embarrassment at a retail outlet and the scars still affect my shopping behaviour today. It shouldn't have done so, but it did, but in saying that, it has saved me heaps of money.

How did it happen?

A teen workmate said that a fashion store in a Sydney arcade was having a sale. We ended up entrapped in a dark strip of a shop run by a garish Turkish woman, with bouffant black hair and shiny crimson lips, smoking pungent ciggies. I bought several frocks on sale, mostly influenced by my workmate and the persistent shop owner, leering like a gargoyle and barging into the changing room making flattering comments.

"What do you think, Mum?" I asked when I got home and spread the purchases on her bed.

Mum pressed her lips in disappointment. "Not suitable, darling, and look, that one seems to have been worn. Look at the burn mark on it."

"Mummy," I wept. "Don't you like the granny print frock? Oh! I hate all the frocks. I'm a stupid shopper. I got talked into it. What shall I do?"

Mum said, "Go back to the store and demand your money back."

The shop owner refused.

"That woman is taking advantage of you. Is she a foreigner? What country? They can be tricky. We will take a bus on Saturday and confront her." And she poured me a tiny sherry. It made me love my mother more. She was going to battle on my behalf.

On Saturday my mother firmly, but politely, confronted the shop owner and the frocks were exchanged for other garments not on sale. Today's generation of women are more assertive and quite savvy when it comes to shopping. They post images of themselves trying on frocks and get instant feedback. It's technology we never dreamed about.

When I was a teenager, parents lived together for the sake of their children. They muddled along despite tiffs that would unravel parents today. There was a saying they adhered to: 'United we stand, divided we fall.' Also, 'You've made your bed, now lie in it.' Only the desperate moved out of their home, but I never knew such a family. Where would the spouses go?

Across Australian and Kiwi households, housewives followed the rules of the week – washing day, ironing day, baking day and so on. Sundays were reserved for church. Clutching a string bag or trundler, women strolled daily to their corner store, mulling over what to cook for their family. Carcasses hanging from hooks, or a frightened bunny with a glass eye, greeted shoppers at butcher shops that had sawdust-sprinkled floors. Rosy-cheeked butchers with bulging biceps, who looked like they could handle today's wayward youths, were busy chopping up the chunks of liver, kidney and bacon that the demure housewife requested for her husband's meal. "I'll have some of your sirloin," was not an attempt to woo the butcher, although a friend's granny made a faux pas in this regard.

The girl was sweet on a young apprentice plumber but too shy to approach him. She sighed to Gran, "He's such a dreamboat with lovely legs," and added wickedly, "I bet he's got lean loins."

A few days later they spied the young man window-shopping. Playing Cupid, Gran marched the girl up to this hunk to make small talk. "So you're a butcher, eh?" He shook his head, puzzled. "That's strange," said Gran, "I heard you had lean loins."

Teens today are bolder when it comes to affairs of the heart. When I was a teen we didn't want to be labelled 'fast' or 'too forward' or a 'tart' by making the first move. It was up to the man. Parties were mostly supervised, and it's a wonder we all arrived home safely as no one wore seat belts. Despite a cry for equality, there was still a gender gap. A young male was entitled, even expected, to sow his wild oats before settling down with a girl of his choice.

Back in the '60s it was a terrible time for pregnant teens, for they were encouraged to place their baby for adoption. It was a stigma for their parents, who were unsupportive, being more concerned about their social standing than the plight of their daughter. When the Domestic Purposes Benefit was granted, the pool of babies available for adoption dried up. Some infertile couples spent years on a waiting list to adopt, before looking overseas for an available child. What were once 'unwanted' babies, now became babies that were very much wanted by their birth mothers, and for those eager to adopt, they were practically unobtainable.

Whenever we adopted a child, we thought about the pain and anguish of the birth mother and the huge decision she had to make. We were, and are, utterly grateful to them. While they created life, they gave us a life and purpose far richer than they could have imagined.

Chapter Six

Food for thought

It's one thing to adopt or foster a child, but quite another when it comes to raising them when they hit puberty. They are bigger, mouthier and more confused than ever, and their actions and reasoning are so extraordinary you'd think you're in the twilight zone. I bet every parent has felt this way. My parents obviously did, but we didn't realise the impact we made on them raising us. No wonder they looked forward to their cocktail hour. Time to reconnect and blot out the stress of work (Dad), housework fatigue (Mum), and teen disappointments (us) before another day dawned. It was civilised, polite and made the end of a working day a celebration.

When our kids became teens, we were curious about their backgrounds. Often, we knew little or nothing about their birth families because it was a closed adoption, or the children were orphaned. When you are given the gift of a child, you are not going to rock the boat by demanding history which families are unwilling to impart unless it's a medical necessity.

Today, parents are required to take courses when it comes to fostering or adopting. It was a lot more relaxed back in the late-'70s and '80s when we adopted four boys. The first was a newborn with a half-Dutch background, the second was a Rarotongan baby, the next was a three-year-old Māori boy, and the last was a baby of Māori heritage. The social workers would say, "I love coming to your house for a cuppa and seeing the children so happy."

And I'd cheekily ask, "Got any more kids for adoption?"

"Wait till they become teenagers," they'd chuckle.

Despite fostering, I felt our family wasn't complete. Bryan agreed and said a daughter to balance out the boys in our family would be a welcome addition now that our niece had left our care. When a friend, Megan, posted magazine articles about abandoned babies, our lives took a dramatic turn. We involved the children in our deliberations, especially the oldest as he was nearly a teenager. "Go for it, Mum," he said. So, with his blessing, I wrote to orphanages in several countries overseas, and they all replied, some sending photos. The situation was more desperate than I'd envisaged.

Being pro-active in encouraging the adoption of abandoned babies from overseas countries, unwittingly put us offside with Social Welfare in New Zealand. The tide had turned as far as adoptions were concerned.

"Mum, why can't you adopt him?" our children asked when I showed a photo of yet another child in Thailand, India, Korea or Colombia desperate for a home. "He can sleep in my room."

The Social Welfare Department's policy was that children should be adopted within their culture, and babies with even a smidgen of Polynesian blood were offered to Māori couples. *Too late*, I thought, wryly. I've got one white and three brown-skinned boys, and the kids we foster are multi-coloured. I mused about Mia Farrow and Josephine Baker with their rainbow-coloured tribe and wondered how they fared. We didn't have a computer then, so I couldn't google their lives – as if I'd had the time anyway. My work was cut out parenting the children in our care and running our kiwifruit orchard.

I continued, though, to field enquiries about adoption, even after I brought home three babies from Romania (girls) (1990 and 1991), and eight-year-old twins (a boy and a girl) from Russia (1995). Then shocked by the plight of children in Sierra Leone whose arms were being hacked off in a civil war, we considered adopting a little girl called Princess. Some New Zealanders had adopted children from there through an American agency. We decided, however, that we had more than enough on our hands with hormonal teenage boys and five children suffering the effects of institutionalisation. I was happy to share information with anyone enquiring about overseas adoption and put that person in contact with I-CANZ (Inter-Country Adoption New Zealand), an organisation that had up-to-date information and was now working closely with Social Welfare. We were amused when our foster daughter waved her arms at the table crying, "More kids. More kids."

"Hang on," I laughed. "Haven't we got enough kids in our family now? How many of us are there?"

The most we had, at one brief time, was twelve, unless there was a party and a sleep over. We had teenagers in two batches. Just as the '80s babies were making their way in the world in 2000 and beyond, the '90s babies were following in their teen footsteps. When the '90s babies became teenagers we rarely fostered. It was evident our younger batch of kids needed more input from us because of their poor start in life.

"How do you cope with so many children?" people asked. "I'd go off my head. Our two run me ragged. Don't know how you do it. Don't they cost the earth to feed and clothe?"

Not to us. Kids need food, warmth, shelter and love. The basics. Before they came to live with us, those we fostered were used to having takeaways for their meals, food shortages, family arguments, and a big dose of TV. The children came to us anxious and stressed. No child wants to be taken from their family and moved into the unknown.

At first, to the new arrival, our house in the country must have looked like an adventure playground with mobs of kids. Teenagers were more cautious. "Of course, you don't have to babysit, love," I said. "And you even have your own room."

"Where do youse all sleep then?"

I still cringe at the use of 'youse' for 'you'. Strangely, some of our adult kids have taken up the vernacular they never uttered as children. When I was a youngster, my mother said, "Speech stamps you. You can tell where a person comes from when they open their mouth. Do you want to marry a lavatory man?"

"No, Mummy," I'd whisper. "But some kids at school speak like that."

"Not you. You were brought up to speak the Queen's English. You don't want to give Daddy a heart attack, do you?"

"No."

"Then don't copy those common children," she said. "No nice man will marry you if you say 'youse' and 'I done it'. It cheapens you."

I had to *uncringe*. My job was not to correct but to be comforting and kind and help an unhappy or surly child coming into our care. They soon thawed, watching the other kids showing off, swinging upside down from trees, or playing football, imploring the new arrival to join in.

We'd show the teen foster child their new bedroom. "We are excited about having you. The girls decorated your room."

But I did admit we were different. We were country folk, not townies. We had an outside loo. It was a little shed by the dahlias, with a can that was emptied daily, next to which was a bucket of sawdust to sprinkle over what you produced.

"Are youse olden-day people?" they wondered. When Bryan tried to explain our waste-water system, their eyes glazed over.

"Don't bother, darls," I said. "Talk straight. Kids are smart and if they don't want to piddle in the loo at night, they can do it under the walnut tree. Lovely fertilizer. Give them a torch, and tell you what, they will see the stars. It might get them interested in astronomy." Hubby hoped so too. He set up a telescope on a wooden picnic table for any unusual happenings in the sky.

"This is an important event. Wake them up," he urged. He didn't want them to feel they'd missed out on comets or eclipses. But they weren't grateful. Sleep was better.

Foul language was discouraged. Once, after my head hurt from their garbage chatter, I was so stressed that I flung those despicable swear words back at them.

"Do you like me saying the 'f' word?" I said. Bryan has never sworn. He came into the back door at dusk with an armful of garden veggies for dinner and must have thought his wife had Tourette's.

The kids were open-mouthed.

"Mummy," they fretted. "Are you having a breakdown? You shouldn't be using those words."

"Well, why are you?" I retorted. "Not nice is it?" And then I became my mother. "Do you want your teachers to think you have slummy parents? Don't you want to marry a nice man?"

"I'm not getting married."

"Why not?"

The girls in our family thought there was no point in it. Old-fashioned. "Anyway, I might end up being a lezzie. Do you know what that means, Mum?"

"I might go bi," said another girl. "Get the best of both worlds."

"God forbid," I muttered. "Where's Daddy? Where's he hidden that bottle of red he bought yesterday for emergencies?" And at dusk, I clumped off to the shed in his oversize gumboots.

"Your mum is so cute. Love rarking her up," said a foster kid.

"Yeah, we do too," agreed the others.

It was easy clothing the kids. Boxes of garments appeared magically on our back porch – some new, most pre-loved. Of course, we bought the kids new clothing, especially the foster children since we got an allowance for them. When the surprise packages turned up there were whoops of joy and a mad scramble to claim what they wanted before frenzied bargaining began. They had the makings of auctioneers or dodgy car sellers. "Mumma, this would suit you," a kid would squeal. "More your oldie generation." Bryan thought the stockings and tiny bras were "just the bee's knees" for tying up the tomatoes. The rest were bundled up to give to charity.

Feeding such a large brood was a full-time job.

We had two large deep freezers and stocked up on specials. Bryan grew a substantial garden and the domestic orchard had an abundance of fruit trees. We traded kiwifruit for honey and meat. One late afternoon, out-of-town friends phoned wanting to visit, so I rashly invited them round for dinner. Rummaging through the freezer in the dark, I found an unfamiliar package labelled 'B.B.' which I assumed stood for braising beef. Bryan wasn't so sure. He thought the phallic-looking slab of frozen meat was geoduck. "Oh, well," I said. "I'll cook us a mystery dinner," and grabbed a few herbs growing outside in disused washing machine tubs. I recalled that whenever my mother had guests and burnt something, or the cat wandered onto the table and licked at party food, she wasn't perturbed. "Cream, darling, hides a multitude of sins. Remember that." I hoped herbs would do the same. Tomato sauce was also an excellent camouflage.

During the meal, our son Tristan breezed in. He was off to go eeling and asked where his bait marked 'B.B.' was. When I enquired what the initials stood for, he revealed the ghastly truth – bull's balls!

There were gasps of "Oh my God. Are you trying to kill us, Mother?" as they lurched outside pretending to gag while the guests scraped their plates into the rubbish bucket.

"This would be a delicacy in another country," I called out to my beloved family. The guests thought it funny but hopped in their car asking where the nearest fish 'n' chip shop was. We didn't know as we never ate out and shops were miles away. Bryan had puked from eating takeaways in the past, which sullied the joy of eating out – as if that was ever possible with so many kids and so far from civilisation.

"Okey-doke, go and get the packet of pies and you can have ice cream after to make up for Mummy's mistake. But don't tell your teachers – or therapists – if any of you go to them."

"Look on the bright side," I said to Bryan when we had the kitchen to ourselves. "That'll teach people to visit us at night when I'm tired from working in the orchard all day."

We lived in a remote part of New Zealand and were a haven for those in need, especially if their car broke down, or they ran out of petrol, or wanted to use the phone. Needy people included runaway kids, local renters having a domestic brawl, or hitchhikers who asked to camp the night because they couldn't get a ride to their destination. Having hitchhiked around the world, I felt grateful to those who took me in. Payback time. However, one foreign couple became a nuisance.

The trouble started when, between bouts of camping in the hills, they'd descend on us at mealtimes. I'd initially encouraged them, hoping the kids would take up a foreign language at school. Might pique their interest and take them out of a small-time country environment, I'd thought. Eventually, it became annoying to hear the plop of their rucksacks on our back porch. The children thought they were entertaining with their juggling skills, but I thought otherwise. Freeloaders came to mind. The younger kids were noisily underfoot one day when hubby affably offered them a home brew. They downed it in one gulp and, as he was pouring seconds, I rushed into the lounge. "Oh no, you haven't given them that tainted beer, have you?" I explained to the perplexed duo that I do the home brewing and that our foster daughter had slipped into the vat after crawling through the kitchen window. I had to fish her out, fully clothed, wearing sandals. The couple looked confused when I said it turned out to be one of my better brews.

"Did the child do anything in it?" wondered the hitchhiker.

"Dunno," I replied. "Did you?" I asked the small culprit.

"Can't *wemember*," she lisped.

The couple put down their glasses.

"Din, din," I called. "Grubs up." Everyone clamoured around the table. The casserole smelt delicious.

"What's that?" a hitchhiker asked.

"Chook," I said. "Home-grown. Organic."

One of our daughters took a mouthful. "It better not be Henny Penny. We're not eating her, are we?"

I shrugged. "They all look the same in the deep freezer." With that she burst into tears and refused to eat. I told our visitors that hubby had knocked off half a dozen hens. "Weren't laying; had gone off the boil," I explained. "They were getting on; a bit like us. No use having old birds cluttering up the place, but this chook is safe to eat, I think."

"Tell them about Henny Penny," begged the children. It was their favourite bedtime story.

I said an Aussie friend had a hen, also called Henny Penny, who got chased by the family Corgi and fluttered into their long-drop toilet because someone had left the lid open. Once retrieved and hosed down, her eyes, now a different colour, were bulging in fright. The unfortunate hen now had psychological problems and went off the lay. "But I'm sure ours didn't land in our toilet – unless any of you kids teased them. You kids been leaving the lid open?"

The guests decided they were vegetarians.

"Mum," growled a son. "You haven't washed the silver beet properly." Sure enough, a fat, green insect lurked out of the food mire and crawled across his plate.

"That's called a stink bug," I said. "They are common at this time of the year. Sorry. I didn't put my glasses on when I washed the silver beet. They are tricky to find because they like hiding. Better check your plate."

"The carrots look fine," they muttered.

"Bad year for grub worm," said Bryan.

"Tomatoes?" they asked, toying with their food.

Bryan said he'd put in a couple of rows of Super Toms, but it had been so muggy they'd all got blight. "You did cut out the bad bits, didn't you, darls?" he asked me.

"Hope so," I replied "Taste and see. But don't tell them about the spuds."

"Potatoes? Did you have an agreeable season?" (I loved their quaint English.)

"Would have, but the creek overflowed in the last big rain and debris leaked onto the plot. We rescued as much as we could."

The kids were confused, but Bryan caught on to my ploy, and nobody ate much. Pretty soon the visitors decided to leave, and when we heard a vehicle picking them and their packs up, we sighed with relief. I got the kids to help me empty the rest of the food into the trash buckets and clear the table. "Seems Mummy stuffed up the dinner tonight, kiddos. Who wants to make pancakes? And anyone who helps with the dishes can have a dab of Dad's Canadian maple syrup on it – if we can remember where we put it," I said. "You might have hidden it in your underpants drawer," I reminded Bryan.

On Sunday evenings Bryan took out the wages book. "Gather around kiddos and tell me what you have done over this week to earn pocket money." He made columns for all the children, including those we fostered, and used a thick pencil and, sometimes, a rubber if a child changed their mind.

"Do we have to include washing-up?" I'd interject. "There are some chores that should be done for free for being part of the family."

"Go away, Mumma," Bryan would quietly respond. "We will sort this out."

"Yes, Mum. Daddy knows what he's doing. You're not going to rip me off are ya, Dad?"

The children looked like little bumblebees, their backsides arched upwards, poring over The Book. Bryan talked in dulcet tones and piqued the kids' interest. I smiled at their enthusiasm and him being a good dad giving them basic accountancy skills. Should stand them in good stead, I hoped. But it didn't turn out like that. Their friends helped them raid their bank accounts. Bryan said it was a learning curve, annoying and disappointing, but hoped they'd see sense later in life.

Wishful thinking.

"Which ones are your real kids?"

Chapter Seven

We have teens in the house

"Don't you wish you could sprinkle fairy dust on your adolescent," sighed a mother down the telephone, "and they re-awake at twenty and become normal?"

"I know what you mean," I laughed. "Not adopting any more are you?"

When I had my earlier round of teenagers, I could ring up friends (costly) or write letters, and I either treasured or ignored their advice or words of comfort. With the advent of computers, it was much easier to network with friends and converse across the globe. I loved them – my brand new American and English friends who'd adopted and were having similar problems, often much worse than mine. I spent nights googling after a doctor, or teacher, or friend said an emotive word that might enlighten me as to my teen's strange behaviour. Most thought the strange behaviour was normal. *But I didn't behave like that,* I reflected. Why is this normal? Is this what my mother put up with?

With friends or family, you go into overdrive trying to justify your child's behaviour.

"I came down hard on my kids and they turned out all right in the end," other friends said, implying we were softer in our parenting style. Some suggested we shouldn't have adopted or fostered so many.

"So which kids shouldn't we have had?" I retorted. And that shut them up. They weren't fostering or adopting but had answers and solutions to teenage problems. *Walk in my shoes,* I silently wished.

I could see their brains saying, "You brought it upon yourselves. You should have been sensible like us and had two point two kids, or none at all." We were happy with our lot, but just wished the kids didn't complicate their lives (and ours) with erratic behaviour.

"I reckon she's getting her hormones," said one of the twins. "Is she, Mum?"

"Are you?" I asked the rampaging teen.

When she said, "Get stuffed" and "You don't know jack shit," we decided it was premature to renovate the house.

"Count our blessings," I reminded Bryan. "The kids are saving us heaps by not fixing up the house. If we do up a nice room for them, they could be smiley now but go bazookas later. No, our job is to give them guidance and the basics. It also cuts out the stress of having builders here when we are busy in the orchard. Plus, you can't subject trades people to foul language. They might quit when they are in the middle of doing dwangs. What are dwangs?"

Once we were awoken at night by a teenager hammering upstairs, putting hinges back on the door that had been kicked in. "Poor old door," I muttered to my sleepy spouse. "I wonder if kids who lived here a century ago behaved like that?"

Bryan thought not because there was no electricity then, and they had to be careful going up and down stairs carrying candles. Perhaps our offspring had the makings of a carpenter. Some of the children were learning woodwork at school, but we wished they'd do their carpentry in the afternoon, not at midnight. While irritable cries of "shuddup" echoed from the other bedrooms were not conducive to sweet sleep, we thought it unwise to confront a deranged teen at night. Like bad behaviour, it would fizzle out. However, when one of the teens snuck a boyfriend upstairs, we removed the door. "This home has an open-door policy," I snarled. "This is our house, not a brothel, and you are underage. Who is your friend with the pink hair? Can't tell in the dark. Boy or girl? We have *standards*," I said, quoting my mother.

"You are so mean, Mum. We were discussing names, and if we ever had a baby girl, we'd call her Jonquil, after you."

"Nice try," I said, "but by the time we let you procreate under our roof, Dad and I might be in a rest home – if we live that long."

"Don't go dramatic on me, Mum. We were only cuddling, weren't we, Honey? Other parents aren't so strict; everyone does it."

Honey squirmed.

"And you are not 'everyone' (Mother's haunting words again). You are very special to us. We are not letting you ruin your future by making us grandparents – we're too young."

"Told you about Mum," sighed the daughter. Honey hitched up his jeans and agreed to sleep in the lounge.

"Make your man a nice big plate of bacon and eggs in the morning," I offered. "And if you are cold in the night, get another blanket. Dad and I are leaving our door open, so no sneaking downstairs. We have big ears and your brother's got a slug gun."

That little incident had me emailing friends for advice. Would they have done the same thing? I recalled having had those feelings, but as an older teen. Underage, they agreed with me. But they said that legal age or not, if they were going to be sleeping together, they preferred their daughter sleeping with her boyfriend under their roof. *Heck no*, I thought. I want them uncomfortable and chaste, and if they couldn't control themselves, then root elsewhere (Australian expression). I was having flashbacks to a young couple who, against my better judgement, grabbed a bed upstairs. During the night I heard stifled moaning. I nudged hubby. "Funny noises overhead. Reckon it's coming from that couple. Oh crumbs, now I'm suspicious about that fish for dinner.

Smelt a bit off." Assuming the lass was nauseous, I charged upstairs with a glass of water and Disprin, and called out, "You alright, love?"

I needn't have bothered. The couple settled down for the night, quiet as church mice.

After Honey left, I told my four teenage daughters they were not having boys for sleepovers in their room, even if they were dressed for the Antarctic. "It's dangerous," I said. "You could get hurt. Something could accidentally poke out at you."

"What?"

"What do you think?"

"Their elbows? Feet?"

"Getting warm, but no. It's a gadget in-between," I said, and when they looked puzzled, I enlightened them. "It's a man's diddlepop. Girls, Mummy is not trying to be rude, but rather telling you something important. A man has two brains: one in his head and the other further south. Bet they don't teach you that at school."

There's a two-year age gap between the oldest and the youngest daughter in our family, with the identical twins sandwiched in-between. The girl twins were premature and emotionally and physically delayed, which gave us breathing space. They were tomboys who preferred riding farm bikes with dogs on the back, thrusting their fingers into their mouths and making piercing whistles. Then I had a brainwave. "You know Daddy and I wouldn't mind one bit if you decided to go lezzo until you leave home. We'd still love you."

"Oh my God," gasped the youngest. "You don't want us to be straight? What sort of mother are you!"

It would seem I flunked the birds and the bees talk, although I did better than my father. He was so irate when my sister and I (as teens) invited 'common' people from a ship to our party and stayed up late playing guitars, that he gave a terse lecture at dinner the next evening. He rose to his full height (which wasn't very tall) and said he hadn't sent us to expensive schools to run around with riff-raff. "Decent people," he said, "speak the Queen's English and mate quietly in the dark." Mum said even the bottle of hock on the table turned sour after that "uncalled for" remark and hoped my sister and I wouldn't need therapy.

When a thirteen-year-old daughter of ours asked to invite a certain John for the night, I got suspicious. "Why would he want to overnight here? Has he fallen out with his parents? And by the way, how old is this John?"

"He's sixteen, Mum, get over it."

"I am trying to, but he's a bit old for you, isn't he?"

"It's not like that."

"Is he a sexual predator?"

"No, Mum. He's English."

"Good. What does he look like?"

"Oh, you'd like him. He's got orange hair."

"Oh, he sounds nice. Has he got freckles? Might prefer him better if he had pustules and zits. Is he a Christian? A nice family boy?"

"No, Mum! He's a virgin."

When my teens made me happy, despite being despicable moments ago, I had to embrace the positive energy almost instantly. While my generation was brought up on delayed gratification, I felt our kids lacked remorse and impulse control, and so I rewarded sparks of niceness if it suited the occasion. "Something lovely happened today," I revealed, "and since you are being pleasant and I haven't heard a swear word in five minutes, I'd like to share something with you."

"Oh, Mummy darling," squealed the youngest. "Did those Liberace videos arrive?"

I nodded happily.

"Can we sit on your bed and watch your lover?"

Our kids were very astute. I told them that when I was younger than they were, I had loved a flamboyant pianist who was on American

TV. If I hadn't married Daddy, then he could have been their father (extremely unlikely), which appalled them all. I didn't tell them he was Mummy's fantasy, a charismatic, powdered queen who was rich, charming and sadly, dead from Aids. Mothers need to grab moments of happiness to de-stress. Liberace was the ultimate in impeccable manners, which is what women dream about, but they are resigned to the brutal truth that men are flawed, and offspring are hard work, but you love them nevertheless because you've invested your heart and life in them.

I said yes, but that Daddy doesn't want to watch Mummy's lover winking and playing the piano, so how do you connect the TV and video? A myopic twin found coloured plugs while another fiddled with the tuning, and another kept shouting "Call Daddy" even though Dad was on the tractor. He wouldn't be pleased to see a row of juvenile backsides on his bed worshipping in the Adoration of the Libby, and nicking snacks he'd hidden in his jumper under the bed. When your children work together as a team, there is a feeling bordering on exhilaration. You forget what went on before, even if you were on the verge of dialling 111 and asking them to put you in jail for a bit of a rest from the kids. While languishing in a cell with drug addicts or worse, someone else did the cooking, and the authorities even offered courses to motivate and entice you back to the family. Then I remembered I had once wanted a family badly, so like any other mother would, I ploughed on and rode the glitches.

When our Russian son walked in and saw his siblings perched on our bed like harrier hawks, the girls cried, "Go away, Misha. You haven't been nice to Mum," and when he said he liked hearing piano playing, I said, "Let him in, but shoosh, kids, Libby is going to wink."

Then Bryan came in, covered in sawdust, and looking overworked. "Has he winked yet?" he asked, glancing at the TV and at the twins sucking their thumbs and rolling bits of the yellow chenille bedspread up their nostrils. "When's dinner, darls?"

"Shoosh," all the kids roared.

When Liberace crooned 'Oh Promise Me', tears sprung to my eyes and I choked back a tiny sob. I realised that in the drudgery of caring for my big family, I was yearning for a spot of sweetness and tenderness.

"Look, Mum's crying," and they all looked, fascinated.

"It's nice to know your mother has feelings," said hubby kindly, and when Misha patted me on the back, Bryan said, "You know, you could look like Libby if you played the piano."

"In your dreams," Misha snorted.

One afternoon the kids came home from school and got the biggest shock of their lives. "Where's the TV?" Since they had become surly about music practices and stayed up late to finish homework, we locked the TV away in the shipping container by the orchard.

"We're doing this for your own good. Believe me, this hurts us more than it hurts you. Besides we want to bond with you."

Two of the boy teens said that normal parents didn't do this to their kids, and they were going to live with friends who watched heaps of TV. Their mothers were much nicer. I suggested they ring up the mothers to see if that could be arranged. "They don't want us," they said dejectedly, but weren't entirely surprised.

Cards, board games, books and indoor activities filled in the time on wet days. Computers and PlayStations were in their infancy. We were the first family in the village to get a Commodore 64, and that had the local children trickling up to our door, mostly to play maths and spelling games. Fine days were taken up with roaring around on paddock cars and bikes, making things in the shed, and after-school activities, such as tap dancing, music lessons, gymnastics, horse riding, netball, football, rugby, hockey and athletics. Sometimes the boys biked 23 kilometres into town to go swimming or to catch up with friends. Or they worked on a neighbouring farm during the calving season. The girls spent half their lives on the telephone until they got cell phones. And anyone who said they were bored or wanted pocket money was told there was plenty of work in the orchard.

The best Christmas present the kids got one year was witnessing the Resurrection of the Box, meaning the unveiling of the TV set under the Christmas tree. We'd bought the *Lord of the Rings* DVD but needed a TV screen to view it and, frankly, I was missing my Liberace-fix. He made the world seem brighter. The kids had forgotten about being deprived and were so excited to see that bit of plasma that they did the dishes and remained cordial. The TV served as an occasional babysitter during the school holidays when Bryan and I were flat out in the orchard, retraining workers who were mutilating our vines.

One evening I was preparing dinner and supervising homework, when one of the older children bounced through the back door and became argumentative. I didn't need uproar at this hour of the day. Fed up, I turned off the stove and told the noisy family I was on strike.
"Go to your room," they said.
"No! You can't make me," I retorted.
Bryan intervened. He knew that it was better to remove oneself from an inflammatory situation. "Go," he said. "I will deal with it."
"Only if you feed me and I can play with the computer in my room."
"Okay."
As I skipped towards my bedroom a childish voice rang out, "She's a bit of a troublemaker, isn't she, Dad."

Two hours passed before a stinging steak and oniony odour wafted down the hallway. The sky had turned from grey to black. On the computer I'd pounded out a meaty chapter for placement in an adoption magazine, explaining why I wanted this family who had banished me to my room. I'd also consumed the dregs of a medium white and devoured emails from delicious friends telling me how vile their kids were. Then I clicked onto eBay. Wow! Someone was selling something I badly wanted, and so did another fan in cyberspace. Feverishly I upped my bid and when the auction closed, a 'Congratulations' flashed across the screen. I was a winner! I screamed with excitement and the kids banged on the door. "Mummy, are you alright in there? You're making a funny noise. We miss you."

"Calm down, Mum," said the youngest son. "We peeked through a crack in the door and you've been gambling, haven't you?"

"Yes," I confessed. "I won some Liberace videos. I'm not a loser but a winner."

"You can come out now, Mum."

"I don't want to. I might cause a fight. Bring the grub in here."

The twins appeared at the doorway, juggling a large platter. "We helped Dad make dinner. Are you feeling better now, Mummy darling?"

Bryan popped his head round the door. "Got the kids eating out of the palm of my hands. They cooked the meal too. Now they're doing their homework."

I was amazed. "What's your secret?"

He wasn't sure. "Perhaps if you're not here they have to deal with me."

"Why, am I a red rag to a bull? Have they got a mother-thing going on?"

"They see you as vulnerable. It's a game. They're teens, trying it on."

"Hmm," I said, and since I was feeling victorious, I embraced my crazy kids. "There's one thing I want to say to all of you. Thank you for being such rotten swines. If you'd all been normal, I'd never have gone to my room and gotten Libby off eBay. Oh, how I love you all."

"Don't you think Mummy is cute sometimes?" said the girls, and we had a group hug.

"Daddy," asked one of the twins, "if Liberace wasn't dead, would he be alive today?"

"I am so happy," I said. "Do you think Libby was gorgeous? Do you think I have good taste in men?"

"Put it this way," said our Russian son, "we're all glad you married Dad instead." And the other kids gave high fives in the air. "I know what we're going to buy you for Christmas."

"Libby videos?" I asked hopefully.

"Nah. Ice cream, coz you give us that to keep us quiet when you let us watch a Liberace video in your room."

Miss Thirteen wrapped her arms around me. "I'm glad you married Dad instead of Liberace coz you wouldn't have adopted me otherwise."

My heart smiled – temporarily.

While the videos were winging their way to me from America, there was a two-week window of uproar. One of the teens had fallen victim to an older girl at school who was leading her astray. I had never spoken to a policeman before I had kids. In fact, every time I spied one, I'd shake with fright and want to grovel with contrition despite having nothing to confess. Now I was giving the visiting cop cups of tea and offering up the kid. "Why don't you shove her in the slammer overnight with only bread and water? You have our permission. We are caring parents."

The cop thought I'd been watching too many action movies and her crime didn't justify that sort of treatment. At a school meeting to get the Wayward One back on track, I was quizzed, "Are you communicating with each other?"

I said we do nothing but talk. Everyone talks in our family; we can't help it. But I think she meant: "Are you listening to each other?"

It didn't help the school situation either when I saw a movie advertised on TV and mentioned to Bryan in front of the kids, "I've worked like a dog in the orchard all day. Mind if I watch it?"

He said, "You deserve it, darls. Might join you."

When one of the kids begged to see it, I said no; it was an AO movie and a school night.

It seems we then missed a phone call from a teacher. "I said you didn't want to be disturbed because you were busy watching a porn movie," explained the teen. And the teachers wonder why we roll up to parent-teacher interview feeling slightly defensive!

Bryan admitted he was glad he was growing kiwifruit now, instead of teaching. "You're your own boss and the plants don't yap back at you," he explained.

We'd both been compliant and studious at school, but with so many children with different needs we had a challenging road ahead.

My mother's motto became mine: "Let's be happy even if it kills us."

Chapter Eight

The babysitter

It is said people come into your life for a reason, and you're only dealt as much as you can handle. Most people were wonderful, like the couple that visited in a white campervan shortly after we'd adopted Tristan, our fourth son, but before we adopted five more from Eastern Europe.

The elderly gent said he was raised in the house we were living in, and had we perhaps come across his gun and saddle in the loft? "No," we said, but "bring in the missus for a cuppa." We were keen to learn more about the history of our historic home. Before the 1900s, it accommodated a dozen young gentlemen who were charged a shilling a night for lodgings, and another shilling to tether their horses.

The buxom, erect wife with white hair tied in a bun, smiled broadly at the new, brown bundle in my arms. "Oh, the little pet," she cooed. "May I hold him?" I tenderly passed Tristan over. "And who are these little devils?" she laughed, pointing to youngsters under the walnut tree, sloshing mud from the recent rains over each other.

"The brown ones are mine, the others we foster," I said. Baby Tristan had snuggled so contentedly into her matronly breasts, like a dormant possum. I airily remarked, "You could be his nana. We're almost family since your husband grew up here."

"Oh, may I?" she pleaded. She explained she'd married late in life, having cared for her mother, and had never had the chance to have children. I said of course she could be their nana, since my mother had died, and my dad was not fond of children.

We were surprised a few weeks later when a large box was delivered to our back door. Inside were baby clothes and gifts for all from our new nana and granddad. I made the children write thank-you notes and added my own epistle, not expecting the relationship to continue. Happily, it did, and for over two decades until they passed away. We wrote regularly and every time we adopted another child, they were at the airport in Auckland to meet us and greet their new grandchild. The value of grandparents can't be overestimated. They can be a wealth of knowledge, help and kindness. Our lives were richer for knowing such a couple and our children benefited hugely from having imported grandparents. It put a positive spin on the meaning of adoption.

On the other hand, seemingly benign people who walk into your life can turn out to be a menace. I mentioned this in my first book, but it bears repeating as a warning to those who are fostering or adopting.

It started innocently enough when an obese woman waddled into our kitchen after dinner one evening. She'd moved into an unpainted house with an overgrown garden down the road, and one of our children invited her up to our house. We were painting the walls and ceiling of our farmhouse kitchen to brighten it up before laying new linoleum. My elderly uncle had heard about my trip to Romania to adopt identical twins, as it had been in the local papers. He offered to pay for the linoleum, and we were thrilled – a nice clean floor for the babies, who'd just learnt to sit by their first birthday after languishing in an orphanage for nine months, unloved, unwanted and highly neglected.

The kitchen was bare except for chairs and paint pots, ladders and a naked light bulb.

We put down our paintbrushes and welcomed our unprepossessing new neighbour (whom I shall name Cora).

She said she'd heard we had lots of children, including babies, and she loved babies.

My son asked if he could take his new sisters out of their cots to show her, but I said no, perhaps another time as they were settled for the night. It was a balmy summer evening and since it was the school holidays, we didn't mind the older children staying up late and kicking a football or playing spotlight in the gathering darkness.

The woman squatted on a wooden seat like a dumpling, legs splayed, and said she'd come to warn us that someone was gossiping about us. Why? What had we done? She pointed to the little cottage next door. Bryan scoffed; that elderly man barely went out of his house. He was lonely, and sometimes the kids helped weed his garden. Occasionally, they put on a concert for him while his Hungarian goulash stewed over the coal range. "He's asking someone in the village to help him write a letter about having your house condemned."

We were aghast. "That can't be true. He's nearly blind. Why would he say that? We've had endless social workers in our house who've inspected the rooms, and they still place foster children with us."

"Silly gossip," said Bryan. "Look, we're painting the kitchen." And he laughed.

While the woman prattled on, I felt distracted and upset, but it was swept aside when there was a knock on the door. The cheerful visitors apologised for calling in at this time of night, but they'd seen the light on in the hallway and were on their way to their beach bach. Our children came rushing in from outside when the couple deposited bags of clothing. The smiling wife said she was the niece of our adopted nana.

"Nan loves your children," she said. "I've sorted out some clothes I thought your boys could use, and books and jigsaw puzzles mine have outgrown." I hugged her. The kids were squealing with excitement. "Nice to see it appreciated and go to a good home," she added.

Good home?

I introduced her to Cora who was ladling sugar into another cup of tea. "We've just heard that the old man next door is reporting us for living in an unfit house," I said.

"Unfit!" she snorted. "My mother and all her brothers and sisters used to live here. They have lots of fond memories of the place, and it's more modern than it was in those days without electricity." She pointed to the lounge where our kids were forming piles of their new clothes, trying them on and exchanging with one another.

"That room used to be a formal dining room which had a mahogany table with a beautiful, heavily embroidered tablecloth, and children weren't allowed in normally. It was reserved for visitors." I thought about the tablecloth; it was a potential fire hazard in a rambling wooden home where candles were used, but she said there had been no accidents.

"This is a wonderful place to raise a family. Perfect in fact. Some people are odd, though; they become envious if someone has a bigger house or more kids." Cora became strangely quiet, and since she lived down the road, our generous visitors gave her a lift home.

Nothing more was mentioned about our house being condemned, and we didn't confront the blind man next door. What was the point? But over the course of the week there was a slight uneasiness as I noticed tins of fruit had been taken from the pantry. "If you kids are hungry, just say so. Don't nick stuff. It's for us all to share. We're a long way from town and we shop once a fortnight. There are plenty of plums, nashi pears and apples in the orchard. Eat those." Of course, the children denied any theft, but I know the difference between full and partly empty shelves.

Besides, I had more urgent matters on my mind. I was dithering about returning to Romania to rescue a year-old boy called Bogdan, who had a turned-in eye. His mother had given me approval to adopt him because she didn't want him, and the father was in jail for rape. It was January 1991, and I'd only been home two months with needy Romanian twins, but the thought of Bogdan stuck in his cot day after day, month after month, tore at my heartstrings. Earlier, my Romanian lawyer said I could lose all the babies if I attempted to bring all three – the twins and Bogdan – back to New Zealand together. I'd be seen as a baby seller. I was shocked at the suggestion and reluctantly agreed when told, "Forget this boy. Take the twins home and give them a good life." But when I got home and watched the baby girls starting to thrive and the joy of the other children, it didn't seem fair not to help another child whom nobody cared about. I told other couples about him when I was in Romania going through the court system, but he was passed over. He was a large, plain-looking little boy who deserved to have someone love him, and if nobody else wanted him, then I would be his mother even though the obstacles were huge.

It would mean Bryan staying home to care for our eight children while I went off to Romania on a rescue mission.

I thought I'd be away three weeks, but instead it was four long, tortuous months during which I cried every day from sheer frustration. I was thwarted by the courts and suffered incompetent lawyers as well as an attempted knife robbery. And all the while I was constantly haunted by images of abandoned babies staring blankly from their cots in orphanages. Maimed beggars with rheumy eyes trailed me and ordinary Romanians in the street implored my help to escape to another country. And I was not allowed to adopt Bogdan. Adoption rules had changed in Romania after negative media reports about some Americans adopting babies and then returning them because the children were not fitting into their new families. They were too damaged by orphanage life. I still think about that little boy.

I returned home in the middle of winter, declaring I'd never go away again, but happy to have adopted another Romanian baby girl instead. One who, although nine months younger, was almost as advanced as her twin sisters. Now we had three babies under eighteen months of age plus several youngsters and teenagers. On top of that, we had to prune 2.4 hectares of kiwifruit, which would take weeks with us doing the work ourselves. Living in an isolated part of the country, it's difficult to find skilled, trained workers, and it takes a while to get them up to scratch, so we did most of the pruning ourselves.

When I got home there was a problem. Bryan had been so busy juggling a lively family that included infant twins, fostering with social welfare, and keeping the orchard ticking, he didn't notice food disappearing from the deep freezer. But I did. It was frustrating expecting to make a nice roast dinner and finding the bag of chicken pieces or the pork chops – bought on special – gone, not to mention packets of bacon, mince, bread and mixed vegetables. "Who's stealing around here?" I thundered. "I'm taking the TV away until I get some answers, and Dad is going to hunt around for a padlock to lock up the freezer. How sad it's come to this."

An older child admitted he felt sorry for the old lady down the road who'd asked if we had any spare food. I was livid. "That Cora the Borer!" After calming down, I said to Bryan that if we employed this woman as a casual babysitter, then she would have money to buy her own food and wouldn't be training the kids to be little thieves. Bryan agreed.

"It's best to know your enemy," I said. I hoped she'd turn into a benign grandmotherly figure. We had learnt too, that she had an adult son who smoked dope and got nasty. I never knew people like this before, and I had no idea what dope looked like. Perhaps this Cora needed a few hours away from home, to be paid, and to feel valued. When you live in a small village in the country it's best to get on with your neighbours for you never know when you might need their help.

We'd just made the biggest mistake of our lives.

Cora seemed plausible, but we did wonder if she was unbalanced. We made spot visits to the house next to the orchard whilst pruning to check on our Romanian toddlers.

"She is odd," I said to Bryan, "but the babies seem fine with her. Let's keep an eye on things." Some days we couldn't work because of wet weather or meetings with Social Welfare, doctors or teachers, and cared for the toddlers ourselves. And some months went by when we could manage the orchard without extra workers, taking turns to mind the toddlers while the other tended to the thousand or more kiwifruit trees.

Through connections with friends, we had youngsters who were travelling the globe call in at our home, and some stayed for a few days or longer. We fed them and showed them around, and they helped out at home, which meant we didn't need Cora. It was a bonus to find a meal made, with lots of excited youngsters chatting and trying a new language. We lent our car to a couple of Dutch girls, but after experiencing three of our teens showing them the sights of Golden Bay, they declared they would never have children! That would have been music to my mother's ears, but I was puzzled. I thought I'd sent them off with the nicest teens!

We had an on and off relationship with this strange neighbour for a couple of years, even employing her surly adult son who was a steady worker. We were a bright, happy family with lots of visitors and lots of laughs. But I wasn't laughing when things turned nasty.

Cora began to have an influence on our youngsters. A teen admitted he felt confused and when another teen broke into our filing cabinet and stole a jar of money, we knew we were dealing with something that needed to be talked about. It escalated when a foster daughter began smoking and stealing to order.

"It's my life. You're not my real mother. I can do what I like," she snarled. She admitted Cora had told her to say that, and she was feeling slightly remorseful. She'd been told to lug up Cora's disgusting rubbish bags and toss them on our kitchen floor, heckling, "This is what Cora thinks of you."

Cora denied everything. "Keep your kids away from me," she cried when I demanded to know why my kids were stealing petrol, detergent, washing-up powder. They even used bolt cutters to unlock the poison cabinet to take weed killer for her. I was later told the cunning old lady would stand outside her run-down cottage with sugary pink buns, waiting for the kids to alight from the school bus.

"Your mother is a slut," she told them. "She can't look after so many kids. I'll foster you and give you ten dollars a week." In quiet moments when I sat on a child's bed at night, the truth was revealed. Yes, they said they were sorry, and that they wouldn't do it again.

Cora was offered a job with a local couple who had a child needing special attention, but she got fired after one day. She was negligent and allowed the little boy to sleep when he needed medication. Now she escalated her resentment.

Unbeknown to us, she enticed one of our young teens and a local woman to take her over the Takaka Hill to go shopping. Instead, she dragged the teen into the local Social Welfare office and said she wanted to foster him. He returned home defiant and threw rocks at the kitchen window. What was this woman saying to feed his rage?

I invited two sympathetic neighbours, who were having similar problems with their teen, for coffee. Cora was the common denominator. It didn't seem normal for teens to become sneaky and defiant overnight.

I rang Social Welfare, the police and a lawyer. One social worker said she seemed a harmless old lady, advising us to just keep the kids away, while another said she was horrified they were having contact with her as she was well known to the Department, but wasn't at liberty to divulge any details.

The lawyer asked if we were giving the kids enough attention and sent her a trespass order. The police investigated money she'd accepted from one of our teens. She'd hidden the stolen coins in a tree stump and had cleverly wiped off the fingerprints. Later we heard she'd stuffed a wad of $20 notes down her cleavage.

Frustrated, I rang the new Anglican minister in our district even though we weren't regular churchgoers. He circled around a spot near the clothes line and said he felt bad vibes. When Cora was babysitting our tots, she'd hung around that area. She took advantage of our good nature and often brought up her own washing to be laundered at our home. He blessed the spot and we hoped it would do the trick.

We decided to quit fostering soon after that experience and concentrate on the rest of our family. I am an upbeat person but felt damaged by the stress. Little things I'd treasured were missing, and it sent me into spasms of weeping. Why would my taped video of adopting my youngest daughter in Romania be important to her? Now my youngest child would never see footage of herself as a baby.

"I don't care if our livelihood suffers when only one of us is working in the orchard," I cried to Bryan. "I trusted her, gave her ample opportunities, but she was hell-bent on ruining our family. Well, guess what! She failed! So let's get on with life." And we did.

The orchard needed us, the children needed us, and as a couple we had to nurture each other. The drama died down, but she had been hugely damaging to us. With adopted children, when things go awry, one is unsure whether it's due to their genetics, feeling vulnerable as a teen, or the influence of their friends. Bryan and I, while busy with the orchard and children, tried to be available, but you have to create the right time to talk.

When the boys brought home runaways, I contacted their parents before allowing the child to stay for a night; I didn't know what we were dealing with. It was nice our boys had a social conscience, but we didn't want to be a haven for kids who didn't like their parents' rules.

While our involvement with Cora proved traumatic, I learned a valuable lesson. Our kids could display behaviour completely foreign to us because they had a poor start in life and lacked empathy. This woman was calculating and undermining us as parents. She'd had her own children taken away from her and felt revengeful. Once, when she shuffled past our gate, I felt like embracing her large, flabby body, saying, "I'm your friend," mostly to protect my family and lessen her hold on some of the teens. I wanted everyone to be happy and normal, but sometimes you seek the impossible. But I didn't trust her after hearing more about her background. She got the message and kept her distance. She'd been warned by the police, social workers and lawyers to stay away from the Graham children.

Bryan and I remained optimistic. Whatever happened in the future, we were parents forever. It is easy to divorce your spouse, but you can't divorce your kids. Perhaps this Cora the Borer did us a favour. She made us tougher in preparation for what lay ahead. And none of our kids, whatever they did, would be as cruelly calculating as she was.

Years later, after she died, an inner voice told me to visit her grave. We intrepidly stood in front of the headstone and read the loving inscription. She had been a mother, a storyteller and friend. Bryan said he felt nothing. I felt a fleeting second of wistfulness and relief that I could manage to step into the cemetery. A soft breeze fluttered, and the plastic flowers stared fixedly. I'd made my peace and I hoped she'd gone to a happy place.

My father's motto was: 'Conquer fear in all its guises.'

I suspect he was probably smiling from heaven too.

Chapter Nine
Puzzling behaviour

Those of us who've fostered and adopted were well aware that the child we were raising might have problems, but believed that with love, commitment and a sense of belonging, they could blossom. Bonding, for the parents involved, started when you first heard about the child available for adoption or fostering – a sweet little human being who'd had it tough. You hoped to heal, or at least lessen the hurt the child suffered, giving some thought to the mother who was relinquishing the child she created.

The children in our care seemed happy enough, so it was hard to put a finger on what was different about them compared to other children. We were devoted and attached to the children, but there was something distant about some of them. One of our foster children squirmed when I cuddled him, and another was a complete mystery. He charmed people by being cute and lovable but on occasions he flipped, and we were the target of his hidden rage. We were flummoxed.

I said to Bryan, "It would be easier to have a child with a physical disability than one who has been abused and neglected. At least you can see it and deal with it. But the way this kid is behaving is odd. It's like he's brain damaged." Earlier I had prayed, "Please God, don't give me a kid with mental problems. I'm not equipped. I don't understand brain-stuff."

I don't think God listened, or if He did, then He thought we'd cope.

And we did, but it wasn't a walk in the park because we didn't have kids like those of our friends, who boasted about their little replica's achievements. When the kids were cheerfully bantering and in good moods, it felt like a celebration. "I love you all when you're like this," I'd cry excitedly. "Bryan, the kids are being nice. Double ice creams for pudding if it lasts."

"Don't hold your breath, Mother. It's stressful being nice to you guys."

We'd never heard of RAD (Reactive Attachment Disorder) until a friend, who'd had four of his own 'genetic' or biological children and then adopted two from overseas orphanages, rang us. He'd read a book on attachment problems and reeled off a list of what he was experiencing since his adopted children had become teenagers. They appeared detached, lacked remorse, and not only were they lying and stealing but also making false allegations against their adoptive parents.

"We are committed to them," cried my friend, "but they are making life difficult and we're at our wit's end. Don't want two extra kids, do you?"

I admitted we were having similar problems. One lad in our care had a traumatic infancy and was shuffled around many foster homes as a toddler. He had chronic ear problems and poor concentration. Whenever we signed him up for a new activity, he would go a few times, then give up, saying it was boring. Now a teen, he was heading down the wrong track and he simply didn't care. Often, we'd have to down tools in the orchard and drive to the school to talk about yet another misdemeanour or attend meetings because he was being stood down.

"There is nothing happening at home to make him unhappy," I said defensively. "I don't know why he does these things. It's a mystery." He was restless, had learning difficulties, and a preoccupation with guns, knives and sharks that was worrying. He smirked at the threat of expulsion or being taken for a visit to the police, and he had no qualms about damaging property or stealing. Other times, he was cheerful, effusive and likeable. What was causing this spasmodic eruption of unacceptable behaviour that was becoming more frequent? Was it due to crazy hormones? Perhaps angry flashbacks about his earlier life? At first, we thought it just a ghastly teen stage and that he'd grow out of it.

We'd heard of ADD (Attention Deficit Disorder) but there was more to him than that. He became decidedly sneaky and reckless and had a phenomenal record of fortuitously finding articles such as money on the road, watches, jewellery – anything small. And he was generous with stuff he found or owned. "He'll grow out of it" and "All kids steal," acquaintances remarked.

He seemed to enjoy trouble and associated with a wide range of people (no fear of strangers or status), including older teens known to the police. It was a relief when the lad was caught red-handed, committing a solo criminal offence. The police talked to him sternly, while the victims wanted to belt him and the school wanted to expel him. Various people, including community and social workers, gave him the idea that he just needed time away from his family – meaning us – the cause of his misbehaviours. The lad was apparently just 'acting out'.

When an exasperated teacher called him 'potential jailbait' and a family doctor said the lad was heading for a crash, we arranged for a referral to a paediatric psychiatrist.

Meanwhile, we ordered and read books on Attachment Disorder, and gasped. The lad ticked all the boxes: lack of cause-and-effect thinking, nonsense chatter, no impulse control, affectionate towards other people but not us (me in particular), plus blatant lies and being light-fingered. He argued, blamed others for his misdeeds and threw wobblies.

"Think my head's a bit crazy at times," he admitted. "Dunno why I do this stuff."

We read that the bond necessary for a child to learn to trust had either been broken or its formation interrupted when his needs weren't met as a baby; therefore, his condition was like a brain injury.

The specialist said, "Of course he's got Attachment Disorder," but that the child was too old to try the controversial 'holding therapy'. Although we were reluctant to let our foster son go, we were advised that he should be boarded with a smaller family closer to the therapy venue. Social Welfare was involved, so we asked them to help us locate suitable accommodation. Bad move. They turned his behavioural issue into a Care and Protection scrap, completely ignoring the diagnoses and the many years we had spent raising him. Like the fiasco with the babysitter, we felt more hurt by the Department's treachery and incompetence than we did by the lad's behaviour. Our battle had just started. We wanted Social Welfare to recognise the disorder he had been diagnosed with. And so did other parents in similar circumstances, as I later found out through networking once we all had computers and could share information.

For readers curious about the outcome – after the lad left our care, he located his birth mother, but it didn't stop his downward spiral. He contacted us some years later and visited us with his wife and baby. He went on to have other relationships and offspring as well. He needs medication for depression, but he is highly likeable and generous. His original anger didn't feel personal, just a primeval cry erupting from a damaged past.

We were determined to enjoy our teenagers, whether adopted or fostered, because everyone has niceness in them, so we'd seek out the good bits and reward that. We had a Pollyanna outlook on life and were often the ambulance at the bottom of the cliff. One of our social workers admitted that she thought we, of all people, could cope and not buckle under pressure.

One of the troubles we encountered was the new unsupported Youth Benefit that was offered in the mid-90s, allowing sixteen- or seventeen-year-olds to claim a weekly benefit payment if they couldn't live with their parents and met certain terms and conditions. It was understandable if school-age teens had a severe breakdown at home and needed to be boarded elsewhere. The new bill, however, caused a flurry of youngsters to claim that they were neglected and didn't get on with their parents, and therefore need to live elsewhere, even if that was untrue. Parents weren't informed because of privacy rules, and youths were thrilled to get free money and a taste of freedom.

The new legislation was being misused and we, like many other couples, felt our parenting was being questioned and undermined. We made a fuss because we didn't want our other teens following suit and leaving home, but later when the legislation was tightened, that was an obstacle we no longer needed to worry about.

"If anything is bothering you, talk about it," we urged. Since we were fostering, we asked visiting social workers for advice, but they didn't have all the answers either.

At one stage our back lawn looked like a caravan park. Some of the teens slept outside to get away from younger siblings. They loved their outdoor accommodation. The twin girls scored too. A young German couple banged urgently on our back door one day, claiming their campervan had broken down in the middle of the road, and that we could have it for free if we towed it off the road. They needed to travel over the hill to Nelson to catch a plane. Luckily, they were given a ride by a sympathetic motorist. The twins thought it was the best present ever, as they could listen to loud music without disturbing anyone, although I did spot checks to make sure village boys weren't snuggled up with them. "It's just the cat," they squealed as I flashed a torch at night. Sometimes the grateful cat sprung out from under the covers like an escaped convict.

"I'd go off my head having all those kids," said a visiting adult.

"Oh, it can be fun at times," I assured the guest.

"But how do you stay sane?"

"Sane? That's debatable," I laughed. "Two things, well three really. First, Bryan is my anchor. If the kids are rowdy, he'll don earphones and listen to the national radio. Sometimes he chuckles to himself. It drives the kids crazy. He's not going to listen to negative behaviour. Second, we have the orchard – our livelihood. The vines need attention just like the kids. We love working out there and when we down tools at dusk, there is a satisfying feeling of achievement. Third, my secret is pretending I'm running a mental institution. If a kid is being obnoxious, I think to myself, 'This is temporary madness; it's not about me but their yukky hormones. Tomorrow is another day.' "

Some of the fun times we had were when the boys brought home their mates. I liked chatting with them and found them respectful and polite. My mother used to say, "You set the standard" and "Don't sink to the lowest common denominator." She'd struggled with my brother as she'd made sacrifices to get him into the Royal Navy. He saw life differently – the waves, his mates and being in the 'now'. He was hell-bent on doing what he wanted, instead of pleasing our parents. This was a big lesson for me. Single-handedly you can't easily change a person's viewpoint, especially not that of a teen. It is stressful and time absorbing to try, and parents need to have a life too. My mother may not have died from disappointment, but it certainly clouded her happiness. She wanted her only biological son to have a brilliant naval career and to be launched on the path to success. My parents wondered if he'd inherited some odd, foreign throwback gene.

One harassed foster mother remarked about her insolent charges: "The trouble is some of these kids have PPG."

"Er, what is that?"

"Piss poor genes."

I was happy to mother the children who came into our home. And since they weren't biologically ours, I learned not to take remarks personally. It helped taking myself out of the equation, and it simplified things. Bryan was Mr Cool. He was usually the good guy.

"I'm so lucky to have you," I hugged him. "I couldn't manage on my own. In fact, I wouldn't have this family if it wasn't for you."

He shrugged. The kids were okay, bit problematic at times, but we could deal with that. "With teens," he advised, "it's softly, softly."

When the kids brought friends home, I was keen to engage. They were using my coffee, sugar and biscuit treats, and there was a chance they'd stay overnight if they had a falling out with parents. I'd tell them they appeared to be a nice person, then ask a few details and go from there. I didn't believe everything that spouted from their juvenile mouths because I'd have phoned the parents if I recognised a name. It was fun to banter with some of our lads' mates.

"Your mum is so cool," they said. Endorphins rush to your head when long-limbed youths straddle the couch while telling witty jokes, some a bit blue in tone. Since they were being so *nice*, I relayed a risqué ditty I remembered:

Old Mother Hubbard went to the cupboard
To fetch her poor doggie a bone.
But when she bent over
Rover took over and gave her a bone of his own.

My son looked startled while his mates fell about laughing. "I'm sorry to be so rude," I admitted, "but I'm trying to bond with you."

"Know any more, Mrs G?"

I became more circumspect when I heard one of the lads got told off for telling the ditty to sniggering boys on a school camp.

Sometimes you need to nip things in the bud. When I spied the teen girls curled up on the couch giggling over a book, I was suspicious. Some of the words sounded saucy. "Give me that sex book," I said, swiping it.

"Mother! We're reading a cookbook – about making hot cross buns."

"Oh," I said faintly, and did a little dance while reading out snippets from the book.

The girls and their friends began laughing uncontrollably. "Oh Mummy, you're so funny and cute. Stop it! We're going to wet our pants." It was a prolonged joyful bonding occasion. A treasured moment until, a short while later, confusion reigned again with some snarling thrown in.

"You were happy before," I reminded a daughter. "We were laughing. We loved each other. You thought I was funny."

She eyeballed me. "We weren't laughing because you were funny, Mother. We were laughing because you were pathetic."

When the kids were young, they'd excitedly greet visitors and drag them in for a cup of tea.

"Mum bought some chocolate biscuits. Where'd you hide them, Mum?" I couldn't admit they were in the wardrobe wrapped in Bryan's silky undies, and that I needed keys to unlock our room. How can you say that to a visiting salesman or a man of the cloth? Once the treasured biscuits appeared, sneaky little fingers would each snatch a couple, leaving an empty plate for the guest and me entertaining someone I'd not invited.

"Don't worry," said the guest. "They're only kids. And I'm on a diet."

No, I thought. *They're impolite little so and so's, taking advantage of squirming Mummy.* In my day it was manners and FHB (family holds back), not grab and run.

If Bryan was in a back paddock, I'd send a tribe of noisy whistling kids to look for him while I was engaging with pedlars selling insurance, fertilizer, brushes and irrigation pipes. So many visitors traipsed through our back door, from streaky-nosed tots with solo mums puffing on ciggies and yuppy salesmen with big attitude, who were probably debt-ridden, to hopefuls like Jehovah Witnesses whom I couldn't turn away. They might have the key to salvaging a teen, for they at least didn't do drugs or drink, and God knows, we were all for purity – which was asking for the impossible.

The lost and lonely found their way to our home, the rich and the poor, the needy and not so, the wannabees, the losers, friends, relatives, villagers, tourists needing the loo or petrol or water or phone directions; even those who wanted to strangle, or praise, or rescue our kids. You name it. It was called 'at-home entertainment'. And we enjoyed them, including those who stole from us, but Bryan said they would come right. Some of these visitors had been to jail, but we looked upon it as their learning experience and we liked the nice part of that person. Besides, I could locate treats as a reward if I could get the low-down from them on what it was like in jail.

On my travels through exotic countries in my youth, I hadn't had the jail experience, except for a brief spell in lockup in France, and was up for inside info. I wanted to know what it felt like being incarcerated – the clanging of heavy metal, sadistic lady wardens with hourglass hips clutching a bunch of keys, peepholes and deprivation. I could always source another sugary treat if the person was entertaining. Perhaps even whistle for the kids to come inside for a bit of education and another biscuit. It might save them choosing incarceration as a career choice.

One middle-aged woman, who had problems with the bottle, dropped in on us now and then, crying, "I need a mother right now." I'd give her a hug and a cup of tea, although she asked for a beer.

Crikey, I'm not much older than you, I thought, as she wept about her miserable life of addiction and loss. How do people get like this? I would muse. Did it go back to poor parenting, abuse, hardship? Or was it a genetic trait mixed up with some trauma? The brain is mercurial. Some people rise above misery and some keep floundering. I couldn't turn this woman with the whiffy breath away even though others wanted nothing to do with her. I would be friendly and available, but I did have boundaries. There was to be no long tirade from her at our evening meal as that was sacred family-time.

When Bryan had to go to hospital to have a prostate operation, we could see that the teens were worried. He was their rock and I merely an outcrop, but I was glad they had feelings. The night before he drove over the hill to get his prostate sorted in hospital, we both frantically worked in the orchard. I was following behind with a wheelbarrow, bopping and bending, and I stumbled. I didn't notice the gnawing pain in my body until after Bryan was being cosseted in hospital because I was busy answering the phone calls we received, some even from overseas well-wishers. "He's still alive," I wept. "Thanks so much for caring."

When the sciatic pain struck me in the middle of the night, it was excruciating. Hubby was an invalid in a hospital, so no soothing backrubs for me. "Shuddup," screeched a voice from another room, but Natasha, one of our Romanian twins, was alarmed. She jumped into my bed and massaged my back and cried when I did. The pain came in bursts and was so violent I could hardly breathe. I told her not to ring her brothers or a doctor. Morphine would have been nice, but we were too far from medical amenities and it was too late at night to seek help.

After Bryan came home to a soldier's welcome, the recipient of flowers and food parcels, the visiting nurse saw me wincing in pain and said I needed physiotherapy.

"What is the pain score from one to ten?" asked the caring physiotherapist. I told her it was four point three when she was administering therapeutic kindness, but otherwise much higher.

During the physiotherapy session, I heard a voice in the next cubicle which sounded familiar, so I boldly called out, "Are you my son, the one who had an accident on the fishing boat when your foot went one way and your body the other on a slippery deck?"

It was.

"Gee, Mum's embarrassing," muttered Miss Thirteen. "She could have been talking to a stranger in that cubicle – you know, stranger-danger." Bryan told her I'd had a codeine fix. "Can you take us to school now? Otherwise she'll want us to feel sorry for her."

I learnt two valuable lessons. No teenage pain and barbs could be as bad as the physical pain I'd endured, and that my beautiful Natasha *did* demonstrate empathy when she crawled into my bed.

It seems strange how you get revelations while prostrate on a pristine, hard bed, not unlike being at a morgue.

I eagerly looked forward to my next physio visit.

"My friends want you to adopt them."

Chapter Ten

Family life

I didn't expect raising a large family would be easy, but it couldn't be too hard, could it?

The children had all the basics needed to make them happy, with two committed parents to nurture and guide them, although puberty changes the rules in this regard. That cute daughter who once ran up to me excitedly when collecting her from school, now said, "When you come to get me, stand outside the gate, and don't hitch your pants up to your tits," adding threateningly, "or I will *look* embarrassed!"

Raising a family meant rules and a timetable. If either of us became indisposed, we missed having the other for backup. Bryan refused to start dinner if the kids had messed up the kitchen. He'd put on headphones, read the paper and sip a glass of red while they moaned and blamed everyone else. I'd lie in bed with a migraine, fretting. Will the kids starve? Have they done their homework and their music practice?

"Stay in bed," he ordered. "I'm doing things my way." And it worked. He helped the children with their maths and reminded them to clean their teeth, but if they didn't do either, they would suffer the consequences. The onus was on them. Like all mothers, I wondered if

I was being too caring by trying to rescue them from foolish mistakes they'd regret.

Few of the kids had dental fillings until after they had left home, and when an adult son complained about his expensive dental treatment, he said it was my fault for not having sweets on tap when he lived with us. His reasoning was that if we'd provided them liberally, he wouldn't have craved them later and overindulged. I privately thought that was baloney and wondered whether he shouldn't have become a lawyer, one dealing in litigation. We didn't condone weed, booze or cigarettes, although some of the teens became sneaky about using these substances with their mates.

When I was growing up, our parents, like many others, had a display cabinet in which the cut-crystal sherry decanter twinkled goldenly, surrounded by elegant glasses – Swedish or Venetian. Wealthier families had a sideboard full of spirits, with perhaps a Qantas flag poking up among the toothpicks. It was an outward show of sophistication. An ostentatious display had foreign labels, like Martini and other Italian vermouth. An Advocaat and cherry-brandy mix was many a teen's undoing at an office party. Imported alcohol conferred more status than did Aussie-made. It never occurred to me to swig from my parents' small but prized booze collection, although my brother topped up Mum's sherry bottle with water now and then. She thought it seemed rather diluted but never accused us outright.

Times had changed when it came to bringing up our teens. They had a voice. If they behaved like idiots, it must be because they had uncaring parents (according to neighbours or gullible social workers), which we strongly disputed. We tried to lessen opportunities for them to inflict silly harm on us and on themselves, so we hid grown-up stuff from them, such as liquor and cash, in a locked filing cabinet, and made sure our bedroom was locked as well. Occasionally, some of the children were tempted to twiddle the keyhole to get into our room and jemmy open the filing cabinet. I went ballistic when this happened because the trust had been broken. Theft is theft however big or small, and if we found out who the culprit was, they had to work it off with paid chores.

"What's gotten into these kids? Are we raising thieves?" But hubby thought it normal for teens to be trying it on. "It's not! I never stole from my parents. Did you?" Bryan said of course not, that it had never occurred to him. "Board meeting in bed when the kids are asleep. Urgent," I said, and hubby smiled at my thoughtful invitation. After a long working day in the orchard, cooking, homework and the usual lively family interaction, we sometimes deferred discussions until the following day. After a good night's sleep, yesterday's indiscretion didn't seem quite so black and white.

After the babysitting fiasco, we padlocked the deep freezers and the pantry when teens, foster or otherwise, became opportunist or even socialist. We were seen as the Land of Plenty, while others were needy. For some of the children, it was an excuse to stay the weekend with a solo mum in return for a parcel of food taken from our home. I said we didn't mind helping, for we had surplus garden vegetables, several fruit trees and an abundance of kiwifruit.

"They don't eat that sort of food," was the reply. "They eat real food like bacon and noodles."

I reminded our teens that some parents might be more liberal than we were, but they were stuck with us, and they could do what they liked when they left home.

"We love you and want you to be safe." And often they agreed after they'd gone away for a weekend to a home with lax attitudes. I was not going to be their weed-smoking, partying, good-time mama. I was nice caring mama who had teens who resented rules when their hormones went AWOL. In my head, I was 'partying '60s girl', who had imaginary fun and a life, and was almost Liberace's wife – if he hadn't been dead. Now I was Responsible Mum of God-knows how many and co-captain of a ship threatening a *Mutiny on the Bounty* incident.

Try as hard as you can, as a mother you can never get it right all the time. There are good and bad times, and your maternal heart discards most of the hurtful memories and latches onto the sweeter moments. It's called self-preservation. Teens are mercurial because they do things backwards. From being delightful little butterflies, they metamorphosise, not exactly into grubs, but close enough, depending how you feel (especially with respect to the state of their bedrooms). Comedy is created from the outcome of teenagers' thinking because their thought processes can be seriously deranged. "I love teenagers," gushed one British comedian. "They're so passionate." I must have missed something here because I'd hoped my teens would be passionate about being nice to mummy, teachers and mankind.

In the '50s and '60s, mothers warned naughty offspring, "Wait until your father gets home," expecting Dad to carry out corporal punishment, which didn't help the bonding process with sons who were left quivering with anticipation. Fathers were more remote then. Our kids were lucky, I reflected, to have a gentle but resilient dad who worked from home, and I was lucky to have a hubby who was actively involved in their upbringing. I didn't have to explain anything to him if a kid had a meltdown; we'd both witnessed it.

Both our mothers had already passed on when it came to us wanting to deport a teen or two to Grandmother's home for a holiday. We were on our own. My elderly father said he wanted peace and quiet but sent money for birthdays, apportioned according to age, so a thirteen-year-old got thirteen dollars. If the kid had been giving us grief, he sent a birthday card without money enclosed and wrote in shaky handwriting 'honour thy mother and father'. The disappointed recipient never found it profound in the least.

"Breakfast is the most important meal of the day," our mothers instilled in us. And, "Never talk to a man on an empty stomach," they said. Wise words.

"Bacon and eggs and unhealthy (white) toast for breakfast, if you've done your homework, and get up straight away with a nice smile on your face tomorrow," I'd offer the kids as they clambered up the staircase, hitching up their pyjamas (they don't make elastic like they did in the olden days). *Poor little mites needed a bit of hope*, I laughed to myself. When dawn broke, Bryan lit the coal range, a heater was turned on in the kitchen, and the sizzling smells enticed a thunder of feet down the stairs. They'd made their own lunches the night before, but if forgotten, I'd sneak in slabs of bread and some luncheon sausage because I didn't want to do a 50 kilometre round trip to deliver lunch, or for them to get into the habit of telling the teachers that Mum doesn't provide lunch, and a bill then being sent to us at the end of each term for emergency pies at the tuck shop.

"You haven't had breakfast," I cried to a teenage son as he was dashing off to catch the school bus. "You can't work without fuel."

"Yes, I have," he said, grabbing his backpack. "I got up at midnight and ate breakfast because I knew I wouldn't get up in time in the morning." How's that for teen logic!

After the children caught the school bus, armed with warnings to behave and be nice to the driver or their life wouldn't be worth living, hubby and I worked on our orchard, sometimes together, sometimes separately in different blocks, depending on what workers we had and what needed doing. When the air brakes on the long, white school bus expressed a noisy sigh at 4 pm, we downed tools to greet the adolescents. Often, we wished we'd waited. Their pent-up frustration from being cooped in a bus for an hour, conflicts at school and uneaten sandwiches, usually led to a noisy, anguished hullabaloo. It could be heard a couple of kilometres away if you weren't hearing impaired, and some of the vocal contents could be X-rated.

"Make love, not war," I'd implore above the jostling and jeering. "This kitchen is a place of love and peace. Daddy and I have had a big day in the orchard. We're tired." Typically, a ratbag kid would sneer that we don't know what real work is. Every time he sees us, one of the kids said, our arms are up in the air, and he mimicked 'hanging-out washing' syndrome. "Our hands have to be above our heads because we're pruning," I snarled, but within ten minutes the kitchen would be in a shambles and everyone cheerful. Bryan and I would head back to work for another hour, saying that anyone who cleaned up would get extra pocket money.

Occasionally the children alighted from the school bus with other kids, so it was confusing when I had unexpected visitors at home. It prompted them to ask, "Are all those kids yours?"

"A couple aren't mine, I think," I'd say, and wait for a "Which are yours?" from any guests we might have.

"Hard to tell," I'd laugh. "I'll feed them and sort out the niceties later."

"His mother doesn't want him," a teen might confess after the feeding frenzy, referring to a stray kid.

"Of course she does. Is he being a bit of a dick?" (I know teen lingo.)

"Sort of, but she's not like you."

"Really? Do you quite like us?" I'd ask, surprised.

"Yeah, I was only being a dick when I said I didn't," a teen admitted.

"Group hug," I said. "Love, love, love."

"It's alright, Mum. Don't be a dick about it."

When you're a mother you are a chameleon. What once worked may need modification, such as in the case of mealtimes. I tried a new experiment: DOA – Dinner on Arrival. It worked for a while, but then the children got hungry again at normal mealtime. It was annoying coming in from work early to attend to meals, but my brain said, "Calm down sacrificial Mother; their feeding needs are greater than trying to squeeze in an extra hour to make a living in the orchard."

Once Bryan and I trooped in together to herald the arrival of the school children, but our pleasant smiles turned to frowns when they bickered at the table. "Please be nice," I implored, but my plea fell on deaf ears. "Daddy," I said turning to the children's father, "I know what the kids are doing. They're trying to split us up."

The kids looked mildly interested. "Well, it's not going to work because, um, Daddy and I are in love." (I remembered that hilarious line from *Muriel's Wedding*). I grabbed Bryan's hand. "Let's run away," and we dashed out past the walnut tree and through the myriad of kiwifruit vines, hearing distant sounds of "They're only joking" and "Come back. We love you." We ducked down near the gurgling creek at the back of the property, breathing heavily and laughing like lunatics. The kids found us, of course, and we were all back on track as a family within minutes.

It helps if one kid is behaving normally because then you know that you haven't damaged a precious life by your parenting. Bullying is rife in school these days despite efforts to clamp down on it. It happened to our kids, and we hoped none of them were bullies, but suspected a couple probably were after they'd been bullied themselves. The local school taught mediation and we practised that at home. Our fourth son had dyslexic tendencies but was outstanding with regard to communication skills, and his younger siblings looked up to him.

One afternoon, as we were digging trenches and laying cables for irrigation after a vicious frost had wiped out most of our kiwifruit, Natasha, one of the twins, yelled urgently. A mate at school was selling his PlayStation and she'd told him she'd buy it. "It's only $400," she screamed above the noise of the tractor. "I'll pay you back."

"Seriously? $400!" I gulped. "No way. What a rip-off."

"Well, last year he was selling it for $180 and you said I could buy it if it was less."

"Hell's bells," I said, "$400 is heaps more than $180."

"I said $100, Mother. Are you deaf? I think it's a rip-off too."

"Oh, so you mean $100, not $400? That's better."

"It's not worth it," she admitted. "But I want it! I want it! I've been the best behaved in the family. I didn't steal and I done – I mean – I did the dishes."

"Offer him $80."

"What, $80?" she shrieked. "No way. I want to give him $120."

"You don't offer a person the max. You start low and work your way up. Have you been skipping maths classes at school?"

"Josh wants $400, I mean $100, but I reckon it's not worth it. I want to give him $120. It's got seventeen games to go with it, and he paid $30 for one of the games out of his milking money."

I can't stand prolonged confrontation.

"Hurry, Mum. It's got to be a cash cheque. He's biking to Cubs soon. Puleeeeze. I promise I'll let you play with it." (As if I'd want to!)

"I'm not happy writing a cash cheque. Josh could lose it," I said, but with all the begging and cajoling we traipsed back to the house. "So, do I write out 'cash', or what?"

"Don't be silly, Mummy. You have to write his name. But don't write his stepfather's name."

When Natasha got the PlayStation (a handover took place in the dark), I spied her clunking a pencil in the remote to get it going.

"So where's the seventeen games?"

She ripped open the black case and counted nine.

"It's still worth it. And, by the way, Mum, he wants the case back. He did heaps of milking to earn that case, so don't you dare ring him. It only cost $100 or $400 or whatever. Just money."

"Take it back," I said. "You've been ripped-off. You should have borrowed it on trial for a night."

Son Tristan and hubby emerged looking tired and hungry. "You're not returning that to Josh," Tristan said. "I know his family and I won't hear the end of it. You made a deal."

Bryan agreed.

Just as I was wondering what sort of family I'd inherited, Natasha's twin squealed excitedly. "It's working. We shoved a fork down the remote bit and it's going. Come and have a look. You'll think it's fun."

In the dark, half a dozen kids were draped around the new acquisition peering at blurry images on the screen with the fork being moved adroitly. The cat was curled up on the Holden blanket, and the room reeked of fuzzy mirth and bonhomie. I didn't know whether to feel confused, complacent or elated. Asking, "Have you done your homework?" might tip the balance.

What is the price of peace? There was no world leader available from whom to seek advice in our remote neck of the woods. I worried about homework, but Bryan said if they didn't complete it, then the onus was on them. I remembered the saying, 'You can lead a horse to water but you can't make it drink.' One horsey daughter said she knew another saying, 'No use shutting the stable door once the horse has bonked.' Stifling my laughter, I said she was nearly right, but it was actually *bolted*.

"Same diff," she shrugged. She had a point: The end result was the same.

There was one unspoken pact Bryan and I had made. We would not be bowed or bent by temporary teenage insanity. An enlightened mother I had come to know, one who had adopted four Russian children and worked in the adoption field, said the hope was always that adoptive parents would keep their sense of humour and look after themselves and wait for sanity to return once the teenage years had passed. Part of the problem, she thought, was that the adoptive parents had been 'good', well-behaved teens themselves, so become alarmed and get a fright when their adopted teens act up and are not quite as good.

Happy times for me were lounging around with the teen daughters, eating home-made pizza and telling jokes or yarns. Their favourite story, apparently true, was about a man who saved a young lad from drowning. The hapless lad had skidded off the road into a lake late at night and was rescued because the passing driver noticed car lights shining in the freezing water. Friends were cheering the hero when there was a knock at the door.

"Are you the man who rescued my son?" asked the woman.

"Yes, ma'am," replied the hero proudly.

"Well then, where's his hat!"

My sister, who lives down the valley on a similar lifestyle block, could make me feel better whenever a kid had been obnoxious. She has that Aussie bluntness that is refreshing – and she's entertaining. Lately, she's been free to travel. At an airport in Thailand, in a queue to go through Customs, an official demanded, "Give me your body part, Madam."

"No," she said.

"Madam! I want your body part!"

"You can't have it," she said, feeling afraid.

A passenger behind my sister tapped her on the shoulder and explained. "He is asking for your boarding pass."

Teens can make you smile for the wrong reasons.

I was thrilled when a son, for the first time, bought me a birthday present, saying, "It cost me five dollars."

"How lovely," I squeaked. "Two packets of incense sticks!"

Soon after, the son sidled up to me and asked, "Mum, do you reckon I could have a couple of those incense sticks? My room smells a bit stale."

It was never dull living with this lively family. When I was a teen, my mother quoted: "Two men looked out from their prison bars. One saw mud, the other saw stars."

We chose to see stars, believing our teens would turn out to be respectable, decent people.

Fingers crossed!

"Yuk! Only healthy food in here. We'll starve."

Chapter Eleven

The orchard

"Kiwifruit is the way to go," said Bryan when he became disenchanted with being a teacher. While our ten-acre block in Golden Bay wasn't ideally situated, since it lost the early and late sun because of the hills, it was possible for us to grow kiwifruit. Once we agreed to change our lifestyle, it was a flurry of activity preparing the ground, jamming in posts and polythene pipes, seeking plants and root stock, putting in shelter belt trees and jacking up a watering system. It was dawn to dusk work. We lived off our savings for a few years until the fruit was marketable.

Growing kiwifruit was like raising kids. Some vines looked needy, requiring extra effort to help them thrive, while others were vigorous, requiring extra pruning to tame them.

When the vines were doubling, then trebling their crop, we needed help for winter pruning. None of our children seemed especially keen to learn and be put on the payroll, although they loved harvest time. We'd been managing on our own, except over harvest, but then it came to the crunch.

"Let's bite the bullet and find pruners." We rang the employment agency hoping for experienced pruners. Alas – none available. They had been snapped up by larger orchards.

"Just send anyone on your books then. Anyone keen to train, and we'll pay above the award rate and petrol money, plus a bonus if they bring someone along in their car."

All sorts of people rang, from yobbos to backpackers, and one year, a one-handed, elderly person. We had to get the winter pruning done before the sap ran in spring but were often beset by wet days. One guy was keen to work, saying he had no experience, and could he bring his mate? They were from a Buddhist retreat. I hoped they had brawn and energy and were not prostrating people limp on eating limpets. Bryan shrugged. "Two workers, let's see how they go."

Next day, when the guys – suitably dressed for the Arctic Circle – turned up in a shiny grey car, I gave a piercing whistle that meant 'danger, visitors or kids running amok'. I hoped hubby was in the shed oiling the pruning tools and not meditating in the outside lav to get onside with the new pruners. Luckily, he was doing the former, but he never hears my two-fingered whistle because he's wearing those jolly purple radio-earmuffs.

"We've got two handsome dudes here," I announced. "They look smart and keen. Let's get the show on the road." And we trundled out the wheelbarrow loaded with pruning shears, snips, leather pouches, black clips, chainsaw and loppers. After giving a demo under the vines, I warned the shorter guy with the Rastafarian hairdo it would be wise to keep his hat on, explaining that birds might mistakenly want to nest in his dreadlocks, or his plaits might lasso themselves around an overhead wire, short-circuiting his life. I didn't know if ACC would cover us for that.

Bryan seemed impressed by these young men asking intelligent questions, while I puzzled over the movements of the shorter guy's Nordic-looking companion who made frequent visits to our northern-facing cryptomeria trees. Was he fascinated by our green shelter belt trees? No, it was Mother Nature at work, and I recalled that people who meditate have marvellous alimentary canals and rapid digestive systems.

"Half an hour break for lunch," I called out, and put on the kettle. I found unhealthy slabs of bread and cheese for hubby and me to gnaw on. Meanwhile, our backyard had been transformed to a yoga delight. Our two workers bopped and bent before gently nibbling from a plastic container of saffron-coloured, coagulated porridgy globs – not unlike the contents of a newborn baby's nappy. "Crikey, I'm feeling guilty. We should go on that health kick," I said, and we hid the white bread. For show, we resurrected the brown, grainy one from the deep freezer. "You guys want a cuppa?" I called out, but they said they didn't like to eat and drink at the same time. I marvelled and felt ashamed. I could eat, drink and yap at the same time.

By mid-afternoon soft rain started falling. We stoically ploughed on as snow plunged onto the peaks of the surrounding mountains. I was looking forward to a pick-me-up beverage at the end of the day, knowing our workers had a long journey ahead, halfway up a mountain to their teepee and damp sleeping bags. Bonding began when I jollied them along with tales of my own meanderings through countries once quaint but now dangerous and less travelled. When rain began falling quite viciously, Bryan said, "Early pack up time. Write down your hours in the book."

"Such lovely lads," I murmured at the end of a long day. "They were respectful, focussed and didn't have a woman-thing like some we've hired."

The phone's message recorder was loaded with enquiries from people wanting work. "Weed out the Poms and some of the locals," I said. "Woman's intuition." But Bryan said no, they all deserve a chance. Suddenly it all became very clear. We didn't need to travel. Just ring up the employment agency and nine times out of ten those looking for work would be foreigners. We could learn about their country, even share recipes. It was like having a free trip overseas while enjoying home comforts. When the two new workers from the Buddhist retreat turned up with orphaned pet lambs, we didn't mind because being vegetarians, they wouldn't eat them. Now, instead of doing yoga in the garden at lunchtime, they were male nurses anxiously thrusting red-nippled bottles of milk down the throats of their new family.

In my day, workers were keen to have a job and arrived minutes earlier than required to impress their employer. Although we shook hands and greeted our new workers, few arrived on the dot of nine, making us feel we should be grateful for employing them. So it was a shock and a surprise when a caveman pulled up in his van and strode towards the house. He looked unkempt, with a beard and steely, matted hair that would have made good insulation for house renovations. An elongated, spotty lad, baby-faced with a vermilion beanie, followed behind. "Hark," I said to myself, "we are going to be working with Chalk and Cheese."

Bryan signed them in and gave them a rundown on pruning, but by the time he finished explaining the life cycle of the ruddy kiwifruit, it was almost smoko break. I left it to him because mostly men applied for the work, and they don't want to listen to a female. I thought they'd bond better with Bryan, and that was not only good for his self-esteem (since the teens had made a dent in it) but it also freed me up to work slavishly and set the pace.

"I think the neighbour's billy goat has escaped again," I said to hubby while he was giving his techy talk. We all looked around before realisation set in. Poignantly, it was emanating from the caveman, and if he hadn't been so old, I would have adopted him and given him rich gifts of shampoo and bath salts, perhaps a spot of sheep drench.

When you are working in close confines with strangers, there is an unspoken bonding taking place. I switched on the radio to serve as a third party. No talking, just connecting with the misery of the outside world whenever the news came on. And you feel happy, the sun is shining, and everyone benefits. Our fruit will get sold on the world market and the workers can expect weekly payments.

Some workers surprised us. Billy goat was an example. Some may not have employed him, but since we were used to lunatic teens, we'd give him a chance. By the end of the first day we hadn't spoken yet, but he wasn't surly, and I felt life may have dealt him a harsh blow. Being aloof and pleasant was all he wanted from us because he was a keen worker. Guys like that gave me pause for thought. How can you make his life better? Bryan said that by us giving him a job, it had made him feel valued. Society can be unfair and judgmental.

While pruning you can't help musing. If stranded on a desert island with this eyes-averting pruner who was reluctant to lather and preen, and whose clothes whiffed recycled mice bedding, would one succumb to carnal pleasures? Perhaps seek out this feculent odour as a source of solace and comfort? Funny how 'no way, Jose' gives way to 'familiarity' syndrome, where shock turns to acceptance and a tenuous relationship, a bit like some relationships with kids these days.

Bryan believes everyone has a bit of goodness in them, while I ask the hard questions, such as – Is he slightly deranged? Perhaps allergic to women? Did he get roughed up as a kid? Plus, I'd throw in bipolar disorder, attachment disorder, ADHD and the DDTs. Son No. 4 said, "Reckon he's real shy. His brain's okay, but he's real hard to know." I wanted to correct his English, like my mother would have: "Say *really*, not real." But I generously kept my mouth shut.

After several weeks, there was something different in the air. I had to tell Bryan, but I couldn't share my insight immediately because one of our sons was revving a chainsaw outside the kitchen door, blocking out the noise of vociferous hungry teens and cats. "I'll share it with you in bed," I promised.

I ventured towards the boudoir where hubby was reading a farming magazine, looking freshly scrubbed and expectant. His side of the family get heart attacks, so I warned him I had something profound to say, but first I needed to check on the teens. One was snoring her head off with Eminem blasting from a stereo, her clothes flung around her room in slatternly disarray. The fuzzy whiff was warm and familiar, a watered-down version of the new worker. Another's room reeked of smelly socks but there was no twin in sight. I located her downstairs in her twin's bed. Four heads lay sleeping on the pillow. It went twin, cat, twin, cat. I was relieved it wasn't twin, village boy, twin, town boy, and smiled in the darkness at the sweetness.

"You know that new worker, Mr Recluse? Guess where his eyes were looking?" I said, cuddling up to Bryan.

"In the biscuit tin?"

Suddenly there was a sharp rap on the door. "Hey, Dad. How do you make rockets and mini bombs?"

If a teen wants to connect, you can't say, "Go away, son, Dad and I are having a board meeting." You embrace the moment even if it's not convenient.

When the lad left, I flung my hands under the blankets and squeezed something large and warm and yanked it up – a hot-water bottle. "Jeeze, thought you put on a bit of weight there for a mo," I said, relieved. "About the new worker, there's been a breakthrough. He made eye contact! Maybe he hasn't got Attachment Disorder. Why do you think the Good Lord sent him to us?"

Hubby is pragmatic. "To make you grateful you have me?"

And since his birthday was coming up, I said that he'd hit the nail on the head.

During harvest one year, an old Aussie boyfriend and his mate came for an overnight stay. We hadn't seen each other in decades, and I was a tad nervous. "Have you been peeking," he asked as we eyed each other soon after they arrived.

"Yes," I blushed. "And you're looking good."

"What do you mean?" He looked confused. He meant had we been 'picking' our kiwifruit. Good old Aussie accent. Generously, I told Bryan he could invite anyone from his past to our home if they were mentally impaired and not too pretty.

"We have enough at home," he quipped.

The teens reminded me I was an embarrassment to their existence when I did 'yummy mummy' style loving and embracing of everyone – even ghastly people who came into our kids' lives. What made them tick? They weren't born like that. If we could be nice to them then they wouldn't make our kids' lives miserable, would they?

Learning to prune requires skill, and some know-alls hacked into the female vines leaving them like vulnerable nuns. It wasn't so bad when this happened with male plants as they sprawl, overpower and darken the orchard, and I was quicker than anyone at pruning them. How so? By visualising boyfriends who'd dumped me and nasty women who'd crossed my path, but since there were so few of those, my mental images were most often of bad leaders of countries, psychos, murderers and critical people.

It's pot luck when employing workers. Ever heard the saying 'works like an Indian'?

Raj was one of the keenest workers I'd known. He'd met our teenage twin daughter Natasha in town, and she offered him work at our property – bit rich coming from her, since she was loath to do any form of orchard work unless her digits were clutching crisps and a cell phone. Raj was a slightly built Indian. "I am a very fast learner," he said, adding that he was used to working ninety hours a week, and smiled at our daughter.

"We're just friends," assured Natasha.

On closer inspection, this beaming chap was not a mere youth. "He looks as old as Dad. At least thirty," I hissed to Natasha.

"Gross," she said, and squatted on the outside picnic table in her pyjamas.

"He better not be shoving his Punjabi around you," I warned. "Tell him you've got five brothers and …"

"Mum! I'm not like that. I'll tell you when I am."

To his credit, the new immigrant didn't seem interested in the slothful teen. Since she was doing work experience (as a school activity) that required her to help us for money, I pointed to the basket of laundry ready to hang on the line, but which was still sitting on the concrete at lunchtime. "See," I said to Raj. "My daughters are not domesticated. Natasha is the worst; not good wife material."

When Natasha smiled, she was achingly beautiful. Growing up with so many brothers, she wanted to be a truck driver. Raj blinked and remained respectful. We weren't used to humble people. Every time we stopped for smoko, he'd ask, "Are you pleased with my work?"

I wanted to cry out that we were overjoyed with his performance compared to the builders who were erecting a shed up the back of the property. He offered to make us a curry if we had turmeric, which was a new ingredient for us; but it has since stained every plate in the kitchen on the nirvana path to being healthy. Sometimes he worked like a maniac, which was puzzling because he was often fasting. "How can you work on an empty stomach? Have you got good mental tricks?" And he smiled like a wiseman. At smoko, I'd serve a plate of biscuits full of carbos and sugary caffeine for the other workers because that was expected of us, but he instead took pleasure in visiting our outside lav, thoroughly washing his hands and sipping water. I wanted his health and goodness to rub off on our kids, but when you have so many teens going to sports practice or church meetings (never sure of the denomination, but it better not condone the use of drugs), or hatching plans and tying up the telephone, it's never a straight run. After a long day in the orchard, you locate the kitchen and start cooking while poor hubby is digging up veggies from the garden in the dark.

Orchardists look forward to harvest and we were no exception. All our kids wanted to stay home, drive the tractors and help out. The school was accommodating and some of their classmates joined the workforce with the permission of their teachers. They mingled with backpackers and others keen to work. We issued them with gloves and picking bags and told them to drop the fruit gently into the bin trailers. Sometimes I had to be mother hen to stop an argument in the orchard, mostly over religion. One Israeli guy wanted to pick a fight, but I could rely on our pretty Romanian-born Natasha, with her green eyes, bouncy black curls and deep throaty laugh, to diffuse a situation. Our teens challenged themselves when it came to who could pick the fastest. While grateful that workers turned up on time, since we are fairly isolated, we were happy our kids pulled together as a family. It was fun but tiring, and we had chirpy times, often insightful ones as well. Some of our teens were not living at home but came to help out during harvest. Family cohesion. It made me reflect on Italian and Greek families with their expectations of one another. Perhaps we were okay as adoptive parents. We were happy for family involvement but never demanded they help out with harvesting. We weren't going to tie a teen down with the burden of feeling they owed us something.

The downside to the pre-harvest period is Mother Nature. Although thwarted by weather, we still managed to unwittingly grow magic mushrooms. We called the police, for we relied on them to straighten out aberrant teens, but now this hallucinogenic drug was establishing itself under the kiwifruit. We'd noticed unusual activity during the night – torches flashing, and strange cars parked outside. And during the day, groups of males were dropped off to fossick for their free drug delight, clutching McDonald's containers filled with scoops of honey.

"What are you boys doing here?" I yelled out one early morning. "Private property." And their pathetic explanation was they wanted kiwifruit. "No," I said. "You are wanting to fry your brains, so rack off." And they did. But more came back. It was a problem. When you want a free drug fix, you travel long distances. Our teens were keen to be policemen, and they jotted down cars' plate numbers and even hunted out suspects at night. It beat watching police stuff on TV at night. We had real action here.

One weekend morning the slothful teens were asleep, but I had a woman's intuition. I crept out at dawn, hitching up my pyjamas, and snuck down to the bottom kiwifruit paddock, a couple of minutes away. Just as I thought: several guys in hoodies scrabbling on the ground. They couldn't see me because of the lush grass and density of the pergola vines, but I noticed a pair of crutches leaning against a post. The guy with crutches was cheating the social welfare system if he was able to climb fences. I grabbed the crutches and ran like a fugitive back to the house. Bryan and the teen boys were not pleased at my bravado and thought it was dangerous. *Phooey*, I thought. *It takes a village to raise a kid.*

When the group of boys came knocking at the door asking for the crutches, we told them we'd taken down the plate number of their car and would have to tell the police. "If you want something, ask for it," I said primly. "But the answer will be no, so tell your mates to keep off our property." Later the police rang and thanked us as the lads were wanted for burglary, both locally and in Wellington.

"Crime doesn't pay," I said to the family emerging into the kitchen. "Mummy's had a big morning. Nearly got a heart attack from that running. I'll make us all a big feed of pancakes, and the rest of you check the orchard for more mushie pickers. I'll try and remember where Dad hid the maple syrup."

Sometimes life with these kids was fun.

Chapter Twelve

Ground control

I imagined running a large family would be like navigating a cruise liner, with hearty meals and an abundance of joy added to the mix. It would be tiring but rewarding, but then reality set in. When the kids were small, it was like steering a tugboat, a bit rocky, but you were heading towards your destination. When the teenage years struck, it was like managing a large barge with a few leaky holes while trying to stay on course – and sane!

"You used to be so nice once," I'd remind a surly teen, and quiz him or her about bullying at school, or girl hormones and whether Mummy needed to run to the shops for Tampax. "And don't think I'll be buying connies (condoms). Keep your legs crossed until you're twenty-one," I warned the girls. The boys gave me withering, disgusted looks. They thought we were too old to know about that sort of thing.

If a kid reported school bullying, Bryan was like a lion protecting his cub and contacted the school. In our day, parents didn't do that, and the child had to learn to cope. When you have so many children from various backgrounds, they all have different personalities. Some internalise and some show aggression. School camps were early in the year so the students could bond and, hopefully, form happy relationships.

"We have to take scroggin," said a son, reeling off the list of camp requirements. It was a new word for us, but a quick phone call to a classmate revealed it was a snack of dried fruit, nuts and chocolate bits. It was chaotic getting the youngster off early for camp and making sure he had everything on the list. When the coach pulled up outside our house to collect the nervous camper, I noticed a packet on the table.

"Quick," I cried to Miss Malaprop, our foster daughter. "The scroggin! Run out to the bus!" Pupils had their faces pressed against the windows as the bus driver re-opened the hissing door. "You forgot your scrotum!" shrieked the daughter to her embarrassed brother.

I urged parents to write down funny things their kid said. Keep a notepad and pen handy in the kitchen, and you'll have a wealth of cute sayings that will serve as fond remembrances for you later in life and will be amusing to the child as an emerging adult. From recorded jottings, I wrote short articles for placement in magazines and newspapers, and when the cheques rolled in, I donated the earnings to overseas orphanages.

"Draw a picture of Nana," I suggested to the youngest. The five-year-old had sketched a portrait of an old lady, but I couldn't work out what the fierce black dots were around the mouth. "Can't you tell?" she huffed. "It's Nana's germs."

Although expensive at the time, we invested in a camcorder so the children could enjoy home movies and recapture their childhood when they were adults. Footage of our adopting from overseas orphanages revealed the giant steps the child had made and how quickly they learned English. They forgot their mother tongues within a year, except for odd words we kept alive. If the Russian twins heard someone speaking Russian, they slunk off and refused to engage. Perhaps they were fearful they'd be returned to the orphanage.

When we were given a camera that produced instant photos, we took silly showing-off snaps, laughing, poking out our tongues and waving our arms. Bryan reluctantly joined in the fun. When a child said she'd taken the photos to school, I hoped the teacher hadn't glimpsed them. She said she'd shown them to classmates.

"What did they say? Did they think we were cute and funny?" I asked.

"Sort of," she replied. "But they wanted to know if my parents were Special Needs!"

We laughed for a week over that. Sometimes our mirth turned to shock because Mother Nature could be cruel.

We've suffered floods, hail, fierce winds and vicious frosts around harvest but learned to be resilient. A year slavishly working in the orchard could be quickly wiped out by elements beyond your control. We've seen kiwifruit growers and farmers have an early demise due to stress, and we didn't want to be victims too. Once the costly sprinkler system was installed, we monitored night frosts, and when the warning beacon flashed red rapidly, it was a sleepless night. We donned gumboots in the dark and checked each of the sprinklers suspended over a thousand vines, and then crawled wearily back into bed. Our vigilance paid off, preventing icicles hanging from the vines and damaging fruit, while dawn revealed cracked shards of ice across the paddocks. Rearing capricious teens was equally exhausting but not as financially ruinous. Saying, "Dad and I were up half the night," did not elicit sympathy from the teens either.

"Mother," said the Russian son. "You have to face life. Don't expect us to pay for your silly mistakes." Instead of being annoyed, we were amused because our kid saw the world differently and had more empathy with animals than with people. You can't be upset with youngsters who have different thought and brain processes. They are themselves, unique, so you learn to cope and accept, and even feel pride in some of their achievements.

When the sun smiled, we happily donned pruning gear and worked in the orchard. It was our stress-free salvation when working side by side. Not so if the employment agency sent reluctant, tattooed youths drawing on pungent roll-yer-owns, who looked dazed and confused. They annoyed me more than aberrant teens. "Can't work with your old lady," said one to Bryan. "Women are too confusing." These guys often didn't turn up the next day, so we'd ask the agency to send someone else. Some had the cheek to return a few days later only to find their job had been filled.

At the end of each day I psyched myself up. What would the kitchen look like after marauding, famished school-teens emptied the fridge and left contents splayed on benches, with a prowling cat grinning through milky whiskers? If I found the kitchen shipshape, I'd nervously wonder what caused this odd behaviour.

"Can't you just accept we can be nice for a change," one daughter said. "Oh, and by the way, I accidentally kicked in the back door and broke a plate. It wasn't my fault. Can I have the phone this evening? You've had all day to spend on the Internet while we've been slaving at school." When broadband came to our area, it was easier to pay extra and not have the phone tied up. You sweat the small stuff and tackle the big issues.

Sometimes you get lucky with adopting and fostering, in cases where the child causes less angst. One of our sons we adopted as a week-old, mixed-race baby, and he slotted perfectly into our family. As a toddler, Tristan followed Bryan around like a mini shadow, and by age two was upturning his tricycle to oil the wheels; his toys were spanners, nails and hammers. When labourers began road works outside our house, he fetched his little spade and dug alongside them and was soon offered rides up and down the valley where they were dumping gravel. We didn't know much about his biological background but later discovered it was in his genes – machinery and a feverish urge to work. School bored him as he struggled with reading, but he could work a chainsaw and drive tractors, and by the age of fifteen had a string of motorbikes and old cars given to him in lieu of pay. His mentoring skills were impressive. "You've been rude to Mum. Write out one hundred lines," he told his younger sisters as a twelve-year-old. And they did. He was unstoppable, working long hours at weekends milking cows, sometimes before school. After doing a forestry course, he worked in the logging industry before starting his own successful contracting business.

The older boys, once they got over their teen blowouts, backed us up. I was grateful when they admitted past transgressions and smiled as they dished out advice to their younger siblings with lots of humour and bantering. So they *did* have a conscience; it hadn't been apparent at times!

"Do come and bring along your lovely family," urged church members. When you have a mishmash of kids with dubious behaviours, it's daunting taking them out in public.

"You'll have yummy food to eat there," I promised as I jammed half a dozen or more kids into the car, accompanied by a couple of piping hot pizzas. "Stop licking the food. Mummy is watching. So is God."

"Keep your eyes on the road, Mum. You're not as good a driver as Dad."

"Well pray then. And by the way, don't nick any coins from the offering bag. God is all-seeing and He wants you to go to your friend's house next weekend, but only if you are a decent person."

Invariably we were late for the service, sneaking up the aisle that could never accommodate all of us on a single, long pew. The kids jostled and tussled over hymn books they couldn't read and stayed seated when they were expected to stand. Sometimes I had a baby or two in my arms, and my pleading, dark look didn't register my inner turmoil, and I'd be crying, *Behave you little ratbags*. Bryan said he was doing God's duty providing for his family by staying home and digging in the garden. The other families had well-behaved offspring. "They're only kids," said the parishioners kindly. Yes, I silently agreed, but I want them to be shining roles of humanity, obedient and respectful. One incident amused us, though.

Our young foster daughter was anxious about food and overindulged to cope with stress. I distracted her by teaching her to read and giving her piano lessons, and eventually we didn't have to tie the refrigerator up with a rope. "We're going to a church luncheon," I said, and glancing at a recipe, suggested, "Let's bake West Virginia's Finest Cookies."

At church, the youngster could barely keep her eyes off the table of goodies. As soon as parishioners said amen, and the shared food was produced amid prayerful thanks, she grabbed the biscuits. When she offered her baking to elderly gents, I noted it was rejected. I was puzzled until I heard her chirp, "Would you like one of Mum's Best Vagina biscuits?"

Raising other people's children gives you the best and the worst of times, but it is survivable when at least one person understands what you are going through – hopefully, your partner who shares the journey. Jarring remarks from professionals, friends and acquaintances didn't count for much because they hadn't walked in our shoes. But those who'd adopted never judged. In fact, some of them were so stressed they sought my advice. How did I keep my sense of humour and not give up?

Good question.

Confusion reigns when other people get involved in your teen's life. One such incident comes to mind. When I heard the crunch of a car's tyres on our gravel and the padding of feet down the steep staircase, I switched on the light. It was 2 am. The headlights of a car reflected off two of our teenage daughters who had snuck out, and who were now talking to a man we'd vaguely met, while his docile fourteen-year-old son lay curled up on the backseat. I made Bryan get out of bed as I donned my dressing gown, irritated he was spending precious seconds combing his hair (what was left of it). "What the hell are you girls doing out here in the middle of the night. Is this a police matter?"

"Go back to bed, Mum. He's a friend. And you can't call yourself a Christian saying 'hell'."

Friend? Friend! It was hard to tell if the guy was spaced out on dope, but the biting wind caught my equally biting tongue while Bryan shone a torch on him to see if we'd ever employed him over harvest. We shivered in the dark while giving him a lecture on leaving our girls alone. And what were they all up to? And what was the name of that black puppy in the passenger seat who was scratching itself?

"You're so embarrassing, Mum," said a daughter. "You're so strict. Don't pretend you care."

Care? Oh, we cared alright!

In the pandemonium, the other daughter began bawling her eyes out. She'd dropped her cell phone, making Bryan act like some dopey sniffer dog circling around in the scratchy gravel in his big gumboots, shining the torch beneath the quarter moon. I inflamed the situation by doing an Agatha Christie. Maybe someone in this circle of trust nicked it?

The crispy air was turning to frost when the weird duo and dog took off to their house truck up the valley. We ushered the girls inside, and they polished off the rest of the pear-cake dessert that had turned brown with fright in the oven. I felt a head cold coming on and didn't know whether it was from ripping into the dad on a wintry night, or whether someone had sneezed in my direction. I was still feeling peeved when Bryan said the magic word.

Pollen.

"It's all around you, darls," and he presented something warm and damp to make me feel better – a cup of tea and an expired 'pollen' pill!

I'd either be dead or alive the next morning but appreciated the thought.

Raising teen boys was somewhat easier even though they exposed themselves to risky activities. They were like fireballs with all this pent-up energy. I reflected on how my mother mothered. Our dream was for our kids to be happy and independent. And we relied on adages to help us in our parenting: 'Stay out of jail', 'Don't spend more than you earn', 'Be kind and caring towards your partner and family', 'If you don't have family it's tough, but if you don't have friends, it is really tough', and 'Stay connected'. We had one for every occasion.

When a son rang and said his missus was expecting, I called his siblings to the phone. "Baby on-board. Say something nice."

"I need to ask her something," said a daughter. "It's urgent. It's about someone famous."

"Put the missus on the phone, son," I said, and before his partner could get a word in, I gushed and gooed and offered her the world before withdrawing.

"Put us down for baby clothes. Op shop or new?"

The daughter grabbed the phone. "Are you related to Che Fu (a New Zealand hip-hop artist)? I hope you are. He is so cool. Coz, if you are, then we are related to him, too."

"We're gonna have a baby," said the excited voice. "You'll be an auntie."

"Yeah, yeah," said the daughter. "But are you related to Che Fu?"

When baby was born, we crammed several daughters and gifts into the car. Our son's boxy abode was littered with kids, inside and out, an assortment of relatives, plus one elongated youth glued to a PlayStation, and a yappy tan-and-white dog. The new father, who was doing the lawns, was looking half-proud, half-jaded. I flung presents at the proud mother who was plumped up on the Dralon couch, cradling the newborn, who was snuffling like a little hedgehog.

Prancing around like a royal-court reporter, snapping photos and demanding a blow-by-blow account of the birth, from contractions to release, I told her about the many congratulatory emails I'd received from well-wishers, and hoped she had received such lavish compliments as well. Seems ironic, doesn't it?

She did all the hard work and now had to smile her way through swollen mammary glands, sleepless nights, nappy rash, split ends and murky complexion, stretch marks and weight gain. Throw in cystitis, mastitis, conjunctivitis and loss of libido, then who is smiling?

Me! Grandma. It wasn't kind to inform the new mum what lay ahead – sickness, tantrums, broken nights, and worse when they are teens – that would have driven her to an emergency snip and zip salon. Gazing at the babe mewing and spewing, I glanced at my own three thirteen-year-olds slumped on the sofa, mouthing, "When can we go?" Would the new baby end up like them, chewing on hubba-bubba, wearing caps back to front, and having attitude?

"Final photo," I said, "so I can do a 'Madonna and Child'. Take the booties off bubba's hands and put your head up."

"Do I have to?" she asked. "I've got a virus. Picked up an infection from the hospital."

"Don't worry. I'm not snapping your nether regions. Head up and smile for posterity's sake."

"I see what you mean," I muttered as she swung her head meekly around. It seems glands under one's nostrils can do funny things when babies get ejected into the world.

"No matter. We think you are the cleverest person in this room, virus and all, isn't she," I said loudly across the room to our daughters.

They replied, "Whaaat!"

"Don't bother," I said. By this time an assortment of kids were hyper on salt 'n' vinegar chips, the spotted dog was leaping around in circles yapping, and the long-limbed youth was still in a trance. I hoped that when this little grandie was older, PlayStations would be obsolete, and it was a return to backyard activities, digging that hole to China, making daisy chains, and exploring nature.

As a parent, you live in hope!

"Are your parents Special Needs?"

Chapter Thirteen

Shopping

"How do you manage to shop and cook for so many children?" visitors asked. I explained we had a large vegetable garden and froze any surplus. We never had a fuss with kids being picky about food, except the odd child who was staying with us who baulked at vegetables.

"Yummy veggies for dins tonight," I gushed, "and roast beef after. You're allowed to lick your plates, little darlings." If the visitor looked stricken, I made a smiley face on his plate with token vegetables, even if it was one pea and a curvy bean. It was an achievable technique for getting them to eat their vegetables, and it wasn't favouring one child over the others.

One of our foster sons told his siblings, "Ya gotta eat ya greens. We had to do that at the last foster home." He shoved a forkful of spinach into his mouth, pinched his nose and gulped a glass of water. His siblings duly copied their big brother. I didn't want food to be an ordeal. It had to be pleasurable, but at the same time I was not going to be a slave to fussy eaters.

Bryan said that if you grow a garden you are halfway to looking after yourself. So after they dug plots, he started the kids off with watermelons. When the fruit galloped to the size of footballs, the little entrepreneurs wheeled them down to the village and knocked on doors to sell their produce, sometimes taking a younger, cute child along for enticement. They always came back jubilant.

"Baked beans on special," Bryan might announce, rattling the *Nelson Mail*. "Reckon we'll go to town tomorrow and stock up as the weather is looking dicey. Look! Ice cream on special too. Have you all been good?"

On wet days, like most farmers, we drove to town – they in their utes and us in a navy-blue hearse. We had purchased this vehicle from the funeral home when my dad was being viewed in his open casket. He took his final ride in it, and when we heard it was being shipped up north, I said we would buy it since it had three rows of seats – if you didn't have to make space for a coffin.

"Are you sure, darls?" Bryan asked.

"Positive," I replied, explaining it would stop kiddy rumbles in the back seat, and my dad would be coming along for the ride, in spirit, when we went shopping.

When you live in the country, it's an excursion going to town. You have to plan the trip, and Bryan was an expert at making notes. When he jotted down words like taps, washers and chainsaw oil, his eyes glazed over at the pleasure of inanimate objects. It beat "Need to see the headmaster. Kid being stood down for three days" as a reason for going into town. I envisaged hubby disappearing into a hardware store, foraging among bolts, plastic drippers and mouse bait, and by the time I located him, he'd be dithering over all-purpose paint with a ponytailed trainee who'd emerged from behind the fertilizer bags.

"You need a day out, darls," he'd encourage. "Might relax you. You're my social butterfly."

Once out of our track pants and gumboots, with Bryan combing strands of hair and me donning lipstick, it felt like a mini holiday motoring down the winding, picturesque country road. Horns tooted in recognition of our hearse. Since we recognised most of the inhabitants, a quick jaunt to town became an adventure.

On one typical trip, while pulling into the kerb of the road at the top of the country town, I spied the youngest daughter. Leaping out of the car, I cried, "What on earth are you doing? Get back to school!"

It wasn't an errant daughter but rather a small Asian lady with similar colouring.

"I thought you were my daughter. She's twelve," I apologised.

"I'm actually fifty," she whispered.

"You're kidding. You look far too young. You mustn't have kids; they age you. You Filipinos have gorgeous skin. What's your secret? Rice and oil?"

The demure figure plucked rogue lint off my navy-blue sweater and said she was Thai. Before long we were embracing cultures and motherhood, and I was practically setting up a dowry, when she said she knew my twins who were in the same class as her son. Plus, one of our lads bought takeaways from her restaurant.

"I have five sons," I replied. "Who do you mean? The nice one or …?"

Her arm dangled around my shoulder like a creeper in our garden. Convolvulus, I think. "All your children are very polite," she murmured.

"Gosh, you're lovely," I said. And I beckoned Bryan, whose backside was poking out onto the traffic while retrieving library books from the back seat, over to us. I didn't fancy returning home from a shopping expedition with half a husband.

"This lady says we have nice kids. Do you think there's been a mix-up?" Bryan laughed and said that teens can be swines at home but pleasant in public. I hugged our new friend. "Hubby and I are going to the lotto shop now, and if we win, we'll take the whole family to eat at your restaurant, even if they don't like rice." It was more affordable than taking them all overseas for a cultural experience.

"It was worth coming to town just to meet that nice lady who said our kids were okay. If I'd popped on my specs, I wouldn't have raced out like a madwoman, telling a middle-aged woman to get back to school. Being half-blind has its advantages."

In country towns the supermarket is a meeting place where you run into people who look familiar, and you yak over the frozen peas section for a catch-up. Sometimes you encounter someone you vaguely know, exchange pleasantries, even embrace. But like pop up ads, they keep reappearing between aisles, so you swing your trolley and reverse. And blow me down if they don't do the same.

"I remember you from computer classes," I said, as a small bright-eyed guy passed, his trolley laden with healthy purchases and a chubby runny-nosed kid. "Is this yours?"

He smiled proudly.

"Nice looking kid. Did you go into those chat rooms and update your computer skills, and find an Uzbekistani bride online?"

He assured me he hadn't.

I was disappointed. "You can tell me if you did; I love ethnicity. Was hoping to practice some Russian, but hey, I believe you if you say so."

He smiled. And heaven forbid, we banged trolleys in the next aisle. I laughed. "Forgot to ask if you updated your formats, inserts and tools. On the computer, I mean." He gave me playful little punches on the arm. "See ya," I said, noticing hubby had swung his alcoholic trolley upwind of the fat-free margarine, heading for the display of Raisin 'n' Nut Forest chocolate, on special.

At the checkout, I was tortured to again find myself trolley-to-trolley with my rediscovered computer-class acquaintance. Hadn't we said our goodbyes? Was he smirking because his trolley held healthy Third World food, while Bryan had topped up with ruinous treats and out-of-date specials, plus two bundles of lavatory paper? Would he think we were in for a severe bout of dysentery? His little kiddy began grizzling, spying the chocolate in our trolley. It was the perfect excuse to say our final goodbyes.

Sometimes we travelled to Nelson, ninety minutes away, aiming to be back before the school bus. Once we took our Russian lad for a specialist appointment in the city, and afterwards we visited the Warehouse, a popular shopping barn. Misha and Bryan were gazing at electronic gadgets when I spied two shabby men carrying string bags. They had that unloved, been-away-from-home-for-months-no-pay look. Obviously, poor Russian seamen off the fishing vessel tied up in port.

"Halt!" I ordered in my best Russian and dashed off to find hubby and son. I was brimming with excitement and told them to come with me urgently. I had a wonderful surprise for them.

I pushed my family into the path of the portly duo who were still rooted to the spot in delayed shock.

"What's the surprise, Mum?" asked Misha.

"Those men. They're Russian. Say something to them."

Misha said he couldn't remember any Russian. "Try," I urged. "It might come back to you. Recovered memory."

While everyone stood looking blankly at each other, I uttered every Russian phrase I remembered. Bryan shrugged. Misha shrugged. And the two men stared like concrete statues. "Speak Ruski?" I asked in a small voice.

"Nyet," they replied. "Polski." And they shuffled off doing corkscrew motions around their heads as if *I* was the crazy one! Misha said he could tell a mile off they weren't Russian, and jeeze, I was embarrassing. Bryan wondered if the poor guys thought I was propositioning them, or that they'd fallen foul of the law.

When shopping with the three Romanians as toddlers, we scooped them into a trolley. People wanted to take photos of them.

"Oh, they're so cute," they gushed. "They must keep you busy."

You don't know the half of it, I thought, what with older kids at school and a big kiwifruit orchard to run.

One cartoon quip amused us. It was of a matronly couple proudly pushing a pram on the footpath. "What a beautiful baby," cooed a passer-by peering into the pram. "Is it adopted?"

I vividly recall a comment an elderly man made once when people were clucking over our babies at the Warehouse. His wife tugged at his sleeve, embarrassed, but he said, shaking his head, "Those babies will break your heart." I wasn't upset but felt empathy towards the couple. He looked like he was recovering from a heart attack, possibly brought on by his teen kids. My little dudes will be fine, I hoped.

Fast forward to the teenage years. What a roller coaster! Shopping, you'd think, would be neutral territory. Shopping per se is not as problematic as the arrival at your intended destination. To illustrate my point with an example … First, you have to check the hearse because something happened that made it go backwards instead of forwards, and you get accused of being a cheapskate because you should have bought a new car. Then you pack a lunch and thermoses because you're not wasting your money on McDonalds. Plus, you know where your hands have been, but what about theirs? And then, once ready to depart, I remind the kids, "You have extra loot to buy at the op shops."

I love those shops, telling ancient volunteers on duty that I could happily camp there and wait for people coming in the door and dropping off unwanted pressies – if they were to look after my large family at home in exchange, but there were no takers.

When an older member of our family was getting married, I said, "Girls, your dreams have come true. We're going shopping for your outfits. Choose something and Mummy will pay." Bryan deposited us at a huge second-hand warehouse for the shopping occasion. When you live in a small country town, everything looks big 'over the hill', and the excited teen girls ran around like they were in a theme park.

"Found something you like, little darlings?" I called between the confusing, long rows of garments. "I've found a skanky top. What do ya reckon? I want to look modern."

The girls were more sober in their tastes. "Black blouse-shirt – are you sure?" I asked a twin. "Bit manly. How about a bit of femininity?"

"Ma," hissed a daughter. "She doesn't know if she's bi, but don't worry."

Bi? Bipolar? Bilingual? Bipartisan?

"Mum," shouted a daughter between the racks as I was excitedly oohing at tops and skirts. "You better not look better than the bride."

The girls were in heaven trying on their stash in cubicles. I was in hell. Neon lights projected cruelly over a tall mirror and I gave a mild shriek.

"You alright, Ma?" called a daughter in the next booth.

"No, I've broken my bra strap and I'm having a heart turn."

Another daughter ran to fetch Bryan who was sitting in the hearse reading a *National Geographic*. He said he didn't need to buy clothes. He could wear the ones he bought a couple of decades ago that hadn't worn out yet.

"What's up?" asked Bryan, jumping the queue ahead of a trickle of customers with armfuls of clothes. "Heard you were having a heart attack."

"I just saw my face in the mirror. It's ghastly. Why didn't you tell me how bad I looked! I always thought I looked quite nice. God, I'm so delusional."

The girls pulled the curtain open, and said, "Don't worry, Mum. We're used to you," and they re-arranged the tight top which had been put on back-to-front in the turmoil.

"Show Dad."

I stepped outside the booth and Bryan muttered low-key approval. He turned to the other shoppers for advice. "At least you have a waist," he said, which was an unfortunate remark as the women in the audience were on the lardy side.

"Forget about the waist, it's my face," I sniffed.

"Don't worry, love," said a kindly woman. "It's called character lines. And that top looks very nice on you."

"I don't want to have that much character," I replied, and since everyone was so nice, I gave quick hugs to my supporters. "Feeling better now. Let's buy Daddy some clothes."

"No fear," he said and darted out of the barn.

"Since Dad is being a tight-arse about shopping, can we buy more clothes?" asked the daughters.

"Sure," I said, "if it's under ten bucks. Isn't shopping fun!"

Travelling to the city to shop took three hours out of our day, made worse if you or your passengers were prone to carsickness. I always took a plastic ice-cream container along just in case the nausea overcame one of us. Years ago, when our three little Romanian girls were all aged about two, I once felt the dreaded waves of nausea as we motored down the side of the winding hill on our way home from the city. On reaching home, I dashed to the rose garden, sick and headachy. When I turned around, wiping my mouth, three fascinated little girls clapped their hands and cried, "Do it again, Mumma!"

Buying presents is an ordeal when you're on a tight budget and with hubby saying people don't need more junk. If they want something, they can buy it themselves, was his opinion. When an acquaintance mentioned getting married for the third time, I fretted over what to buy her. She was a bit of a snob and liked nice things. While Bryan was going starry-eyed in the plumbing supplies shop, I nipped next door to an antique cum second-hand shop. It was dark inside, but in a murky corner I spotted the perfect gift – a small, boxy coffee table for four dollars. I purchased my prize quickly, before the owner realised his mistake.

However, the laugh was on me for, when jogging up the road in brilliant sunlight to the car park, a small door on the borer-ridden cabinet flung open and a secret panel slid out, bruising my face. My bargain was an old-fashioned commode!

Undaunted, I sanded and varnished the 'coffee table' and the snobby lass was delighted. But she doesn't know why I decline to accept refreshments from a table that once housed an old lady's potty!

Shopping expeditions can be ruined by one wondering what thoughtful gift to buy. For instance, when I needed to select a gift for a newly engaged couple when it's also the woman's birthday and she is expecting. It's daunting when you spend most of your life staring at cows, kiwifruit and kids' yukky bedrooms. It's tricky buying perfume because it might be the wrong brand, and she'd think I was forcing her to be fragranced 'to order'.

As a teen, I was often given a fragrance from the new range available – Jonquille perfume! So that was a no-brainer, especially for boyfriends. My sniffer buds had eventually gone off the boil after gathering teens' clothing lying on the floor and washing them. Only to be rewarded by getting abused when the kid says it was clean clothing, and now they will have to go mufti at school. And what was I doing in their room? Snooping? Haven't I got anything better to do with my life?

Thumbs down to jewellery as a gift for her as well because it would go on Trade Me, and I don't know her taste in music or romance books. Kitchenware was too boring, and baby clothes would be for baby and not her personally. A 'no' as well to smokes and booze, or a breadmaker appliance because she might be tempted to only make the white flour variety. People don't knit or embroider much these days, so crafts are out. I saw a funny cartoon book on how to avoid having babies, but it's too late now. They already learnt their lesson!

Young couples these days have TV sets as big as walls, unstained coffee mugs and freezers with processed food. So it's also a 'no' to a basket of fruit and veggies because some complain they are allergic to nature's produce. Plus, it reeks of interference from a sage older person.

The best solution I found was stapling a cheque to a handmade card, after crossing out some noughts, and telling her to spend it on herself as this was her last gasp of being a carefree maiden. The rest of her life would be spent thinking about her kids, partner and extended family. Come to think of it, I should have sent a bereavement card instead and upped the cheque.

Although itching to get home after shopping excursions, we had to make time to call in to see a bed-ridden lady who'd been moved to a rest home. "We'll all be old and crotchety one day," I explained to our teen son, who was sporting wild, woolly orange-and-green hair.

Sometimes he shaved it, prompting a neighbour up the valley to remark, "When you visit you either look like Bob Marley or the pope!"

Under sufferance we entered the old woman's bedroom. It resembled a religious shrine. "Why don't you cut your hair, boy?" she moaned. "You look like a girl."

Our son pointed to a picture of Jesus, and said, "That guy's got long hair."

For once we were speechless.

"What a beautiful child. Is it adopted?"

Chapter Fourteen

Pets

We never bought pets. They came to us, a surprise – like acquiring kids. At first, we resisted, having dealt with a runaway horse and with sheep that needed crutching or that wouldn't look after their offspring. We were given other people's hens, ducks and turkeys, but when they appeared on the dinner table, everyone went vegetarian. We especially choked on Miss Piggy. Trapping wekas and setting them free was a popular pastime, but they found their way back to our property along with possums who made jeering noises up the walnut tree.

When a fourteen-year-old foster child arrived with pet rats, it was hard to say no to him keeping them. He seemed bonded to them, and they did look cute in an albino-twitchy kind of way as they slithered around his neck and dived for cover inside his shirt. "Aren't you worried about them doing poopsy-bang on your clothes?" I asked.

Our kids translated. "Mum means 'shit on you'."

"Gross," I admonished the kids. "We have a nice young man here. He mightn't know that sort of lingo."

"Nah, it's alright," he said. "I've trained them."

We found a disused budgie cage and play equipment the right size for rats. It was fascinating watching them pedalling crazily, non-stop on the little treadmill. I wanted to ask if they were on speed but changed my mind. No need mentioning the word 'drugs' as we'd had problems with marauding louts coming onto our property looking for magic mushrooms that grew brazenly and unwanted in certain spots – like some teen behaviour. The rats didn't last long after the new lad climbed the magnolia tree with his rodent companions, and they plunged to a miserable demise. He acquired more rats at school but they, too, came to a sticky end. He didn't seem remorseful, so here was another kid with attachment problems that we had to deal with.

Once, as the skies heralded a new dawn, one of our sons knocked on our bedroom door, asking, "Can I come in? There's someone who wants to meet you."

"Only if it is urgent," I replied. Then I heard scuffling, panting sounds.

Tristan said he'd just finished milking for the neighbours, and he'd been given something nobody wanted. "I know you'll say no, but you'll love it. It's called Puppy."

He opened the door and a large, wet dog leapt up onto the bed, pinning me down, it's salivating tongue dripping goblets of spittle. The dog looked old despite its exuberance and, more impressively, everything was erect – and I mean everything!

"This is no puppy," I gasped. "It's a mini lion and it's got domination tendencies."

"Get down, Puppy," ordered Tristan, but the dog took no notice and began licking my face in a pleading way. "See it likes you. Can I keep it? I'm the only one in the family who's helpful."

The dog was on trial for a day, but it wasn't going to work. We lived on a main road with open gates on our property. Besides, dogs chase sheep and we weren't going to antagonise the local farmers. Tristan ended up getting several motorbikes, and cars were given to him in lieu of pay, despite being too young for a licence. At one stage, our gravelled entrance resembled a second-hand car dealer's yard.

Cats turned up at our house and stayed, usually one at a time. When Black Magic fell under the wheels of a big semi hurtling down the road one dark, wet night, we vowed never to have another cat. Our stance softened when birds became a problem. Sparrows were attacking the flower buds of our gold kiwifruit crop, and they had begun pecking the tomatoes for the first time as well. We covered the nashi pear tree, but black birds kept falling into the net, causing the kids to run out with scissors to rescue them, and they ended up making gaping holes in the netting.

We enquired about a Burmese cat from the cattery up the road because they were classy, and it would be the first time we chose a cat, although the price put us off. When I heard they were devoted and faithful, I asked the cattery lady, "Could I train the cat to love only me and not the kids?" I explained that if the cat loved one kid more than me, it might follow the child up to the bus stop, and perhaps even want to hop onto the school bus. She laughed and said she couldn't guarantee that. I couldn't bear another squashed cat on the road while its bowl of kitty biscuits at the back door stood as a sad reminder of someone never returning home again.

The twins pleaded for a kitten, from a local lady, that was destined to go to the SPCA. We said no. I reminded them that the lady's cat kept having litters year after year, and that she should take care of her cat's sexuality. "Is that all you think about, Mum? Sex, sex, sex." I opened my mouth like a codfish.

"No, I don't," I retorted. "What's the kitty like? And, if it's a boy, call it Lorenzo. I love that name." The twins hotfooted down the road and returned cradling two kittens called Sox and Diana.

"I said one, not two, and what are they?"

The girls chose a cat each and upturned them, unsure where to look. Diana (who had a royal birthmark on her furry forehead) was renamed Possum, and Natasha said, "Mumma, I'll call my cat

Lorenzo if we can keep both kitties. I can't see the sticky-out bit, but what if it's a girl?"

"They'll both get a little botty-fix at the vet's when they're older," I said. "Start saving your pocket money. It's a big job owning a pet. Are you up to it?"

The thirteen-year-old twins nodded. While I loved their infectious enthusiasm, I got distracted, caught up on the phone. A friend was having marital problems.

"What's wrong? Is hubby seeing other women? Is he being disgusting?" She said that, in fact, no, he wasn't being disgusting enough. "Gotta go," I said after a while. "We've got two more additions to the family."

"What? You've got more foster kids? Are you crazy?"

"Just two little kitties," I said. "We'll see if the girls keep their bedrooms tidy now."

The first night was bliss, barely a profane word was uttered. The twins set up litter boxes in the study and used my best towels to cuddle the kittens. Natasha called, "Mummy come here quickly. My kitty's doing a poo," and her twin retorted, "My cat has lovely manners. Better manners than your cat, Natasha."

"Mummy," called Natasha again, urgently, while I was cooking wiener schnitzel – similar to a flattened cat carcass we'd seen on the main road. "Look! My kitty has growed [sic]. Its legs are twitching."

The kittens were playful, and the euphoria continued when the girls returned from school each day. I took a home video of the girls dangling wool from the staircase as the kitties cavorted playfully, but I felt somewhat dismayed that viewers might hone in on the dust particles circling the pets, making little halos around their furry heads in the brilliant sunshine.

When one of the kids brought a sad-looking dog home, called Worm, we said, "Sorry, but no. And tell the owner to rename it; that might give the dog a better chance of being rehomed." When orphaned lambs arrived, Tristan built a shelter around the walnut tree and bossed his sisters about, ordering material comforts, such as old bedspreads and bottles with red teats.

The grassy backyard became a place of excitement and yes, excrement, but with such joy and bonding going on, we even agreed to a pet calf joining the family. Like a teenager, the bobby calf grew bolshy, but the daughter said it's because he's lonely. So we got another to keep him company. "Go on. Fall in love," demanded the daughter. She'd made us laugh earlier when she was tossing a basketball to a sibling, and it landed heavily on her chest. "Ouch," she yelled. "That hurt my udder."

There's something magical about being in the country at night when the stars come out, the moon is peeping coyly, wekas are rustling in the bushes and it's *All Quiet on the Western Front*. Especially when the teens are outside playing cricket in the dark or hanging upside down in the walnut tree. You know tomorrow might be different, but tonight was a good night. Enjoy the now.

Several months after the arrival of Possum and Lorenzo, tragedy struck. The twins were so concerned about their kitties running away, they slept with them at night, and heaven knows how their sheets weren't stained with cat debris because they fiercely clutched them. I expect they had remarkable bladders. It was hard keeping them locked up for their own safety, as we worked all day in the orchard while the girls were at school, and cats like their freedom.

But one day Lorenzo ate his last supper and never came in for breakfast. Natasha and I were scouring the orchard, offering him all sorts of rewards if he would just miaow. We went to church and sang joyous hymns and even had a happy barbecue with parishioners, unaware that Lorenzo had met his Maker. He was a victim of a hit-and-run accident. Bryan was spraying under the shelter belt trees and found the large black-and-white cat spreadeagled under the front hedge. It would seem the cat had staggered off the road and laid his furry body to rest in a quiet place. Even headless chooks have a minute of running around to find solitude before dying.

After locating the cat's corpse, which appeared similar to stretched out cardboard, the teenage son of the cat's grandmother turned up looking like Mr Cool, dangling a ciggie, with a Walkman wrapped around his head. He had parent issues, so he wouldn't understand that Lorenzo, despite growing twice the size of his feline sister, for he was a glutton, was special. The cat had wormed his way into our hearts. He'd been a bit wormy himself but megabucks at the supermarket and pills from the vet cured his affliction. We understood his affection was conditional on being fed, but when his needs were met, he purred like a V8 motor. He loved his sister, Possum, but would gobble up her dinner too. Often brother and sister kitty lay entwined, so it was hard to know which paws belonged to whom. He and his sibling would nip, lick and caress each other, and we allowed this pre-puberty play once they'd had their snip and zip.

"Come here," I would call our twins. "See something beautiful. Your kitties are getting on so lovingly. They are teaching us a lesson."

It was heartbreaking for Natasha. She cut off fur from Lorenzo's body and popped it into a plastic bag. Then she dug a hole at a spot across the creek, where brother Tristan's wrecked cars were lined up. He had a noisy barbecue in progress, and they didn't notice a furtive little figure wearing a cap turned back to front, digging and silently weeping.

Then Natasha thought about the cat's sister. She put Lorenzo's sibling on her expensive Holden minky blanket, along with a bowl of food and water, which was normally a no-no, but rules are bent on tragic days.

"Possum is looking sad," she said. "Look what I've done, Mumma." She'd placed the tiny parcel of Lorenzo's fur close to the surviving cat and next to a photo of both cats wearing shawls and sunglasses that I'd taken earlier. "That's so Possum remembers," she explained.

I came in from the orchard to hear Bryan's low decibel bellow about someone having been in the shed and leaving his tools and nails lying around. I'd heard vigorous hammering earlier and hoped someone was building a new outside lavatory.

But no. "Look at this Mumma. Do you reckon he'll like it?"

Natasha had sawn up a piece of wood and filed it so it could be stuck into the ground. "It's a cross. Now I'm going to decorate it. How do you spell 'Lorenzo'?"

We trooped across the paddock, plucking sprigs of festive buttercup for the grave, barely aware of the clanging of beer bottles and muted guffaws of a happier celebration taking place close by. Natasha had stapled a note to the cross, with the inscription 'We all loved you' written in green and yellow highlighter ink and decorated with hearts that looked like tears. The poignancy made the sunblock on my face run and it stung my eyes, the effect resembling full-blown grief.

"Natasha, maybe we should give Lorenzo a double blessing, just to make sure he gets to heaven?" She blinked and wiped her nose on the cuff of her hoodie. Not meaning to add to her pain, I said that the cat had been a greedy guts, sneaking Possum's food, and I doubted he was remorseful about it.

The minister who'd married us years before sent occasional letters whenever we were mentioned in the local paper, and he was on hand when there was a health crisis in the family. He and his wife drove over the hill twice to perform a healing session for one of us, demanding that the cancer in our bodies depart henceforth. The cells got a fright and obeyed the man of the cloth. More recently, we'd taken over a box of kiwifruit to share with his parishioners and to thank him for past kindnesses. When he opened the door, looking frail and vague, I pecked this dear man on his cheek. We had a pleasant little chat before our goodbyes. "Er … by the way, who are you?" he asked.

"Perhaps you shouldn't kiss men who don't recognise you," chuckled Bryan.

That night we lit a candle to our dearly departed furry feline and hoped Possum was coping without her brother. In fact, she grew large without the threat of bro nicking her food and purred non-stop with the extra attention.

Animals are like teens. They can behave objectionably but have endearing qualities. When a neighbour's rampant billy goat escaped into our paddock and bailed me up against the hedge, I wasn't sure what part of his body was more dangerous. I scrambled up and over the hedge, crying, "Shoo, naughty goat. Go back to your owner." There was an impasse where man (well, woman) meets beast, eyes locked, where one old goat meets another (me). Sweaty, scratched and hyperventilating from the adrenalin rush, I crawled along the top of the hedge and vaulted into the garden. Bryan wasn't particularly sympathetic. He said he knew I could look after myself but did ring the owner who eventually collected her escaped beast.

The air was colourful as the neighbour retrieved the escapee. "Like bloody kids," she said.

"I can attest to that," I laughed. "Give 'em an inch and they'll take a mile."

When people adopt, especially babies, they seem flawless; the same happens with animals.

A friend of mine, and three of her friends, were each given a female pup from the same litter. The hairless mutts looked like a cross between a black pig and a bandicoot and had no redeeming features, but they were much loved. The ladies met regularly and, with their dogs perched on their knees, sipped coffee and swapped doggy foibles. "I'm sure my Josephine is on heat," said my friend. "We'd better take our little girls to the vet and get their tubes tied."

In the vet's waiting room, the teary-eyed ladies cuddled and soothed their pooches. They were weepier still when a voice boomed out, "Now which bitch wants to be spayed first?"

One evening, one of our youngsters retrieved a harrier hawk hit by a car outside our house and brought it into the kitchen.

"Din-din delayed," I cried. "Bird in need. Who's done first aid?"

The family gathered around crying, "Give it splints. Give it mince. No, you don't do it this way. You do it like this."

It reminded me of the time Bryan went up to the local community hall, which is a centre of social activity. I asked a teen son of ours to pop up to the hall and deliver a message to his dad. He returned quickly, looking disgusted. "I'm not going in there," he said. "People are lying on the floor. Dad's doing yoga with a bunch of old ladies!"

I went up to investigate. Apparently, St John's Ambulance staff were demonstrating a CPR course.

The harrier hawk survived the night, just like the rescued hedgehogs brought in and given leftovers and splashes of water in my best bowls. "You have to release animals into the wild," I told them. "Just like Daddy and I will release you when you know how to keep your room tidy, learn to save money, and not go gangbusters when your hormones go AWOL. Get my drift?"

They did, but still didn't like being reminded. Who would?

The hawk was given breakfast, and while several of us gathered on the back porch to admire its return to health, it suddenly flew off with not so much as a backward glance. My mother always said she would come back as a bird. "Maybe that was Grandma turned into a harrier hawk, and she wanted to spend a night with us?" And no one said phooey.

An acquaintance of mine admitted that looking after other people's pets is hazardous, even disastrous. Neighbours were going on holiday and had asked if she could keep an eye on their pet goldfish and feed the cat.

The day before the couple were due to return, the neighbour popped next door to tend to the pets and was shocked to find the goldfish dead. The bubbler in the fish tank was disconnected after the well-meaning neighbour had been vacuuming, and she had forgotten to reconnect it. So, she hurried to a pet shop and bought a replacement fish, hoping the couple wouldn't notice the substitute.

When the oldies returned, they said the cat looked good but Tipsy, the goldfish, seemed to have shrunk and changed colour. To allay her doubts, the neighbour told a white lie. "Perhaps Tipsy missed you. I've heard fish get stressed when their owners go away!"

Pets are like teens. They give you the run around, but you still love them!

"Puppy wants to live with us."

Chapter Fifteen

Gifts

Every Christmas Bryan says, "Keep it simple." It was easier when the kids were little. If they got a pillowcase full of presents, they were happy. And if they didn't get their wish, then Santa was the nasty dude.

One December I got shingles and couldn't go shopping. Earlier we'd bought cell phones for the girls but as Christmas neared, their behaviour deteriorated. So I told them the shocking news. "You've been ghastly to poor Daddy and me. No pressies this year. We love you but not your behaviour. Amen."

They were gobsmacked. I told them about a Christian family down the valley who had many children. "They love each other so much they don't need to exchange presents. Can't we be full of love and enjoy mankind and the reason for Christmas?"

"Stuff that," they said.

Come Christmas Day, I suspect that the relatives holidaying in the tent on our back lawn held an emergency prayer meeting to avoid the fireworks in our home. "Where's my frickin' cell phone?" demanded a kid.

The others were philosophical. Their birthdays were coming up and there was a good chance they'd get a cell phone if they toned down their language and upped their helpfulness. Better still, they could work for it.

Santa remembered the cat, though. She got a nice packet of worm tablets.

When the disappointed teen swore in front of our gentle religious guests, I threw up my hands in despair. "What would you do?" I asked, "And by the way, Happy Christmas."

"It's beyond our realm," they replied.

The deprived teens scooted upstairs and drowned out Christmas carols with their rap music until big brothers, partners, kids and hangers-on arrived, tooting their horns and flinging packets of crisps into the air. I lunged at the mob, crying, "You're the first normal people we've seen in weeks," which offended the campers on our property. In all the excitement, the disgruntled daughter slipped away. She returned as we were noisily tucking into a barbecue under the walnut tree. She said she'd hitched to town to raise money for the poor people.

"What poor people?"

"Me," she said. "You didn't give me a cell phone." The rellies were astonished, but Bryan gave her credit for lateral thinking.

When the girls eventually got their cell phones (which were a newish device then and expensive), three ended up going to a watery demise (a bath, a toilet, a swimming pool) and one flew off the roof of a moving car.

Another of our Christmases had a hygiene theme. I gave everyone boxed toiletries because the girls were always running out. They sprayed perfume and deodorant over their clothes, not under them! Instead of "Thank you, dear Mother, how thoughtful," the girls swapped their gifts. I can't remember what the boys got – probably a book on *Investing* and *How to Save* – which would languish unread and be used as a doorstop. One of our sons got a seized-up concrete mixer as a gift. That year the cat and grandkids were somewhat miserable when a hyped-up dog chased them and sank its fangs into the rubber toys they'd received as presents. In the dog's defence, one of the twins said, "The dog can't help it. I reckon it's got ADD."

Despite a broken caravan window, littered lawns, dog piddle down the hallway, and a sink full of dishes, we hugged our big family. "What fun we've had. Come again next year."

When they all left, Bryan reiterated, "Next Christmas keep it simple. Let's just give people our best wishes."

One Christmas Eve I suffered a panic attack. The doctor had prescribed pills for my sciatica, but the body went into revolt, and the side effects spaced me out. A large G and T might have been safer, plus a sign on the letter box: 'Lovely couple, now unwell with Lunatic Teens and Desperately Busy in their kiwifruit orchard, seeks solace'. But doctors don't prescribe that. So I paid a small fortune to be rigged up to a machine only to find my heart more normal that the teens' behaviour. "I'm going to survive," I hugged my husband. "Help me hobble into the supermarket and we'll splash out on some treats."

Bryan said he'd discovered a box of biscuits under the bed but was not sure how long they'd been there. "No, we can't be 'cheapos'," I said, and reminded him about a dying man who'd staggered into the kitchen where his wife was baking. He reached for a freshly baked cookie, but his missus smacked his hand. "Buzz off," she said. "These are for your funeral."

Back home once more, I joined our American employee in the orchard for summer pruning and told the kids to look out for visiting rellies. When a noisy car roared into the paddock, full of waving people who seemed vaguely familiar, and one of our sons leapt out so happily, I wondered if he was on drugs. He hoofed out a gust of 'mouth wind' (no bad smell there) and said he left our presents on the table, but that there was a problem. He'd spent all his funds buying Christmas presents and the cheque we gave his family wouldn't clear until early

January. We made a deal: Take one of the girls for a few days of the school holidays and we'd help out financially. "Thought you were splitting up and landing us with the missus and kids," I said, relieved.

"Nah, Mum, what do you take me for? I wouldn't do that to you. Got any magic mushrooms? Just kidding."

"You can come too," I said to the American employee. "Smoko break."

The back lawn was littered with cars, a couple of tattooed, skinny ladies with shiny blue studs in their noses and chins, and kids running wild – most of them in singlets and disposable nappies – and a mongrel dog chewing the Christmas tree being retrieved from the house by a dark-skinned man. Squealing youngsters were fed lemonade in bottles ("Aw, Mum, it's Christmas"), but tooth rot was the last thing on my mind. The American employee was so excited to be in a home atmosphere he extended his smoko break to the extent that it ran into another. "Hey, Yankee-doodle," yelled the children. "Wanta play baseball?" Of course he did.

Finally, it was all love and hugs after I found presents labelled 'Emergencies for People who Give and Expect to Receive'. When a teen agreed to go with the extended family for a few nights, I located the suspect biscuits in a dark recess and added meat from the deep freezer to make up a package for them to take home. Later, when we went to collect her, the daughter said she'd had a great time, adding, "You're not going to like one thing I'm gonna tell you." I braced myself. Body piercing? Biological troubles? Watching AO movies? "Promise you won't go off your head?"

I promised.

"I didn't eat vegetables for a week."

I was so relieved. She had had her dream holiday, but she shouldn't expect that holiday to last at home. "I know," she said happily. "I feel like I want a big feed of greens now."

Despite having sciatica, I knew my ticker could survive another exuberant family visit planned for the following day. The atmosphere turns festive when cars draw up, horns blaring, and shouts of "Merry Christmas" ring across the gravel driveway, accompanied by yapping dogs.

"Tricked ya, Mum. Thought you weren't getting a pressie, didn't ya," said a son's partner. Everyone called out for Dad, who was stubbornly staying in the orchard for some peace. I waddled out to him in a sciatic way to remind him he was a beloved member of our family, and despite being told not to, they had bought presents.

"They're all happy," I said. "Join in the festive spirit for a few minutes, even if it kills you." I had written out cheques for the boys but when I saw their generosity, I enticed Bryan back into the bedroom. "The kids are being all grown-up and generous. Reckon I should add another zero?" One gift we received was a picnic set for two. "You can do dummy runs being on your own," the son said.

Whenever we went to the city the day was jam-packed with things to do, so we never had time to eat out. We preferred sitting in the boot of the hearse, nibbling our lunch and drinking from thermoses in a car park, often facing a restaurant. It was like having a front seat in a movie theatre. Some diners were businessmen with florid complexions, perhaps having a tête-à-tête with a junior office-worker. At least we didn't have guilty consciences and have to worry about a bout of salmonella or an STD.

The older boys always enjoy yarning around a barbie with a few beers, whether it's at Christmas or some other family get-together. "What are you all talking about?" I enquired once, after hearing hearty guffaws.

I felt misty-eyed when they said, "The olden days." So they *did* remember some of the stories we'd told them. "Not your olden days," they retorted. "Our olden days!"

But mothers can get things wrong.

As a gift, I once gave a fifteen-year-old a rugby top. He was a keen rugby player, but I worried about the high number of injuries in that sport. When I spotted bruising on his neck, I suggested he might find a less dangerous game to play. Rather sheepishly, he admitted the bruising had not come from the rugby field but from his girlfriend during their night at the movies. I decided rugby was safer after all!

My biggest gripe about gift giving is that after you've gone to the trouble of posting a parcel off to someone, its receipt is not acknowledged. Excuses are made that the recipient was busy. When I was a kid, Boxing Day was the day to write a thank-you note, often to overseas relatives, for gifts and greetings received, perhaps adding a little drawing as well. Mothers oversaw this activity, and when finished, you were free to go out and play. It was called good manners. I thanked my mother-in-law when she sent me stained aprons, old tea towels, and an out-of-date lotto ticket. It's the thought that counts.

Pity the pensioner shopping for her grandchildren. The effort involved is vexatious. She has to get to the shops, maybe by public transport, be confused about what to buy when youngsters have so much these days, wrap up the parcel, and totter back to the post office. Older people love receiving mail, and how sad is it to wait by the letterbox expecting a handwritten card in childish print. I was taken aback when talking to a Christian friend of mine. She said when you give, that should be your reward. Yes, but parcels can get lost in the mail, and one frets about it. Bryan said, "Next time send a hanky and a card, and after that, zilch."

Some Christian people believe they are a gift in themselves, like the evangelists who visited us one wet day. Bryan had been feeling peaky, and I thought their presence might enhance his well-being as they had a more direct line to the Maker, so invited them in for a cuppa. The guy and his large wife were off to do mission work overseas. After an hour-long monologue on their part, I seized the moment when he was dunking his biscuit in his teacup. I was curious. "What's it like being touched by God?"

He eyeballed me. "Like having an orgasm."

My eyes nearly shot out of my head. What sort of tea party was I hosting? Once the kitchen sink came back into focus, I stared at my chunky guests who resembled large, hungry caterpillars buoyed up on my chocolate Afghans and the joy of living.

When they left, I repeated a phrase my mother quoted, "What sort of elements have come into our abode?"

Bryan laughed. He reckoned the guy had been practising that line. Good shock tactic.

If it hadn't been so early in the afternoon, I'd have had a sip of another kind of spirit to aid recovery. "Just as well the kids weren't here," I said. "This is a house of decorum – or it was until we had those unexpected guests on a high." I joined Bryan digging holes to replace vines that had died. We would get our own highs on nature.

A real gift came to us in the form of Bryan's cousin, Jenny, and her husband, who lived on a large farm in South Canterbury. They offered to board one of our teenage daughters, who had spent a holiday with them and had been given a horse to ride at their farm. It was an answer to a prayer because our daughter was easily influenced and underachieved at school. Local farmers were sending their kids to boarding school, but this was a much better option. It helped her grow up safely within a loving family structure, and in a setting where she attended church and was home-schooled. We rang often and she came home for school holidays. When I asked Bryan what sort of gift I should send her, he said, "How about a packet of sunflower seeds? I received some free samples in the mail." He said it was a practical gift and she could start her own garden.

"Be realistic, love," I said. (My mother said using the endearment 'love' was common, so I never said it until she had departed this earth). "The only time I've ever seen her in the garden was ducking down behind the asparagus when the dishes needed doing." I asked the other kids to put on their thinking caps, but their suggestions were outrageous. No, I was not going to send her that ratbag boy down the road!

The next day I found the perfect gift and emailed the daughter. She immediately rang up. "What's my present? Will I like it? Is it embarrassing?"

I said it was kind of oblong, useful, and she would look at it over and over again.

"Mum, is it p … ?" she whispered.

"Speak up, love. I can't hear you. My ears are a bit wonky."

By this time the family were gathered around the speakerphone, keen to talk with her.

She whispered louder. "My present. Is it pads for when I get my you-know-what?"

How I laughed. "Mummy," she asked in a faint voice. "Are you alone?"

I had to tell her the truth. "No man is an island, my child. I am surrounded by people who truly love you – your family."

"Um, did they hear what I said?"

"You've lived in this family for years, little darls. Who listens to whom? Hark! I hear a large bang in the village; probably another car running into a telegraph pole, or a domestic. Gotta go, love."

I felt a tad guilty hanging up on that pleading little voice. She would get her awaited gift when I could be bothered hunting for wrapping paper.

"Thanks, Mum. It's an okay present. Love ya," she emailed a few days later. I hoped the gift would be her confidante and best friend, and that she could use it to see how much she had achieved living away from home.

Okay, I'll tell you: it was a diary.

Some gifts backfire. One particular year I felt that one of our teen sons had been disrespectful and insulting leading up to Christmas. I told him that even though I'd bought him an expensive present, he could forget about receiving it until he shaped up.

On Christmas Day he tapped politely on our bedroom door, wished us a Merry Christmas, and he handed me a parcel wrapped in newspaper. It was a set of Asian bowls I knew I'd never use. But I was so touched I gave my lovable lout his pressie. But I wasn't so thrilled when my son received a final demand letter. It was sent in an attempt to collect payment for the set of little bowls. And since he was underage, we had to cough up!

Another time, on the eve of Father's Day, I awoke to a terrible pong. I shoved hubby in the ribs. "Wake up, you've been disgusting." He came to from a deep sleep, snorted (like men do) and muttered, "Not me. Must have been you."

I was up in arms. He was in denial. "Hmmmph. The air is too foul in here. I'm getting myself a cuppa," and with that I grabbed my dressing gown and strode down the hallway. Strangely, the smell grew stronger. Light blazed out from under a crack in the kitchen door. I flung it open. Who on earth was that trespasser in my kitchen? However, there was no demented old neighbour or vagrant before me, but a teenage son. He had a knife in his hand, and his fuzzy, curly head of hair was bent over a green plastic bowl.

"What on earth are you doing up at this hour?" I cried, suddenly awake.

"What do you think?" he growled. "It's Father's Day tomorrow. I'm making garlic bread."

The garlic was heaped up like a pile of dead maggots. I could see the son didn't do things by halves and was catering for the whole family. I couldn't go back and apologise profusely to hubby as I didn't want to spoil his Father's Day surprise. I meekly crawled back to bed, infinitely relieved, and whispered, "Glad to see the air has cleared a little. Night, night, love."

When my penfriend, Megan, suggested contributing short articles for magazines that paid well, I was one happy little writer. Working in the orchard gave me hours of memory recall if I wasn't busy rarking up the teens or, to a lesser extent, the slack lads we'd employed.

I was thrilled to win an expensive-looking bottle of shampoo from one magazine. Our teen son kept begging to try the shampoo because of his split ends. "Nope," I said. "This is far too precious to use on your mop. Buy your own." The next day, I was dismayed to find the same product selling cheaply at a supermarket. Somehow my win didn't seem so special any more. But I bought one for my hirsute son. He'd be none the wiser when he got it for Christmas. He wouldn't care that Santa gave him nothing else for Christmas; he'd just be happy to get an expensive gift he once coveted!

One wet morning, Bryan and I were lazing in bed like a pair of old sows when we heard a crunch on the gravel outside. Like coiled springs we leapt up in unison and rushed out to greet the new arrival. Too late! It was a courier van doing a wide U-turn in our yard and hightailing it up the road. There on the outside picnic table was a gift of great prettiness – a bunch of flowers wrapped in lime-and-purple coloured paper and adorned with a saffron-coloured ribbon.

I clutched the bouquet with extreme excitement. Who'd give us flowers – and they weren't even plastic! I felt cherished. "Hurry up and read the message," I urged hubby. "It'll take me half an hour to find my specs."

"What's the hurry? I wonder who they're from?"

"Probably a mistake, or one of the boys apologising for I know not what."

It was from the courier lady. Yesterday we needed her services to send some parcels away, and we gave her a bag of large, second-grade kiwifruit. It was only a small gesture, but she was so delighted she gave me a quick hug of thanks.

My spirits were so uplifted I willingly performed a thankless but necessary task. I flung myself under the teens' beds and lay in the missionary position collecting detritus – empty cans of condensed milk, spoons with dried dollops of Milo, noodle packets, mouldy lunches and worse. I didn't need the sick bucket this time. The heady scent of the gift, freshly percolated coffee, heavy rain, no orchard work, teens away for the day, and a pleasant husband – the effect was like having my own personal biblical revival. Utter joy.

Problem was the flowers contrasted with the shabbiness of the kitchen.

Time to talk about renovations.

"Just feel blessed the kids want to spend Xmas with us."

Chapter Sixteen
Other people's kids

Late one afternoon I heard a piercing whistle, followed by a bellow. "Where are you, Ma? There's a man on the phone with a funny voice. He wants you."

"What sort of voice? Foreign?" If so, it would be a telemarketer saying I had a computer virus or that someone wanted to de-bug our house for insects, but I thought we'd put those guys off by saying, "How do you know we have a computer?" and "We like our spiders."

I'd spent the day pruning in the orchard and was on the cusp of packing up loppers, secateurs, sunglasses, clips, twine, bucket and transistor radio. "Hurry, Ma! And why are you hitching up your tits?"

"I like being fancy-free in the orchard. I'm sick of over-shoulder-boulder-holders." (Meaning bras.)

"Gross," she said.

"Sorry to keep you waiting," I breathed down the phone.

"Is zat you, Jonquille?"

"Yes," I assured him, intrigued. I hoped it wasn't an old boyfriend I'd met on my hitchhiking adventures years before. The kids made sure I had wrinkles and crinkles in places men adore, and besides, I had my own man, maturing weather-wise like me.

"And you are da mudda of six adopted keeds?"

"Nine," I corrected.

"And you adopted a keed from Russia?"

"Twins," I again corrected.

"Aw, soree, may I haff a few minutes of your time. I need advice about my leedle boy we adopt from Russia. My wife, she weeps a lot. I think we return za boy back to za orphanage."

"Wait," I cried. "Let's talk this through. I'll help you. You mustn't give up. Where are you ringing from?"

It was France. I didn't know anyone from that country.

I spied potatoes in the sink that needed peeling and mince thawing on the stainless-steel sink. I couldn't worry about dinner being delayed, I justified to myself, and took the cordless phone into the bedroom where it was quieter. The wily cat would probably jump up and nibble what's on the bench, but what was more important – a desperado or our hungry teens? This poor man was in a crisis and the future of his son in limbo. The boy could go back to the orphanage to a bleak life, or I could tweak this man's affections for his adopted son with comforting words and by sharing my experience of raising nearly thirty children.

Upstairs, rap music was blasting from a stereo and two teens were arguing in the lounge. The crunching sound of a vehicle on the gravel heralded the arrival of another son who'd been milking at a neighbouring farm. He'd be especially hungry, like the rest of the family, but right now I had priorities. I was not going to tell the desperate man who sought me out from the other side of the world, "You've rung at an inconvenient time and it's pretty noisy around here." I'd let him talk because if I could encourage him to see his newly adopted child in a different light, then the child might have a brighter future.

As I was talking, Bryan wandered into the bedroom wanting to know what was happening in the kitchen department, and where were his tractor keys? He poured himself a slug of wine from a cardboard cask stored in a hiding place, away from the kids. I told the French guy my husband had arrived, and since he was the father of all our adopted kids, would he like to talk to him?

It was a positive *oui*. Yes.

The men talked man to man, father to new father.

I spend a fair amount of time on the phone taking calls from people I don't know. They want reassurances their adopted kid will normalise, that life will be happy, that it was all worthwhile in the end.

I love new parents for their fervour and commitment to a child who may not otherwise have had a future – those who wanted to create a family and those who wanted to add to it. In reality, if you adopt a child from another country, another environment, dubious parentage and so on, you need to consider whether it will damage your relationship with the person you most wanted in your life initially – your spouse.

Bryan was talking so sensibly to this man that I gave him a squeeze, topped up his glass and fetched myself one. It was exciting hearing a quaint, anguished accent coming from the other side of the world. After an hour, and an obviously expensive call, we felt bonded to this man, to each other and even our feral kids.

"We're lucky," I reminded Bryan. "We're survivors, still talking to each other, even enjoying the kids – mostly. I feel a bit sorry for the French couple as they wanted a child to treasure, but he's acting out." I know how they felt, but we didn't have the same expectations.

When we emerged from the bedroom, slightly jaded from sharing our wealth of experience, the rap music had died down.

"Are you kids dead or alive upstairs?" I called. "Daddy and I had an important phone call – an international one! Have you cooked us a nice meal? We've got the munchies."

"Nah," wafted a sound bite down the stairwell. "There was nothing to eat so we picked the lock on the pantry and found some tinned spaghetti."

What did they mean nothing to eat? What a silly thing to say. It was all out on the bench unless the cat had clawed at the plastic packages.

"We didn't feel like eating your kind of food. We've gone off healthy crap."

"Well, goodnight then. Love you too," I called back and grinned at Bryan. Not worth making a fuss about that.

When I told the slouching son in the kitchen why dinner was late, he was surly and made a derogatory comment about me giving advice to other people. In fact, said Bryan, *he* had done most of the talking during the telephone call. "Oh, that's alright then," he said.

Our son was having his *mother thing*. I had a choice. Tell him to quit being disrespectful, flounce out of the room in high dudgeon, or do subtle probing. "Son," I said. "Hear me out for one minute of your busy life. If you don't interrupt, I'll give you one of Dad's chocolates."

"No fear," said Bryan. "They're too good for him."

"Nothing's too good for our son if he keeps his mouth shut for one minute. Time it on the kitchen clock. In fact, we'll give him two chocolates if I go over the time limit."

Bryan looked stricken.

In fifty-eight seconds, I reminded our son that when we adopted him at the same age as the little boy, whom we were discussing on the call, was now, we didn't send him back to the orphanage. And *I* was the one who initially chose him. He could do anything he liked in life now, except become a murderer. So he should be happy he has a family who loves him, and if the man rang again, would he like to speak with him? Or better still, would he like to go back to his birth country for a visit?

"No way," he said. "I've seen it. Why would I want to go back?"

"Because it's your history, your culture. It's got lovely churches."

"Nah. Rather stay here. A minute's up. Where's my chocolate?"

Some days later, I got my Mother's Day reward even though it wasn't Mother's Day. We were lounging on the sofas after dinner, licking ice creams, when I mused, "I love Russian ice creams, not too sweet, not too thick, just right. Did you have any at the orphanage?"

The floodgates of his memory opened for our lad. You can't beat Russian ice creams, best in the world. And he rambled on about his pre-orphanage life, telling us where he and his twin were taken from, starving and neglected. No one cared about him, he said, so he jumped on trams and buses and wandered in the woods, even seeing wolves, and came home when he felt like it. Once he lit a fire and enjoyed the excitement of people trying to extinguish it. His days were spent either looking after his twin in a cramped apartment with abusive caregivers or sneaking out and exploring. He said Kiwi kids need to toughen up, for he alone would survive a catastrophe as he had survival skills. I smiled gently as he spoke in a strident voice about why he was vegetarian, wouldn't smoke or drink, banked all his pay, and shared his thoughts on discipline.

"You two have brought it all on yourselves," he said, shaking his curly head. "You wouldn't be having trouble with the kids if you brought them up like Genghis Khan."

"But he was cruel and blood-thirsty," I protested. "We like to raise kids with love and …"

"Mother," he said. "You have to learn to toughen up. Those Mongols knew how to control thousands of people. No one would walk over them; they'd be dead if they tried."

"So, son," I asked. "Are you going to raise your kids like that?"

"Hell, no," he replied. "I'm not getting married and have my life ruined like yours. I've got better things to do."

Bryan and I didn't need to go out for entertainment. We were in our own movie being with the kids – a mixture of comedy, light relief and drama. I'd fantasised about having twins, never expecting to adopt two sets. Both pairs were close and never took offence at the other's remarks. The Russian son could be paternal, bantering with his twin sister. She was, by then, living away from home. The twins were passionate about horses. "Hey, sis," I overheard. "How's it going? Orright? What's this I hear about you smoking? It's no good for you. Dirty, dirty! If you continue down that track, you'll end up in a dark hole." And, "What courses are you doing? Only Grade Three? You're not wagging, are you? Are you sure about that? You know you can't go on the dole forever." And then he gave her sage advice about saving.

Where did he learn all that? I wondered. Was it inbuilt or was he picking up snippets from his dad?

"What are you going to do with your life, sis? When you say you don't know, that is not an answer. You have to think about being a leader. Good to talk with you. I hope you get back on track again instead of wandering off. See ya."

I grabbed the phone. "Sorry about your bro," I said. She was bubbly and giggly and said it was fine.

"How are you, Mummy darling?" she sweetly asked. "No, I don't want anything for my birthday. Oh alright, if you insist – just your best wishes and maybe a flower."

One of my New Years' resolutions was to be nice and understanding with teenagers. Sure, it's a big ask, but I thought, *Hey, who's the adult here? I can do that.*

Confusion reigns when a familiar teen arrives in a noisy car jam-packed with kids of indeterminate breed, and then wants to know why I have a suspicious look on my face. I reply that it's my normal look for teens, and have they come home because they love us? Or do they want something? They're all hungry. Their friends have been kicked out of home, they inform me, and could they borrow a tent and camp at our place? It seems their parents are awful and don't understand them, and we are much nicer, which is news to us. The newcomers drape themselves over chairs, slurping sugary cups of coffee while one of our daughters dashes upstairs to put on loud music and another peers into the refrigerator, saying, "Yuk. There's nothing to eat here – only healthy food. We'll starve."

I tell them that if they stay, there are ground rules to follow – no swearing, no entwined sleeping, and no chucking ciggie butts on the lawn. I doubt they're listening because everyone is texting, even to each other in the same room, and the girls emit high-pitched squeals. Just when I'm bonding and loving humanity again, I have to open my big mouth. "Anyone got a job yet?"

"Oh, so you're on about that again! What sort of mother are you? We were having a good time before and then you go and spoil it."

By the time Bryan fetches a newspaper with job offer listings, and reminds them that we have plenty of work in the orchard and our country is having to import people from overseas because of staff shortages, they're stomping out the door, still texting and blowing smoke, crying, "We came for a peaceful visit, but you guys just cause drama." Strangely, they all want to hug us goodbye and say "love youse" before roaring out of the driveway to our faint cries of "Good luck finding a job."

When we discovered a teen village-lad had been sleeping in one of our disused cars at the back of our property, we felt sorry for him, but not enough to invite him to live with us. If he had a fall-out with his mother, then it was for them to work out between themselves. I had enough on my hands with hormonal girls in our home. We fed the lad in the morning and last saw him with his swag as we headed off to the orchard.

We were shocked to learn later in the day that the lad had sawn off the lock on our son's caravan, stolen his laptop and hitched out of town. The police came and took fingerprints. The culprit was arrested, and when he rang us, I asked the big "Why?" He admitted he did it to impress fifteen-year-old Natasha because he really, *really* liked her. "Are you on drugs or just plain off your head?" I roared down the phone. "Stealing from Natasha's brother, who worked his butt off to get that laptop? And you think you can win her love? What planet are you on? Planet Crazy?"

Misha, the victim, was much calmer when I handed him the phone.

"Goodaye, mate. How ya doing? I hear there's been a spot of bother 'bout you taking my laptop. Can you tell me the password on it?" He chatted amicably before delivering a veiled warning. "Hey, mate. Did you know there are two roads in life – the right road and the wrong one? I wouldn't want to see you go down the wrong path. Your choice, mate. Just get me back my laptop and it'll be as sweet as."

We were proud of our lad. Despite devouring books on savage heroes of the past, he had come to a peaceful solution.

We didn't feel particularly alone raising our teens with their up and down behaviour because I reached out for advice and support. We were friendly with the kids' teachers, youth aides, neighbours, truant officers, police and anyone who rung up with a complaint, justified or not.

While Bryan was cooking dinner, I emailed friends with adopted kids to get a balanced view on any dilemma I had raised for discussion. "Emails are flooding in, love. Can you give me another ten minutes?" I tapped out a reply and then had to call it quits. It was tiring working in the orchard and worrying about other people's problems, but after a glass of wine, theirs seemed larger than ours.

I was intrigued about how other adoptive parents coped. They all had one thing in common: They weren't giving up but needed to vent their frustrations. I felt mothers especially needed nurturing. Since I had experience with the older batch of teens (who were launched from home already), but was still dealing with the younger ones, I hoped to give them reassurance. Hang in there, buddy. It's survivable.

I mentioned amusing things our kids said or did to lighten the mood when interacting with other adoptive parents. Every day is fluid, I reminded them. Don't hang on to what happened yesterday. I was no expert but advised finding time for their partner. You are stronger together.

One parent emailed from Australia. She wondered if adopted kids had a memory gap that served as an emotional tool, one that humans have for self-preservation. If the brain is exposed to unbearable physical and emotional trauma, she suggested, it automatically forgets incidents. She cited what happened in World War Two when children would unconsciously wipe out harsh memories of the blitz or their family backgrounds when they were obliged, even forced, to re-locate from their homes.

She wondered whether adopted kids with emotional trauma were searching for people or incidents in their lives to make up for what they experience as a gap in their early memories. Or was it related to the habitual behaviour displayed by abused kids, patterns they were locked into. For example, in their lives they repeatedly look for abusive relationships because that is normal to them. Or maybe a pre-traumatised adoptive kid looks for trouble because being happy is not normal, and they think they are unworthy of happiness. Or is it a grief response?

We knew that some teens go through a phase of having dark, reflective thoughts and suggested ours keep a diary. It could be their confidante, their quiet friend. This didn't suit the boys because they were boldly being macho teens and didn't daydream. Our saving grace was living in the country, where they roared around on motorbikes, practised being firemen, and even climbing onto the two-storey roof then abseiling out a window.

We didn't turn a blind eye to all their activities, though. Once when we suspected a teen was being secretive in his bedroom, we unlocked the door while he was at school and stumbled over trip wires. Tiny dope seedlings were maturing under a blanketed table, with a burning light bulb providing warmth. My gut instinct possibly saved us from a potential fire.

I rang my sister. She was a source of advice and information because her kids were older, and she knew of several locals who grew their own weed. Instead of dealing with a confrontational, angry schoolboy, I devised a plan. As soon as the bus turned up, I rang my sister and handed the phone to the lad. "Your aunt wants to talk with you. Something about a police raid. They're canvassing our area. You haven't done anything illegal, have you?"

The son bolted upstairs, grabbed his seedlings and charged out the door in panic.

The police, of course, didn't turn up, but it gave him a fright, and Bryan hid all the keys to the upstairs rooms after this incident.

The lad learned a lesson, and we learned to be more vigilant.

Chapter Seventeen

Muddling along

When our kids were younger, they were less complicated. They were never bored on our ten acres and amused themselves sliding down the hill up the back on sheets of cardboard, making huts, rearing orphaned animals, and wading in the creek looking for gold. Plus, everyone was given a bike for their seventh birthday.

They were co-operative whenever a journalist from a newspaper or magazine visited – even the kids who weren't living at home. The visit was usually to do with adoption. This was a chance to raise awareness about children needing families and to inform those who wanted to adopt but didn't know where to start. It was never an attempt to showcase our family. Someone had to keep plugging for these kids and, hopefully, the media would highlight their plight. If I saw an opportunity to help, I felt it selfish to disconnect. It would have been easy to do so, but what I saw in Romania still haunted me.

Children do not belong in an orphanage. They need a loving family who will commit to them.

Although we had a home computer, it was limited to applications for the teens' schoolwork since Facebook was not available then. It's dismaying today, to find that the screen is more important than visitors coming to your back door. Our kids greeted people enthusiastically. "I love coming here," said an older person we unofficially adopted. "My own family treat me like I'm an old cabbage."

"You're special," I cried. "You've lived an interesting life. Pop on the kettle, kids," and I whispered that I'd find some snacks if they joined us. "Tell the kids about your travels or what it was like in the war," I suggested. "You are living history."

I hoped she didn't have incontinence problems because we still had the outside loo by the herb garden. I'd warn the kids that if they saw a walking stick outside the lav, then a lovely lady was in residence. And not to be rude like I was once when out in the garden, weeding. From a distance I spied someone darting out of the loo and heading down the side of the house. Presuming it was one of our teens, I yelled out, "Hey! Wash your hands. Don't be a filthy pig." Bryan tried to shush me. It wasn't a kid but a desperate passer-by in urgent need.

"Sorry," I apologised. "It's my eyesight. It goes wonky in brilliant sunlight."

We were grateful to those outside our family who took an interest in our children. Our Russian son was refusing to conform at school, and his teacher's aide, Chris Pomeroy, went above and beyond the call of duty to help him. He was like a big brother. He took him fishing, where they could engage in man stuff away from the classroom. Once the excited son came home and said his stomach ached. Was he ill?

"Can't you guess why?" he said. I couldn't.

"Think about it, Mother. I'm too excited from catching all that fish!"

Another mentor, Kris Russell, a farrier, introduced him to horses, an interest which is still ongoing. Her late husband helped him build a boat and took him sailing across Cook Strait. These people were invaluable in helping a lad who was floundering, and challenging, at the time.

It's awkward 'getting inside' the feelings of your teen child, for they are secretive, and even they don't know why they feel the way they do.

Kids can't imagine their own parents being teenagers. As the years pass, my vivid memories don't fade – especially those about my own teenage feelings. Flashbacks helped me reconnect with our growing youngsters.

Decades ago, when a boyfriend casually knocked on the door late one night and asked me out, it was a firm 'no' from my parents. What horrible mean parents! I loved him. I'd die if I couldn't go. What did they know about love!

"If you venture out that door," warned Mother, "then don't bother coming home. Ever."

The boyfriend loped off, maybe into another girl's arms. I bawled my eyes out, emitting small shrieks of rage that had my siblings tumbling down the staircase. Dad bellowed, "For Chrissakes. Stop that confounded noise! I've got a busy day at the office tomorrow. I'll shoot any bastard who comes around at an indecent hour."

Mum said worriedly, "Should I ring the lunatic asylum?"

My brother gleefully replied that it could be arranged; his surfing mate worked there – which appalled Mum as she didn't want our family to be associated with 'those types'. Shocked by his betrayal, I shouted, "You don't understand how I feel. You want to ruin my life. Bet I'm adopted."

"Oh, for heaven's sake," said Mum. "Who in their right mind would have children, especially other peoples?"

My father was making exaggerated snoring noises. Mum added to the sting. "Why would you think you're adopted? You've got the Washbourn legs." (Mother's side of the family.)

"Like upturned beer bottles!" I wept and darted upstairs, flinging myself under the frilly nylon bedspread. Liberace's face smiled sweetly from the posters lining my attic wall. *Life is so bloody cruel. Sorry to say 'bloody', my darling. But you understand. And where was God when I needed him?*

It's a fact of life, isn't it, that teens lash out verbally. It's not intended to wound; it's just juvenile frustration.

One stout mum I spoke to admitted she once received a backhanded compliment from her adopted child. "I'm so glad you adopted me," said her teen daughter, throwing her arms around her. "Coz if you were my real (birth) mother, I would've had your thick ankles."

De-bonding can also happen if the adopted child is away from home for any length of time.

At the suggestion of health professionals, we agreed to our Russian twins going on a trip to a health camp for underprivileged kids. We didn't think ours were, but it was another experience for them. It was an airplane ride away and all-expenses paid. I had my doubts but bowed to their wisdom. The daughter was fine and co-operative, although not sure how much she benefited from the camp. The son went crazy the first night, being cooped up in what appeared to be an institution. It reminded him of the orphanage in Russia with its high windows. The next night he was put in a corridor for being disruptive, and the following day was put on a plane and sent home. The carers said they'd never experienced a child quite like that. He beamed broadly when we fetched him from the airport. He was happy to be back in our family. We didn't know much about post-traumatic stress disorder but resolved to rely on gut instinct in future.

Another gut feeling to rely on relates to being cautious about adults who come into your life, seemingly benign, well meaning, even lavish in their attention to our children. We take people at face value, but this particular guy we once met was too good to be true, and we soon felt uncomfortable about the interaction between him and our young pre-teens. He loved animals, and he was generously bringing unhealthy snacks and treats to our home. He seemed like a lost soul but was pleasant and articulate and fancied himself as a grandfather figure.

I was perturbed when a couple of daughters scrawled on the wall in felt pens, saying they wanted to live with him. We were concerned he was undermining our values and parenting, while the kids thought they could get money out of him. It was hard to ask him not to visit so often – and hurtful. We didn't want the kids extracting and accepting favours from this elderly gentleman who overindulged them. I could talk about our dilemma with Internet friends who'd also adopted.

I received letters from people who'd adopted children from overseas countries. One of whom wrote that her adopted son was displaying behaviour that was damaging to his three siblings whom they had also adopted. Would I consider taking him on? It was tricky, even tempting, but it meant involving Social Welfare. Usually problems like these are resolved, and in this case, relatives agreed to take the child who would still be living near the family who had initially adopted him and with whom his siblings lived. He would benefit from ongoing contact with his siblings, something we could not have offered him as we lived much, much further away.

Going to RDA (Riding for the Disabled) was a bonus for several of our kids. They weren't intellectually disabled, but it was a programme offered by the school for those who didn't fit into the category of 'more able' students. It was a confidence booster, and since our kids loved horses, it was a happy time out of class. Often, we had to down tools in the orchard and take them to and fro between classes at school. It's no wonder we got behind in orchard work. If someone volunteered to ferry them, we were grateful and keen to know how the day went. When one of our young teens said there was a new kid in the riding group that day, I asked what disability the child had. Down syndrome? Autism? Missing limb? The teen shook her head. "There must be something different," I urged. "What do you think it could be?"

The youngster thought deeply, and said, "Well, he's got blonde hair."

As teens, our life wasn't worth living being cheeky or impertinent to our parents. Nowadays the younger generation have a voice – they have support through schools and agencies. We took one of the teens in our care to a counsellor because she was being kicked out of school. The counsellor asked about what was happening at home. Miss Teen swore, and said she wanted more freedom and that she needed to de-stress with a ciggie. I wanted to cry, "We don't bring our kids up this way," but it wasn't about us. It was about making the teen happy and finding a solution. We were silently fuming, but open to suggestions, and the kid held the balance of power. When the well-meaning social worker sent out a questionnaire regarding her abilities as a professional, as she was moving on from her present role, I tore up the paper. She hadn't cautioned the teen about being rude and disrespectful. We had left the interview room with a smirking kid in tow.

"Just because I've been a bitch to you doesn't mean I can't have a birthday celebration," she said later. I wasn't offended by that remark. I was delighted for it meant she had a conscience.

Birthday presents did not mean having a boy sleep overnight in her room, but one guy turned up anyway, which thrilled Miss Fifteen. He said he had a Mother's Day gift for me even though that was months away. He darted out to his car in torrential rain and handed over an expensive bottle of Galliano liqueur. I gushed, "Oh you poor little thing. Don't go wasting your money on me. Drink it yourself." Then I withdrew the offer since he was only sixteen. "How'd you manage to afford this? Did you nick it?"

The daughter wailed, "Ma! He's got money. His parents are rich."

I said, "What's that got to do with the price of eggs?" but nobody knew what it meant. I hesitantly accepted the gift, and since there was some missing from the top, I said he could stay half the time upstairs and sleep in the spare room when we went to bed.

"Not doing anything yukky upstairs are you, lil' darlings?" I'd call up like a sergeant major. It was a tongue-in-cheek remark I'd come up with since reading the biography of an iconic Kiwi artist, a latent 'gay', who'd married and had several children. His dour old-fashioned mother had her suspicions about her son, for she asked after his wedding, "And have you done the horrible thing yet?" What a thing to say to your child!

"Nah, we don't do that anymore," the daughter called back. "We're looking at photos of me when I was a baby. Jeeze, I was cute."

A friend said she allowed her fifteen-year-old to have the boyfriend for regular sleepovers. I wasn't sure about being so liberal but chuckled when she said her daughter had been annoyingly grouchy because the boyfriend had to go away for a few days. The boyfriend's grandmother was on her deathbed, and he and his family travelled a long distance to spend time with her during her last moments. The lass missed her boyfriend and moaned to her mother, "I wish his grandmother would hurry up and cark it. I have my needs too!"

While I was laughing, another mum emailed about a recent wedding she attended as her small son was a pageboy at the ceremony. As the bride bent over, he said loudly, "I can see right down your front. But don't worry," he whispered behind a cupped hand, "I only saw the white bits, not the orange bits!"

One year we enrolled Miss Thirteen in Tides – a programme involving young ladies being mentored by several older women to ease their transition from girlhood to womanhood. It was held at a camp in a wilderness setting near the sea. We hoped it would enrich the daughter as she was becoming precocious. It was back to basics and the ultimate in organised freedom, with outdoor baths, organic food, chanting, talks and other activities. When the camp finished after a few days, we were invited to collect our daughters, and a ceremony was performed welcoming the girls' parents. We suffered sunburnt faces clutching hands in a circle as people made speeches.

One by one the teachers spoke a few words, and then there was a pregnant silence with people uncertainly eyeing one another. Some were shuffling their feet. My brain said, "Be proactive." I broke away from the outer circle and joined the teachers. "Hello. My name is Jonquil. I brought my daughter here for some mentoring and fun and I want to thank you. And I would like to introduce her father, Bryan with a Y. Come and join us, Bryan."

The leader, a Mother Earth woman with long, damp undergrowth in her armpits, which reminded me of rain forests in the Amazon, looked blank. She wondered whether I would like to take over, but I politely declined. There was more touchy-feely stuff before Bryan suggested we head off into the hills and admire the new subdivisions. A man on a steamroller frantically waved at us, but Bryan charged on, waving back. The road got steeper and rougher until we ended up facing crumbling granite rock, but the views were spectacular. The girls and I alighted from the hearse and shouted instructions to Bryan who was gingerly reversing.

"Dad's not a loser, just misguided," I said once we settled back into the vehicle. "Did you have a wonderful time? Did you learn Māori? Did you cook the kai (food)?" When the camp daughter shrugged, I persisted.

"Friggin' hell, you're so nosy," she snapped.

My mother said you never talk to a man on an empty stomach or when he's tired. Let him unwind first. Same with teens back from camp I learnt.

When shooting pains started in my head, Bryan ordered me to bed. It had been a gruelling time for me, getting phone calls from Australia about messed-up people who'd had kids removed from their homes, or the Filipino Internet bride who became hysterical – screaming and bawling down the phone, pleading for help and money. Some of our orchard workers thought we could solve their problems for them, too.

Since I felt so miserable, I obeyed hubby and watched dated Liberace videos. That hunky spunk perked me up, and eventually I was able to receive food and compliments in bed – when I managed to take my eyes off the screen. Bryan made chicken soup – which is what his mother used to do. Misha gave me a backhanded compliment. Apparently, it was nice of me to try and help stuffed up people when, instead, I should be sorting out my own life. I said I was perfectly happy, thank you, except for my poor aching head, and that he was blocking my view of Mummy's idol tinkling the ivories.

When I heard jogging was a good way to relieve stress, I jogged for so long one day the family was about to send out a search party. It was hard to tell what time it was with daylight saving in effect. "Mummy's here," screamed the kids. "You're not dead!"

"Never felt better," I snorted as moisture discharged from cracks and crevices too indecent to mention.

When a twin jogged with me down a country lane, I cautioned, "Don't look at what that rude bull is doing in the paddock. The cows were perfectly happy until Mr Randy came along." We laughed so much my body made violent, involuntary gurgles. "Pretend those noises are from a Walkman attached to my bod," I spluttered as we zigzagged.

As we jogged back, the exhausted bull had wandered off, leaving a paddock of smiling cows, similar to a polygamous cult, I imagined.

Once when Miss Teen was ranting, I got a brainwave. "Satan," I demanded. "Get out of my daughter's body. You have no business being there."

The daughter swore. "I'm not talking to you," I said. "Hey, Satan. Did you hear me? You leave my beautiful daughter alone."

Confused, the daughter retreated. "And don't think I won't tell Satan off in front of your friends if you get lippy again," I said.

Today's kids don't ask what it was like in their parents' time. One evening we were watching a documentary about Australian immigration in the '50s and '60s when a clip showed a young European family alighting from a ship in Melbourne. I screamed, "That's my movie!"

"Calm down, Mother. It couldn't be you. You're not a movie star."

The phone rang. It was my sister. "We were on TV," she said excitedly.

As youngsters, my siblings and I auditioned for *The Way we Live* (1959) movie and got the role of migrant children. It was a promotional movie depicting the Australian way of life for prospective immigrant families in Europe who were keen to make a new life in the 'lucky country'. We were holidaying in London when the movie premiered and never got to see it. "I'm going to track the movie down if it's the last thing I do," I assured Sis.

The *Nelson Mail* was helpful and sent out a reporter who covered the story on their front page – 'Old footage shocks *star* from her seat.' It was picked up by the *Christchurch Press* and went viral.

"This is the BBC," said a clipped voice when the phone rang at midnight. I thought it was a hoax. We were used to teen jargon, not a polished, refined voice coming from the other side of the world. The caller set up an interview for the next day. It meant clearing the house of teens and rash promises of rewards if they stayed outside, otherwise that nice BBC man would think he'd reached an asylum. After the interview, he wished me luck tracking down the film, but did he have to ask, "Are you sure you were in that movie? It was forty years ago, you know"?

"Young man," I said indignantly, "to me it was like yesterday. I can remember every scene I was in. And besides, I can recall being twenty months old. My mother said she'd buy me a doll's pram if I stopped wetting my bed. It was a cane pram wrapped up in brown paper, which I pushed up a Sydney city street." The guy hung up the phone: information overload.

After phoning the film archive in Canberra, the movie was sent to me, and I shared it with my family.

"See, I was quite nice once, wasn't I?" My teens retreated halfway from the room for the bouncy soundtrack music was irritating, and the movie did seem dated. Baby boomers, however, find it a fascinating slice of Aussie history.

In quieter moments I reflected on my own sunny childhood, recalling the saying: 'Stolen moments, sweeter for the theft!'

Chapter Eighteen

Book launch

One of the sweetest books I ever read was *The Family Nobody Wanted* by Helen Doss. It's a 1954 memoir, the story of a minister and his wife who adopted twelve children of various nationalities in the '40s and '50s in America. The dog-eared paperback was posted to me by my penfriend, Megan, who was encouraging during our endeavour to adopt from overseas. I read the book in one gulp, then read it again. We were already parents to four adopted boys of Dutch, Rarotongan and Māori heritage. We didn't initially plan for an international or intercountry adoption, but when Megan sent articles about abandoned babies left in orphanages in certain overseas countries, it stirred my heartstrings. Yes, we did have capacity to bring another child into our family. I couldn't ignore what I read.

Luckily, Bryan agreed to my going ahead and enquiring from orphanages across the world, especially if we could find a little girl to complete the family. Privately, I thought that we should be open-minded and flexible. And Bryan smiled when I said, "What if we are offered twins?" never believing that would happen, let alone us eventually adopting 'triplets', and then twins. He thought that was just fine. I knew I'd married a special man.

Once we had adopted five more children from Eastern Europe

(between 1990 and 1995), I decided to ring Helen Doss in America. There was a Telecom special offer available at the time, and I could chat internationally for an unlimited time for ten dollars. When you are raising many children, you are on a budget, so I took advantage of the offer.

Bryan said, "Go for it" and told the kids that Mummy was busy and not to be bothered, since she was talking to friends across the globe. For me, it was a marathon twelve hours with barely a loo stop. The kids were amazed I knew so many people. I was too. But I had to ring the author of this beloved book knowing she would be in her late eighties. Her reedy little voice reached across the airwaves as she told me about her family, and when I said I was writing about my family, she was gracious and encouraging. She said she was visiting Donny, her oldest adopted child, and since she wasn't computer savvy, she would ask him to get in touch with me.

Donny and his wife, Sharon, live in California and stay in contact with their surviving siblings. I was keen to know how adopted siblings 'gel' and what happened to their relationships with one another when they grew up and had their own families. I hoped mine would all be friends once they left home. The Doss children have personalities as diverse and different as those of our children, and some formed closer relationships with a particular brother or sister than another, which happens in any family. Donny married a gem, for Sharon is a connector and is genuinely sweet, generous and perceptive. Quite frankly, she is one of the nicest people on this earth, and we haven't yet met in person! Whenever I had problems or was bothered, she was available by email, and we've had lengthy correspondence and exchanged gifts. She put me in touch with others who had adopted. I always felt better after talking with these American mothers for our experiences were universal.

On the other side of the world, especially in the UK, I found new friends and support through my cousin, Joanna. She, too, is one in a million. Joanna flew out to Romania three times when I was adopting my three babies on two separate trips, and she helped me financially. We hadn't been in touch for years, but Romania was close to her heart after hearing about the thousands of children languishing in orphanages. When I wrote I was going to Romania, she impulsively hopped on a plane thinking she'd find me there – the long lost cuzzy. She doggedly found me after ten days, with only a day to spare before catching her own flight home. This was before emails, so it was a huge effort on her part. I told cousin Joanna I would love her to be godmother to my Romanian babies and that when I was in a position to do so, I would fly her out to New Zealand. "I owe you big time, cuz."

The opportunity came when I submitted a manuscript to Chris Cole Catley, a pioneering writer, broadcaster and publisher, who co-founded Parents Centres New Zealand, and was made a Dame in 2006 with the Dame Companion of The New Zealand Order of Merit (DCNZM) in recognition of her services to literature.

Chris and her second husband, Doug Catley, set up their own publishing house in 1973, Cape Catley Press. Chris, who was an octogenarian when I submitted my work, said she rejected a lot of manuscripts, but she couldn't reject mine. "To me," she wrote, "it is ludicrous and PC in the extreme to put a child's culture before its need for a family. Monstrous I say!" She wanted to know what motivated us, and how we managed emotionally and financially. I hadn't thought too deeply about that. We coped because we learned from our parents about saving and recycling and never buying anything we couldn't afford. She was old-school, for that was how she was raised, too. She ended her first letter asking, "To put it bluntly, are you two big-hearted but batty people???" I knew we'd get on well.

We exchanged letters before she sent me a contract. Having a publisher takes away the stress of extra editing and marketing. When she said the book was being released in time for Mother's Day, I sent tickets to my cousin and her son for them to come out to New Zealand. "Just paying you back, cuz, and you can see your god-daughters and some Kiwi scenery."

It was a whirlwind of radio, TV and media talks around New Zealand, which continued after the pair flew back to England.

"Mum's talking on the radio this afternoon," Bryan would warn a teenager. He said if they stayed away from the house for an hour, I might cook their favourite meal.

"Oh, Mum, can you make mine?" pleaded Natasha. She had trouble describing it. "You know what I like. It's that fish shit."

She meant Hunza pie. It is whipped up rice, eggs, cheese and spinach, baked in the oven, topped with buttered crispy bread. Not a whiff of fish in that dish!

Dame Chris and I kept in touch. She said she laughed over my emails about giving talks to various women's groups and libraries. Not used to public speaking, I always felt anxious and would hit the google button to research 'confident speaking'. The helpful advice, as I recall, was to pretend your audience was naked.

Happily, erotica was far from my mind when I next spouted forth in the cosy confines of a warm library, one filled with a sea of white-and-grey heads and a sprinkle of fake gold, brunette and black-haired heads. In other words, I was going to yap to a rainbow audience.

My confidence was restored when I found a new purple bra that I'd bought earlier for the book launch. Bryan mentioned I needed an uplift and he was surprised to be dragged into a lingerie shop. He said he meant in terms of self-esteem. My family noticed something different about me but couldn't quite pinpoint it. One of the teens begged to come along to the talk, and even did the dishes. I caved in, saying she could if she didn't smoke, swear or cough. She was almost perfect. I had cut my own hair and was ready to party. Bryan, the wayward daughter and I set off over the hill in the dark, and we called in briefly to see another one of our young teens who was holed up with the boyfriend and his old landlord. The daughter was thrilled to see us, shouting into the night, "My parents are here. My lovely mum and dad! Hey, Mum, are you wearing my bra?"

I cut to the chase. "Just called in to see if you're on the pill, and can we use the lav?"

The landlord bellowed from the smoke-riddled lounge out the back, "Who's using the shower?"

"It's all right," yelled the daughter. "Just my parents using the toilet. Come and meet them." But he chose not to. Wise man.

The boyfriend said, "I've got a job starting Monday," which was a nice thing to hear, even if it was wishful thinking.

And then we headed off for the talk.

And something lovely happened to Bryan. It was expected, of course, but the question was 'when' it would occur.

A largish woman lunged at him. She had read my book and to her, he was a star. I was happy he was being attacked in such a delicious way because, to be frank, I might go to my demise before him, and he needed experience with the fuller figure.

Another woman, with grey roots, urged us onto the speaking stand and waved the book in front of the compliant audience, saying she'd read my book in the library, then bought a copy for herself. "It's a love story," she cried. "A New Zealand love story," and she said so many nice things I felt a bit damp – but full of adrenalin.

I started off with a raunchy story and before long it was coffee and biscuit time with nice-smelling ladies opening up their handbags. I told them my profits would go to a charity, but they didn't care. They gladly parted with their coins to get a whiff of hubby.

Another thing that I expected could happen someday, eventually did. The birth grandmother of one of our boys introduced herself to us. Over the years, she had kept every magazine and newspaper article on our family. She was sending a copy of the book to her daughter in Australia, our son's birth mother. I hugged her hard, a bit like what the women were doing to my husband.

"I can never thank your daughter enough for allowing us to parent your grandson. We have to stay in touch." And we all have.

Delivering a talk to a receptive audience gives you a high. It certainly spilled over to the next day when we alighted from our ailing hearse, me wearing my new purple uplift. A local, who normally crosses the road in our country town when she sees us, spied me looking glam, and she wondered if we were joining the Probus Club lecture. Bryan wickedly told her if she played her cards right, I might be persuaded to give a talk to the Probus Club. When I reached to embrace her, she said, "Better not touch, darling. Might smear our lipstick." After that I was happy to return to the orchard, to being a peasant again, and to the familiarity of family.

In Motueka I gave a talk to forty or so lovely dears at the Country Women's Institute. They fussed over Bryan and made cauldrons of veggie and pumpkin soup, delicate sandwiches and cakes. Many were widows. I said to one attractive woman, "You look too young to be here. Are you somebody's daughter?" She laughed and said she was seventy-seven. I didn't like to comment, but replied that her face must never have seen the sun, or had she had a facelift?

"You're so pretty. You must have had some nice men in your life," I added. Indeed, she'd buried two husbands. She wasn't sure what to say when I said she'd have more chance finding a man than most, including me. Anyone who bought my book got a squeeze of grateful thanks, but this little poppet waltzed away. It made me wonder whose arms would be reaching out for her on these long, cold South Island nights.

The meeting was held in the rooms of the local fire station, and when some burly six-foot-two firemen barged in to fix up a blocked sink, the ladies let out a throaty applause. After that I decided to keep a close watch on hubby, the only man in the room with women who, collectively, had known more men and action than I'd see in a lifetime under the kiwifruit vines. I told them that being in a room with so many nice people saying lovely things about me, was like attending my own funeral. After they stopped laughing, I cut the talk short in case they'd ask about our teens.

On the return trip, we again visited the daughter flatting in a cold house with the boyfriend, although we couldn't understand why the landlord was away getting a cancerous growth removed from his neck when it was known that the junior doctors were on strike. We told the couple to keep looking for work, buy a ten-years' supply of connies (condoms), and not rip the landlord off by keeping the heater on all day. Teens don't take offence; it's all love and kisses when you leave.

At the Warehouse we bumped into the local truancy officer who looked so familiar I wondered if she was at the talk I'd delivered. We updated her about the kids. And blow me down if we didn't see her again at a supermarket, lurking behind the Sauvignon Blanc in the liquor aisle. She looked a tad guilty as our trolley only held washing-up liquid, so when she scurried down the aisle, we nipped back to the grog department and bought a nice red. How strange, I reflected, this police officer and I could end up in the same rest home, imbibing sherry through a nose drip and reminiscing. I bet she has a few stories in her.

Shortly after, I gave a talk to the Friends of the Library, in Nelson. As the library door flapped open, two pairs of outstretched hands greeted us. One pair we weren't allowed to shake; they were stained pink and off-limits. The owner of the crimson paws said she had a lurgy. Her mouth was swathed in a nylon scarf, like Michael Jackson was wont to do. She said she would introduce us before running home to bed. The other, a silvery gent, said he was gobsmacked by my book, but he smiled widely, and his big, warm hands smelt fragrantly soapy.

Intimate. That's how I'd describe the room we were ushered into. Paying guests were already seated like obedient pupils. She, with the crimson hands, said we'd better get cracking, and once the introductions were made, she took off like a Bedouin in the desert, making little coughs with the nylon scarf about to throttle her in full flight.

I told the sea of upturned faces about the different authors I encountered as a child. One of whom was a stooped, middle-aged Jewish bachelor who my family and I met on a ship sailing to England in the 1960s. He was a concert pianist and writer, and he fancied my mother. It sent my father into spasms of inner turmoil and suppressed rage. He lent my mother a manuscript of his latest book. The paper looked pristine and pure, but the words were not. The second sentence read: 'He cupped her white bosom in his hand.'

"Mummy," I cried. "You shouldn't be reading this filth." All the way from Marseille to Dover, I worried as fifteen-year-olds do. Will Mother be safe? Will he be cupping his hairy mitts around poor Mummy when she is writhing in bed, seasick?

The audience was appreciative and told me to speak up. I find it helps focussing on one or two people while you're yabbering on. One old biddy had a strained look, so I wasn't sure whether it was the pickles in the sandwich spread that gave her suppressed flatulence, or if she'd dropped her hearing aid. Others had wide upturned smiles and nodding heads, and when I ground to a halt amid (sorry to sound vain) applause, I told the audience that I should be the one clapping. How kind of them to listen – my teens never listen to me! The man with the soapy hands invited us to lunch, but Bryan wanted to buy thermals and look at tractors instead. I thought, *Okay, that sounds manly; I'll go with what I know.*

When we got home that cold evening, Bryan and I were standing in the lounge with our backsides to the wood-burning stove, trying to get warm. Misha came in from milking cows and asked how the talk went. I told him that one old gal kept leaning forward. "Bet she wasn't interested in your talk, Mum. She was trying to perve at Dad's legs, aye Dad?"

Momentarily I wished I hadn't heaped generous praise, in the past, on Bryan's pins which are strong, brown, vibrant – definitely his best feature compared to the albino-veined 'see-thru' legs of some of his contemporaries. But I was gracious, and said, "Misha, Daddy was a star."

And everyone was happy.

You get the odd person who challenges you once you become a public figure. I agreed to talks because it raised the plight of orphans, but it was always an ordeal preparing for one. A friend, who'd adopted two Romanian daughters, thought I needed smartening up since my usual apparel was gumboots, old clothes, a sunhat and lashings of sunblock. We agreed to meet in town during her lunch hour because, being a businesswoman, she knew about fashion. She flung items of clothing into the changing room, but the style just wasn't *me*. Some items I paraded back-to-front. "You are hopeless," she cried, flinging herself onto a mannequin in the display window and retrieving a garment that I wouldn't be happy wearing at my demise. "This has been the worst experience for me," she complained, and I said it had been pretty bad for me, too.

After, I said to Bryan. "Let's go to the op shop," and I came away smiling. So did Bryan: his wallet didn't have a big dent in it.

I love a bargain. Who doesn't! Since we were thinking of renovating, I found an enormous rimu window going for fifty cents and put in a bid on Trade Me, hoping someone would outbid me – then I wouldn't have to think about it again. "We have to pick it up," I told Bryan. "You need to get your shoulder x-rayed in Nelson, and we can nip into demolition yards while we're there." Good naturedly, he revved up the hearse and we took off over the hill with our thermos and sandwiches.

The seller was Irish, with a lilting accent. I told her we didn't actually need or want the window, but it was worth coming just to hear her gorgeous accent. Her complexion deepened to a delightful crimson as she and hubby heaved the white elephant onto the trailer in drizzling rain. While he was trying to avoid sideswiping her pot plants down the driveway, Bryan muttered that he didn't need any more bargains. I told him to be happy we weren't towing an empty trailer back over the Takaka Hill. He wisely said nothing.

When we got home, Tristan said, "Mum, did you know we were in the paper?"

My heart sank as I rummaged through the police round-up section, and said, "Doesn't look like any of the kids have gone to jail. Tristan, your dad and I have had a big day looking at shower units and gazing into lavatory bowls. Don't tease. Worry about your poor dad who has a crook shoulder."

But there it was: page 31 of the *Nelson Mail* – a lovely review of my book with a photo, titled *An Extraordinary Family*.

"Let's do something more extraordinary and be serious," I said to hubby. "Call the local architect tomorrow about renovating the house. It's time to up our standards."

Chapter Nineteen

Renovations

"Now I've written my book, darls, it's time to think of renovating this old house. The older kids have left home, are even procreating. And, surprisingly, one even got married before having a kid."

Bryan laughed. He thought they were basically good kids and had absorbed some of our values. "Pour us a red and we'll draw up ideas to discuss with the architect."

Our brains became imaginative and productive. No wonder our parents looked forward to 'tincture time' when they relaxed and celebrated the survival of another day of teens.

The Russian son barged in through the back door, kicking off the cow-pong gumboots and peeling back his blue plastic gloves that may have been inside a birthing cow, but we didn't like to ask. "Dinner's slightly delayed, son," I said. "Daddy and I are going modern. We're getting this house renovated and, wait for it – adding an inside loo!"

"You're not getting rid of the outside one, are you?" he asked horrified. "Don't you realise inside toilets can be dirty, dirty things."

So glad I got that lad from Russia, I mused. His remarks could be stinging but always entertaining – if you were in the right frame of mind. And right now, my mind was on frames, the wooden type.

Bryan said he was also partial to the outside lav, with its warm wooden seat and the occasional cheeky weka popping its inquisitive beak in the door. Also, it was a temporary respite from argumentative teens. Call it a poor man's holiday, if you will. It was useful for the pruners we employed, although some took advantage of the distance if we were working in a far-off block, for once they'd visited the lav, they ambled back slowly to pick up their pruning tools. "They should have done their business before they left home, aye Ma," offered a teen. That remark sounded like one of my father's, who'd been a military man.

Dad was regimented when it came to daily routine: a cup of tea (preferably British), a run around the block to get the intestines working, showering (initially cold, followed by the treat of a hot one), and a sit-down on the outside throne – all before facing a three-course breakfast. He timed himself with a fob watch, making sure we teens were not at the breakfast table at the same time because, he said, his mind was on beauty, and not on that foreign muck we kids listened to on the radio. Mum would ask, "Had any beautiful thoughts today, dear?" That got him out of his chair quickly and off to catch the early bus, his briefcase bulging with one of the encyclopedias he'd bought for us to improve our minds, but which were barely touched, except for when we teens opened them to glimpse the nude paintings and statues illustrated within.

In Australia, land of my childhood, my mother's greatest thrill was planning and decorating any house we moved into. I would have loved her input for what we were about to undertake, but she had been 'gathered' – a '50s euphemism for passing into the next world. She was in her element when it came to bathroom tiles, and even got Dad to convert the big empty space upstairs in our Collaroy beach bungalow to an office and three bedrooms. Most people would have thought it suitable only as a crawl space for marauding marsupials. She received a handsome cheque from *Home and Garden* magazine for an article she wrote about the renovations, which was spent on roses to beautify the garden. My father, however, carelessly mowed them over, calling anything not lawn 'bloody weeds'.

I emailed friends, telling them the big news: we are renovating. Got any advice? Some replies were disappointing, suggesting we torch the place and start afresh. Others said it was a lovely old house but renovations cost heaps. In the local supermarket, when people enquired about our kids, I couldn't help myself. It was like telling someone you're pregnant or who'd died. I said we are doing the Big R (renovating). Trolleys jammed up aisles as shoppers offered advice. I'd touched on a subject where everyone's an expert – or so they thought – and they revealed intimacies about their shower nozzles, lazy Susans, taps and light fittings. Bryan scribbled copious notes, which only encouraged those stacking shelves to join in.

But first things first: we retrieved sketches of what we envisaged from the filing cabinet. Some were so old they had moth nibbles in them, possible BC (before children). Two decades earlier, we had asked visiting rellies to submit ideas for doing up our house; some contributions were thoughtful, if somewhat impractical. It was now time to bite the bullet. We chose a certain ponytailed architect because he was local and had a nice, earthy feel about him – unlike the city dude who visited, looked at the house, and said he didn't think we could afford his services!

The architect liked our concept but modified it. The back of the house had to be pulled down, but the steep staircase was to remain. He would be adding a verandah to the north side and replacing the original verandah in front of the house that had been removed because it was rotting. I wanted a large kitchen, overlooking the massive back lawn, to accommodate the expanding family. Nothing is worse than poor Mother in a poky kitchen, drenched in sweat and splatters from frying something unhealthy (but which the kids liked as a treat), and a beefy person reaching past her protruding butt to gather ice-cold beer from the fridge. No! The kitchen had to be large and work friendly. Perhaps modern too, with melamine, which was a new word for us country bumpkins. We visited display houses for ideas, but the sophisticated neutral colours weren't true to the character of our house.

Timber from our small block up the back was milled and cut into slabs, and a local librarian said we could have doors from her 1870s house as it was being demolished. Another librarian's brother offered casement windows from the Cobb Valley – very old. I wanted to hug them all for caring about our home but thought I better keep my paws to myself.

When word came through that the architect's plans had been approved and that a representative of Heritage New Zealand's Historic Houses division, a lady, would be visiting, we downed tools in the orchard, put pansies in the outside lav in case she had a 'moment', and awaited her arrival. I told the teens to buzz off as we couldn't jeopardise our project. We even bribed them, and they hitched off to town with a few bucks, thrilled and shouting out, "Love you so much, Mum and Dad. You're awesome parents." We were taken aback when the Historic Houses lady from the city, dressed in black, glanced around the house, and said, "Shocker. When do you want to start the renovations? Yesterday?"

It was a thrilling moment. Full steam ahead!

Now that we had approval, it consumed our thoughts. Daily we worked in the orchard, and at night I again sought advice from email friends, printing out their replies. "If you had to do up your house, what is absolutely necessary?" I asked. Many said a dishwasher and a heated towel-rail, which we bought but never used. The dishwasher was noisy, long-winded and wasted power, so it remained a storage for extra plates. And a heating rail for towels was too luxurious and non-essential. No one suggested solar panels; we thought of them ourselves.

For our project, we chose a couple of local builders who couldn't start immediately, which suited us as Son No. 3 (but No. 2 in order of adoption) was getting married. There'd been a muck-up at his brother's wedding when we got stuck shopping in the Warehouse and couldn't find all the kids. "We're here," I cried as we dashed into the venue for his wedding, where music blared, and tattooed guests milled around with noisy kids sliding down the railings. "Start the wedding." But the groom said it was too late – we had missed the ceremony; the celebrant couldn't hang around. And he continued smooching his bride on the dance floor.

"Don't worry about it, Mum," he said good-naturedly. "Grab yourself a beer."

That's my boy, I thought. *Easy come; easy go.*

This time, the new groom-to-be said, the wedding would be held locally, on the beach, and we had no excuse to miss it. When we asked if he was sure about getting married, he quipped, "It's all good. I'm into extreme sports!"

We ploughed on with summer pruning until it turned to autumn, which is harvest time. When Tristan mentioned going to Australia to see his birth mum and find work over there, we were encouraging of the idea. We had both travelled and wanted our kids to experience life outside New Zealand.

After the bins of kiwifruit were trucked away and the workers paid, Tristan climbed into a digger and smashed down the back of the house and dismantled the brick chimney. Where the jaws of the digger entered the kitchen, he dug up the concrete, yanking out the coal range.

He and his new partner had barely arrived in Australia, when he phoned, "Comin' home." Why so? we wanted to know. "Too busy," he said, referring to city life and the bustling motorways in Queensland. We urged him to give it a try, but the young couple returned a fortnight or so later with huge smiles on their faces. He ambled around the renovations, arms folded, and periodically popped a gold kiwifruit into his girlfriend's mouth to immobilise her jaw so we couldn't quiz her. Our son has always been a lateral thinker.

Since we had no kitchen, we lived like old pioneers for months, cooking on a gas ring in the shed. The cat didn't know where it lived, and the kids complained they couldn't find food because it was concealed in mice-proof containers. We boiled up water for washing dishes and bathing, and we shivered as the days got shorter and frost crackled on the ground. We sighed when the younger set of twins arose early, hoed into the bacon, left tops off coffee jars, and disabled the toaster by lighting their ciggies from it before hitching off to town.

On Day Three of the renovation project, the builders arrived in their utes whistling, and said manly things, such as "four be twos", "she's level – good as gold" and "can ya put a sight on that, mate, box of fluffy ducks". Bryan and I grabbed spades and dug trenches while the twins turned up their stereos, fought and giggled uncontrollably when reminded the builders were nice people; one was even a Christian. When the chief builder needed several copies of the amended working plan and dimensions for a toilet – S-trap as opposed to P-trap – we told the girls to hop in the hearse for a trip. The builders needed a rest from us. When we returned, a young lad on work experience was digging trenches – which encouraged the twins to pitch in. "I'll be your girlfriend if you like," offered twin Natasha when she asked if he had one.

He said, "No" and "No, thanks."

She smiled prettily and shrugged, "Okay, that's cool."

Nights could be lethal for me, tripping over ropes, mounds of dirt, ditches, tools and gumboots by torchlight, traipsing from the shed to half a house, balancing plates of food for the family gathered around the TV in our bedroom. The front door was out of action, so climbing through the open kitchen window with the wind whistling through was a faster entry. When the teens complained there were stink bugs in their evening meal from the silver beet, I told them off. Who else works all day in the orchard, and then, on the same day, has to deal with a building inspector, the concrete man, the plumber, the electrician, the solar panel man, the kitchen joinery duo, and other trades people? Did they have to deal with an orchard worker who was on the go-slow because he's fasting, as well as *lunatic* teens? Did they have to go to the frosty garden in the dark, digging for their tucker, then wash the veggies under a tap that was starting to freeze over, and cook a meal in the shed stumbling over chainsaws, ladders and cement bags? "You are a bunch of ungrateful wretches," I snapped, "complaining about one little stink bug."

"There were several," said Bryan quietly. "I'll wash the veggies in future, darls. Your eyes aren't up to it."

"Plus," I added, "your oldest brother rang with upsetting news. I could have pruned a row of kiwifruit in the time I spent consoling him."

"What's his prob? Is his girlfriend leaving him?"

"Worse. The baby has nappy rash," I said, and gave a tiny smile. The family chuckled with relief. "And your sister," I told the children (she was boarding away from home but periodically returned when things got difficult), "sent a text reminding us we were still her parents and should pay for everything. She said, 'Can you chuck in another twenty bucks; I've run out of smokes.' "

We laughed so hard the poor old house began vibrating.

Sometimes it pays to be 'mummy-explosive'. The next day I cooked a vegetarian meal to please a son. Nothing grand – just brown rice, three slightly burnt fish cakes with an egg, mixed veggies sprinkled with chilli sauce, and possibly a bit of dirt since I tripped over the wheelbarrow in the dark.

"Mum," the son said, patting my shoulder as he entered the shed.

"This is beeyootiful. You are a legend. This is five-star cooking."

"You're kidding," I gulped.

"Nope," he said. "You have to believe in yourself. You're a good cook."

I suppressed giggles, like unleashed butane gas, while sloshing through the mud and over the concrete pad, finding my way into our bedroom with a torch. Bryan was lying down like a war vet, black beanie on his head, looking at the rugby. I told him our son had been nice to me. "Was he unwell?" I asked. Bryan said our son was simply growing up. I said I felt like celebrating, and hubby said he did, too. We hunted under the bed for a celebratory chocolate but were out of luck.

We hoped it would rain the next day, which meant a trip to the city to stock up on emergency treats and cheap bread, and to visit junk yards. We knew how to have fun! The trick was to sneak out of the house early, before slothful teens arose and wanted to come with us. Any time they came along it was mayhem, although one twin came with us when we collected our refurbished claw-foot bath, knowing it would barely be used as we are on well water, not town supply.

It was confusing looking at lavatories (a word my mother used because it sounded posh). Selling us a toilet was like selling Marmite to a nomad in an African desert. I was happy as long as it flushed, and preferably, had blue dolphins emblazoned on the plastic lid. The loos were lined up like contestants when it came to choosing one. Were we catering for round butts, square butts, fat butts? Since we were used to our outside lav, I told Bryan that ultimately, it was his decision. Think about the depth of the bowl and the squirting capacity with city dudes in mind, I suggested, since guys around where we lived opted for the bushes. The Dutch salesperson was no use; he was laughing too much about our dilemma.

Renovating in winter is tricky when tarpaulins are covering newly poured concrete and Mother Nature is gushing rain from heaven, but it left us slightly excited. We couldn't work in the orchard and neither could our workers, so we merrily ripped up floorboards or did preparatory work for whatever job the builders were going to do. It was like a mini reprieve – just us and a teen or three. We talked and bonded, but still needed to cook in the shed, and we took occasional showers in the cottage next door that our son rented.

While the builders tore down walls and banged in nails, we still had to prune. One of our kids yo-yoed back and forth between living at home and elsewhere, and since she was seventeen, but immature, she strengthened our resolve to hang in there. We refused to bow down to dismal teen behaviour; the same with our orchard. The trees showed promise, but some became frail, whether through a fungal disease or something we didn't know about. We expected them to come right in the end.

Weeks after the renos started, Bryan got a lurgy. It was scary seeing him looking like a frozen pixie, developing a rash and saying he couldn't get warm. I ran around like a demented nun, praying profusely, *God take me. I am the most useless person in this family* (although I didn't believe it – just trying to be humble). *My poor sick hubby is better at cooking leftovers, he is good at doing farm accounts, and when the kids are scrapping, he says it's just a phase. He is one chilled-out guy. Exchange him for me. He has a fifty-fifty chance of meeting someone nice compared to my chances.*

Someone still had to do the male-vine pruning and supervise the workers. If I was annoyed because some were too slow, or was presented with a difficult vine, I thought of old boyfriends who had dumped me. And when I ran out of caddish beaus, I thought of all the nasty women who'd crossed my path, but since they were so few in number, my thoughts turned to bad leaders of countries, psychos and people who bashed their kids. It never occurred to me to include wrongdoings committed by my own children. A mother's love overlooks transgressions, and teen behaviour is temporary, although it doesn't feel like it at the time.

When Bryan arose from his deathbed, after my fervent prayers and being fed food our mothers served when we were kids recovering from an illness – chicken soup, 'googie' eggs and 'soldiers' (the Australian terms for boiled eggs and strips of buttered bread), I got the lurgy. Now it was his turn to deal with the workers, teens moaning about making appointments for showers next door (they had to be supervised in case someone got light-fingered or made toll calls), sharpening work tools, saying hello to the builders who arrived at dawn, telling the twins to quit smoking and get a job, fetching water, greeting trades people, and soothing a son's black mood. His computer went blank because the switchboard in the shed couldn't cope with the electric jug, microwave and computer all being on at the same time.

By Week Ten of the renovation project, going into the house was like walking inside an elephant's guts, with exposed pink batts bulging from walls and ceilings. There was no kitchen, no bathroom and no privacy. I wanted to collapse on my sickbed, but the builders zinged and banged noisily. It was also hazardous – men's thighs up ladders hammering away in the hallway, or stumbling over electricians' cords, cables and huge torch lamps. No one brought me googie eggs or soldiers in bed. It wasn't worth being ill. Did I detect a spooky whisper from above: "Wake up, woman! Hubby is alive. Go forth and do an honest day's work."

I thought of my mother eons ago wearily buffing up the linoleum on her hands and knees and arising like a praying mantis for a cuppa. She couldn't afford to be ill. She had a bad-tempered husband and three *wild* teens. I had a good-tempered spouse and several *mad* teens.

If she could do it, so could I.

The renovations went on for months. We had survived and more importantly, the builders were on speaking terms with us after it was finished.

You can't get a better result than that!

Chapter Twenty

Occasions

After several weeks the builders were practically family. They could see how we got on with our lives despite living in poor accommodation, pumping water from the well, cooking in a freezing shed by the tractor, and dealing with noisy outbursts from the teens. And surprise! No marital fusses. When a daughter had one of her fits, chucking tools, papers and chairs, crying and swearing, we rang the cops. As the builders drew up at our house, I told them they weren't under arrest, but the daughter was being taken away to calm down. Hoping they didn't think it was a couple of lunatics who were raising the teens, we extended their smoko break, justifying to them why we called the man in blue, who was also beginning to feel like family with his occasional visits.

Although it was beyond the builders' experiences, we told them about the teen girls' backgrounds, their poor start in life in the orphanage, and how deprivation in terms of food and nurturing affects the brain. The daughter who had been taken away to calm down, struggled at school and said she was bullied. She had 'brain surges' which most thought was simply naughty behaviour, but her condition was never officially diagnosed because every time we made an appointment, she would buzz off. We said we loved her, and so we could put up with it most of the time, but sometimes it was too much. For example, she knew people who grew dope. Bryan said, "You don't fight fire with fire." He was like a horse whisperer and could generally calm her down. He also said that if she wanted money, then there was plenty of work here at home. She was an energetic worker when it suited her, splitting wood with the log splitter, mowing the vast lawns on the ride-on, pitching hay – anything physical. The old ladies in the rest home loved her as she noisily enquired about their health and what they'd been up to and hugged them all.

"Come here, you scallywag," they would call. Even if they were new patients, she would go up to them and say, "You doing alright?" And when you are practically bedridden, who wouldn't like visitors!

Sometimes she was the sweetest of all the kids. When we took her and her sisters on a week's holiday to meet other adopted children around the South Island, I later asked the girls what they remembered about the trip. One recalled a bloated cow lying in a paddock with its legs sticking up, and another said she liked that fizzy drink someone gave her. "I found happiness," replied this particular daughter. Once when I told her why I wasn't going into town, pointing to a vicious mark across my lip where a kiwifruit branch had snapped against my face, she soothed, "Don't worry about it, Mum. Tell people you've got a cold sore!"

The builders remained a source of normality in my life, and they hammered on. If we had to return stuff, which they thought was unsuitable, to the suppliers in town, we'd combine it with picking up a twin or two who'd hitched over the hill and wanted a ride home. We could be tough-love parents but also worried, caring parents, and no one wants a lecture on their parenting style. We did what we felt was right at the time. Every few minutes a twin texted from her cell phone, "were r u now?", "hurry up", "we bored", "we getting wet" – and worse! "We're losing weight from walking."

The twins were relieved to have a ride home. "Girls, we have to look after our complexions," I said. "It's a bit late for Mummy, but you've got a fighting chance." Then Bryan swung into the main fruit and veggie store that was bursting with garden goodness. And since that went well, we drove to Pak 'n' Save to stock up.

When Natasha dumped a packet of crinkly crisps on top of the healthy food, I said, "No, darling, we love you too much to let you eat that high-fat salty muck. It'll hurt your brain cells and make your lovely body explode." Strangely, I noticed other shoppers within earshot replacing their indulgences back onto the chip shelf, too – although I betcha as soon as we ducked down to another aisle, they recovered their chips, covering them up with toilet paper and bread!

The twins spied a teacher with a cute toddler, but not-so-cute partner. He looked like a builder whose head had concertinaed from planks of heavy gib board landing on it, although it could have been genetic or a car accident. I was more interested in glimpsing into a teacher's trolley. "Alright," I said to the twins. "You've been pleasant, so you can dash back and get one bag of crisps – and make it last a week." The girls came back with one each. It was a small price to pay for pleasantness, and we had a long drive home. It was easier to sweat the small stuff and not be too lecturing.

"If the teacher's not looking, duck back and get us a vino on special," I suggested. Bryan said he didn't care what anyone thought and for good measure he got several, since he loves a bargain and he enjoys being a bit perverse. He deliberately trolleyed past the nice teacher and gave a happy wave. "You are such a lovely, brave man," I said. "You give me strength to face the world. Isn't Daddy just the best, girls," I said to the twins. But they'd disappeared down the aisle for feminine monthly products, knowing Dad wouldn't venture there and they could toss packets into the trolley without comment. Our little girls were growing up.

Soon after, on a wintry night, a carload of kids turned up, including a daughter and her boyfriend. "We've come to bond with you and stay the night."

"Couldn't you bond somewhere else? It's messy here with the builders and um, we're boring and um, we're old and tired." They did take off in the dark but then returned an hour later. No one wanted them. "Oh, alright," I said, as half a dozen teens in hoodies landed on the back porch. It didn't feel safe driving over the hill at night, and it wasn't clear if the driver was on a restricted licence since teens mumble. They could get a lecture in the morning, which was Bryan's forte. "Are you guys or chicks?" I asked. I was unsure with their unisex clothing. "Sorry to be rude, but we do have a rule in this house. It's a no-bonking zone, so separate rooms for boys and girls." And, to reinforce the rule, I added, "It's in print. In my book."

"What page?" a suspicious daughter asked.

"Oh my God," gasped a teen with red and purple hair. "Are you a published author?" I nodded. She said that she wanted to be one, too, and flashed me a look of renewed respect.

I was starting to warm to this little sextet and generously suggested the daughters make coffee for everyone and offer them baked beans as well. But they said they'd had takeaways in town and were keen to hit the sack. I couldn't tell if anyone was cheating on the rules as they lumbered up the stairs to the empty bedrooms.

The next morning Natasha said she'd had a dreadful sleep. "Those lezzos were noisy."

I muttered my sympathies and in response to my probing, she assured me that in no way was she involved in a *ménage à trois*.

"Yuk, what do you take me for, Mother!"

I recalled my mother's words: "Choose your friends wisely."

Whenever anyone invited us out, it was an occasion. Truly, who wants a weary mum and dad escorting a tribe of kids of all shapes and sizes? The older teens were happy to be dropped off at their friends along the way, but the younger ones came along for the ride. A friend of my mother's was celebrating her eightieth birthday with a party, and her sister, aged eighty-seven, was putting on a bit of a bash. I couldn't imagine being that age.

Now these two elderly sisters had something that I thought completely unfair (apart from longevity). They had brown hair. Not an itty-bitty strand of grey between them. Of course, when the oldest sister told me they didn't dive into the dye bottle, I was suspicious. Instead of remarking, "Pull the other leg," I remained respectful, but every time I passed her rocker to surreptitiously get another cuppa, I peered at her scalp. She seemed to be telling the truth. I couldn't bear the suspense, and asked, "Are you real?"

She was taken aback, and said, "What do you mean, dearie?"

"Look at my poor spouse," I said. "Look what the kids and I did to him."

She was confused – normal for a person her age. But so was hubby. "What are you talking about, darls?" he asked.

"You've gone grey," I said accusingly. "And so have I, to some extent. Why hasn't she?" And I enviously glared at her.

The old girl laughed. "It's hereditary, dearie. My mother kept her hair until she was a hundred."

It reminded me of that American Clairol advert which said, "Only her hairdresser knows for sure."

In our family we cut our own hair and do wonderful things with our locks. We must all have throwback genes, making us want to snip at things within close range. It was more pleasant seeing the girls cutting one another's hair than snarling at each other. I overly praised any such hair grooming behaviour because they could be on the path to getting a hairdressing job once they left school. They'd come a long way since the youngest snipped her hair, aged five or six, and left gaping gaps. I did the best I could to make her presentable for school.

"The kids laughed at me," she said when I asked how her day went. I wondered what the teacher thought. "She told the kids to be nice to me. She said, 'How would you like it if your mother gave you a haircut like that!' "

Hubby cuts his own hair. "Don't cut it too short, darls," I'd plead. "You'll look like a convict." Once I emptied a bucket of kitchen scraps onto the compost and gave a mild shriek. There were bits of fluff, corrugated iron in colour, littered amongst the whiffy composting school lunches, tea bags and back-of-the-fridge stuff. "Come here kids," I called out excitedly. "I think your kitties have caught a skunk."

The girls darted out. "Where's the body?" We gingerly prodded in the steaming mire of rotting food and grass clippings. Maybe it wasn't a skunk. Could it be from a dead bird, or, I offered, a mouse's fur coat? Perhaps they could take it to school for science class. "Daaaaad," we yelled in unison since we thought he knew everything. "What's this funny grey stuff in the compost?"

Bryan materialised out of his cubbyhole (which he calls the shed), and we gasped.

"Don't bother walking over," I called out. "We know what it is now." I added to the sting, "You look like a deserter from the army with that haircut." Bryan did a half wave and returned to his little boy's stable. "Even if Daddy looks half-witted, you will still love your poor father, won't you? I'm going to try."

They answered, "Okay, Mummy darling – if you let us watch that AO movie tonight."

There were some days when our only companions, apart from the teens, were bored cows who'd swish their tails and amble off doing desultory plops. Or the neighbour's goats that greeted us with strong whiffs and butted against the boundary fence. The road close by is busy, and one morning I discovered why semis and milk tankers cheerfully sounded their horns passing our little cottage next door, where one of our sons resided. I went out to investigate and found lumpy tourists clambering out of campervans with a battery of cameras around their enlarged goitres. The son had carved two large phallic symbols and nailed them to the front swing-gate. Someone had tacked a sign underneath saying, *Farmer's Weekly* – the name taken from the throwaway farming magazine. I didn't get the joke initially and told the son how proud I was he could carve such quaint little oriental figures. And with such skills, why was he driving dangerous diggers and logging trees that reached the sky? He could take up sculpturing and work for us for a pittance. To which he quite rightly replied, "Get lost." I blushed when the pun was explained and became the laughing stock of his hunting mates.

Some days are riddled with visitors. A knock on the open door revealed a figure from the past. Sunlight was pouring into the back porch, and the guy's hair glinted orange with grey flecks. "Hello," I greeted him. "You're out."

He looked puzzled. "I'm not gay."

"No, I mean you're not in."

"In what?"

"Incarcerated."

"Nope, that was years ago. Been out for ages."

I had barely asked him if he'd been in for DV (domestic violence) or DD (drink drive), when a couple of odd bods materialised beside him. "Who are these handsome dudes?"

They were Asian students and they were all going fishing. "I love Asian people," I cried.

"Why?"

"Because they can sign my visitor's book with their funny writing. It's a thrill to see people from a faraway land. Come and have a cuppa."

No sooner had the trio left when there was a mild hullabaloo on the back porch. "It's your son," said a son. "I've brought the whānau (family)."

"You're only allowed in if you've brought my gorgeous granddaughter," I teased.

"Course," he said, and once we had disentangled from our greetings, he loped to the car parked under the walnut tree. "You'll have to wait, Mum. She's busy."

How could a baby be busy?

She was on the breast. "Give her a good feed," I said bossily, "and a good burp, because I want a long, long cuddle. Now introduce me to your whānau." People of all shapes and sizes were clambering out of the shiny vehicle, some carsick. There were so many relatives it was confusing.

"How's the veggie garden? Got any pūhā?" asked the Māori son.

Bryan swirled down the gravel driveway on the rusty blue tractor, looking like Mr Magoo.

"You've got visitors," I called out. "They've brought the baby, so be nice."

He got off the tractor and greeted them. "We love being related to them, don't we, darls?" I said.

Bryan grunted, "Very nice," and offered to put on the kettle.

Bryan worried that his whānau didn't eat properly, so dug up half the garden for them while I gooed over the new grandie. She wailed and I was treated to violent nappy eruptions. "What are you feeding this kid?" The proud mother said she was on solids now, at eight weeks: half a teaspoon a day. And we all marvelled.

Just then another visitor turned up. He looked different. "Crikey, you're looking better than when we last met. In fact, you're quite a nice-looking man." He admitted he had also been in the slammer. It was hard engaging with him because the baby was puking, the visitors were guffawing under the walnut tree, the kids were running under the sprinkler, and two dogs of indeterminate breed were sinking their teeth into soccer balls. The guy said he might be living under a bridge now because of his loser missus. Distracted, I quickly gave a positive reply, "At least you'll get a good view of the water" when, holy moly, another guy turned up. He was stranded and wanted to borrow our phone to ring the AA, which I thought was Alcoholic Anonymous, but he meant the Automobile Association, the outfit that rescues people when their cars have broken down. These days people have cell phones – much more convenient.

Bryan came in and said, "Oh, you're from DOC (Department of Conservation)," while I mused that I'd like to dock his hair. He had a grey, corkscrew ponytail and a snorting jolliness. I imagined him in deep bushy terrain, lost and calling for help, but with no yellow rescue helicopters around – just a few nanny goats wondering if they had sniffed some long-lost rellie.

I was on the verge of enjoying myself with a pre-dinner tincture, when the twins turned up on bicycles with a man in tow. "We found him down the road. Can his friend use the phone?"

"Which friend?"

"A lady that talks funny. They moved in down the road," and they pointed to the house where a neighbour had recently changed addresses from Upper Takaka to c/- Her Majesty's Prison.

The friend soon arrived and when I learnt the lady was Korean, I grabbed the visitor's book and told her to write something. While she was writing little squares and squiggles, an older kid ambled into the kitchen.

"Who are you?" I asked. The twins said she was another friend but didn't know her name. "She'd better sign the book, too." When the kid scrawled, I whispered to the twins, "She's ruining my book. Is she on dope?"

They shrugged. "She's cool, isn't she." And I glared with confusion.

The Korean lady had a serene demeanour, so serene I wondered if she was a Buddhist lady monk going incognito. She hummed and chatted on the phone in her own language, bit like techno music, which made the twins giggle.

"Shoosh, don't be insensitive, girls. She can't help how she speaks," which caused further mirth. When Bryan came in for a tipple, since it was dusk, he hoped he wouldn't be indebted to Telecom for the rest of his life, paying other people's bills.

It seemed our mercurial little Korean friend had contacted a person from the medico, and left a message, and he duly rang back. But by then she'd returned home with the twins on their bikes. The phone caller had the loveliest baritone voice, rich and rolling, almost mesmerising. He revealed the Korean lady was in a delicate state and learning to open up and be receptive to the world around her.

"Is she mad?" I asked. "She looks harmless. Is she a needy little person?"

"Well, she could do with a friend."

I said okay, she could have my twins, but the telephone went dead. When the twins cycled back home, I was going to offer them some noodles and mention that they could learn Korean cooking and, perhaps, a bit of serenity from our new neighbour.

"Do you realise the world came to us today," I said to Bryan as we turned out the lights. "We've had Chinese, Korean, a big Maori whānau, beneficiaries, a homeless person, a bushman and the odd misfit at our home today. But there's good in everyone."

"We're the biggest misfits of the lot." he chuckled.

I could see he had a point.

"Are your friends boys, girls, or otherwise?"

Chapter Twenty-One

Holidays

When the house seemed almost childless, Bryan said something astonishing. "How about going somewhere after harvest for a couple of weeks. Where'd you like to go?"

"Australia," I cried. "Where I was raised. Do you really mean it?"

"Of course," he smiled. "We can hire a campervan and have that honeymoon we never had."

I was thrilled. We'd never been on a holiday together. I spent months on the Internet googling vans to hire, air fares, getting passports and emailing anyone I vaguely knew decades ago.

Then I remembered we had kids who boomeranged home for a sleep, food and unwanted advice. "What about the girls?" I said. "They might have abandonment issues if we buzz off without telling them. But if we tell them too soon, they'll tell their mates and we don't want no-hopers helping themselves to our fridge and daughters."

Bryan said, "First things first." We could do dummy runs over the Takaka Hill to Nelson without them so they could learn to live a few hours on their own. After all, they were eighteen, and Social Welfare wasn't going to put us in jail for that.

When the girls heard the car starting up early one morning, they wailed so loudly I felt guilty, and said, "Oh, alright, but behave!" But once we were on our way, the trip was embattled with urgent stops for a ciggie (since our talk stressed them), junk food (because they were allergic to our unprocessed food), reaching over the driver's seat to sound the horn at every truck, and leaning out the window crying, "Hi, bro" to road diggers, solo mums pushing strollers, ex-teachers, pensioners, and a couple of cops. Strangely, everyone waved back in recognition and gave them high fives. Later, one of the girls threw a wobbly outside Mitre 10, causing staff to crane their necks to witness the commotion. I cried, "I'm going to end up in a mental home," so Bryan pulled out his wallet and told the feral kid to find her own way back home.

On another occasion, I checked the girls' rooms before we made plans. Nope, no sleeping beauties, just whiffy scent from discarded jeans and socks. As we were edging out the farm gate, a vehicle drew up and a kid said, "Where are you going? We want to come."

"Step on the gas," I shrieked to Bryan, and we shot up the hill like a couple of adrenalin-crazed bank robbers. An hour later we pulled into a rest area for you-know-what, when a car drew alongside.

"Trying to get away from us?" giggled the girls, jumping into our car. We were gutted. That day was a hazy mixture of disbelief, faint amusement and chaos.

The next time we pretended to be normal. We snuck out of the house in our dressing gowns and changed into city clothes while concealed between tractors and bags of fertilizer at a farming depot in Motueka.

When a tiny packet arrived in the mail from Trade Me, I confessed that Daddy and I were off to Australia, and that Mummy had no decent underwear. I said my own mother told me, as a teen, that you had to wear clean knickers because you might be in a car crash, and what would the doctors trying to save your life think when you're wearing big, stained undies with floppy elastic?

"Gross," said the girls, examining the bits of frippery that looked like they'd been ripped from a discarded bridal veil. "Exactly what kind of holiday are you going on?"

I slunk off to the orchard like a depraved hussy, saying, "Not to worry. I'll give it to the cat for Christmas. Might look nice around her kitty bowl. Or look festive on the Christmas tree."

We flew to Australia with a clear conscience, although I was a bit miffed to find Bryan packing only half an hour before we set off. He said, "You only need a change of clothing, your passport and tickets, what's the big deal?" Tacked to the fridge was our busy itinerary and phone numbers except for during one activity, which read: 'Probably camping in the bush, dunno where.' The Russian son said he'd be upset if we didn't get on the plane soon; this was his holiday – not having us at home!

When I was in Australia, I reflected how it would be for our Romanian and Russian children returning to their respective lands of birth. I wondered if they'd be excited seeing things familiar to them in their ice-covered part of the world. It was a such a thrill hearing kookaburras laughing at dawn, watching wallabies leaping around gum trees and seeing the crashing waves on golden sands. I went to visit my old homes and school, culminating with a school reunion where everyone bought my book. I was in danger of exploding with happiness. Except that the congested and confusing motorways spoilt that. I told hubby I'd never go on any more honeymoons with him if he uttered another snide remark about my navigational skills.

The best thing about a holiday is it clears your head. You are happy to return home and see your funny little family who help you carry in the duty-free items and squeal over cheap souvenirs made in China. Then we gathered them in our arms, saying, "Missed ya, did you miss us?" And we said warm fuzzy things to each other because we are family – a created family. Though born in different parts of the world, we are connected by an invisible rope. Occasionally the rope gets frayed, but mostly it feels strong and never-ending. But we, and they, know we will never ever run from the family we wanted so much.

Now we'd had a taste of adventure, we opted to return to Australia the following year, after harvest and before winter pruning. Staying in hotels is not adventurous. The rougher the better; so it was campgrounds and cheap campervans for us. The major problem was what to wear.

Disliking what I found in my wardrobe, we opened the shipping container out the back of the property, in which I had stored boxes of clothing either given to us or that the kids had outgrown. It wasn't worth taking a day off work trudging miserably around the city for a couple of items to impress the Aussies who didn't care because they didn't know us! I found a pair of red, flowery board pants that I'd saved to give to one of the boys years ago but had forgotten about. Then I rifled through the girls' clothing upstairs and found an immodest top from the youngest, smelling of stale perfume. Perfect.

"Do I look quite nice in these?" I asked my men folk. Bryan was sitting at the table doing his tax, and the Russian son had his head draped over a bowl of muesli, ready to bring up a scoff.

"Mother," he said. "I don't want you walking around Queensland looking like a prostitute. I'll be embarrassed."

"Son," I said. "You're not even coming with us. It's Dad who'll be embarrassed."

"Mother! You should dress to your age. In order to get respect, you must give it. Dad, you tell her. She won't listen."

Bryan said, "Son, you should be proud of your mother. Not many people her age have a waist. Wear what you like, darls. Australia's a big country. They can take it."

Clothes were the last worry on my mind a day before we left. An older woman from a commune rang, snarling about our teen daughter taking off down the West Coast with her man, a middle-aged pig hunter. "We can't go on holiday. We have to find our daughter," I wailed. "What sort of beast would take her away and not tell her parents?" Bryan agreed she was slack not telling us, but she probably ran out of credit on her cell phone. I rang the police, who rang the commune. He said the woman was a nutter, and since our daughter was eighteen, she was a consenting adult. I told them she was immature for her age and vulnerable. The sons had a go at me. One asked what kind of mother was I to even consider going overseas when his sister could be kidnapped, even getting murdered. The son at home said his holiday was ruined if we didn't go to Australia and give him some peace at home. Another said, "She'll be right" and that we could use his ute if we wanted a holiday at home spent looking for her.

"That's it," I said. "We're not going. Unpack your bags."

Just hours before we were due to catch our flight, the police rang. She'd been located and was as happy as Larry. It seems it was all above board. Breathing a sigh of relief, we grabbed our bags and started up the hill in the hearse, which developed an electrical fault. "Our daughter's sending a psychic message that we're not meant to go. The plane is going to crash," I said. Bryan thought that was rubbish and got on the phone and bought a second-hand car from a friend to get us to the airport.

Once we reached Cairns, we dined with hippies in cheap dives, chatted to locals, swam, explored every botanical garden and zoo, and bonded with surfie dudes who thought we were cool for oldies and shimmied up trees to fetch us coconuts. My cup was overflowing, so to speak.

"This is the real life," I said, as we clinked glasses in the dark around a bonfire with my Aussie friend. We were laughing like drains, recalling being teenagers in the '60s, roaring around in a sports car, dangling bikini tops out the window. Bryan learnt a bit about me that I hadn't told him, but he was happy and relaxed too.

"I feel young again. How about a facelift?" I said. My friend cried she wanted one but had to wait until she sold her waterfront property. Her friend up the road said she wanted a face job too. I said we could have a 'girlie experience' getting our faces cut up at the same time, and that Bryan could be our toy boy and carry our bags. We rang my sister back in New Zealand, and she said, "Can I come with you?"

"Nothing wrong with your dial, sis," I said.

"True. But I'd be up for a tummy tuck."

In the cold light of day, I talked to my brain that whispered, "To thine own self be true." Much of our savings had gone, spent on adopting kids and doing up the house, so this was a frivolous idea, and what for? Who cared? Who am I trying to impress? The kids didn't care; neither did hubby. If you work outside in the sun for several decades and fret over teenage behaviour, you're bound to get character lines. No! I would put that money towards a trip for the teens who wanted to reconnect with their birth families overseas, and towards supporting orphanages because life is cruel to abandoned children, who need a family to love them. My new face could get re-arranged in a car accident anyway.

Bryan was relieved I'd saved him the angst of escorting three lovely dames overseas, since he'd rather be in the garden growing surplus veggies for the teens, who yo-yoed back and forth from home, and for the community workers who had a list of needy families.

It was a wayward teen daughter who sealed the decision. We'd barely arrived home, when she turned up on our doorstep with a solo mum. "I'm so happy to see you," I cried lunging at her. "Give me a big hug. I want to know if you're real."

When the smallish daughter's nose came up for air, she said, "Hey Mum. I'm as tall as you. You're shrinking."

"Keep cuddling," I urged.

"Hey Mum, I need some undergruts (underpants). Is my cat still alive?"

Then she said something astonishing. "Hey Mum. You're looking good. You been doing all right?"

"How could you say that," I exclaimed. "Poor Mummy's face has gone terribly old and crumpled, like a sunken ship that got hauled up and lots of sharks attacked it. I need a facelift."

"I wouldn't bother," she said. "Where's my cat?"

"Bryan," I called down the hallway. "Your daughter's here with a nice person. She said I looked okay. She has saved you heaps. We don't have to fly to Asia now for my stupid face. Let's reward her. Shall we give her a couple of packets of biscuits when she leaves?"

"Haven't you got healthy food?" asked the daughter.

"But you young people love junk. I've got some leftover savoury pies. You can have them," I generously offered. "It'll stick to your guts when you have a session."

The visitor giggled.

The daughter said, "Don't worry. Mum doesn't know what a session is."

"Yes, I do. It's when you go all psychedelic and go like this." And I did a silly dance with arm flinging. The girls were doubled over, laughing.

Feeling guilty that what we called treats, was a staple diet for the young, I ventured out to the big shed and filled up boxes of kiwifruit and apples, and I made up a packet of meat too, as I was feeling generous and appreciated. Meanwhile, the daughter was foraging in the bathroom for deodorant and a toothbrush. I was happy she was into hygiene. Then the daughter said, "Hey Dad, I've lost my glasses. I can't see so good."

"I can't either. We're like twins. I hate wearing them. You've got nice eyes," I said to the daughter's friend. "What's the world like?"

The friend giggled again as they hauled their food parcels to her car, which Bryan had filled with petrol. "Lovely seeing you beautiful ladies," I said. "Good luck with job hunting."

Since becoming somewhat myopic, I didn't know if the daughter's gesture in the passenger seat was giving me the fingers, or if she had her digits curled around a ciggie. Although lethal for one's health, I chose the latter. It was a much more pleasant send-off choosing that option.

"It takes a holiday for one to return to normality," I reminded Bryan. "The house didn't burn down while we were away and not much has been nicked from the deep freezer. And some of the kids want to visit to know we're still alive. Let's count our blessings."

When my brother suddenly died in Australia a few months after our holiday, I returned with my sister, her daughter and the daughter's daughter. Four fab women, the youngest only seven, but she knew about flash hotels with swimming pools, coffee shops and Asian food. It was an eye-opener after travelling on a shoestring with hubby; both versions of the holiday experience were fun, but with hubby you came home with more cash in your wallet. Bryan said he could manage the teens at home and no need to bring back souvenirs. The kids don't need them, and the world is full of plastic junk.

The best part about travelling is your thoughts are not focussed on what your teens are doing. They become somewhat abstract because your mind is telling you to deal with the now. Which is probably a healthy way of existing. I was in a state of nervous excitement. Of course, I was sad about my brother, but the adrenalin of being free from immediate teen worries was intoxicating. We almost didn't make it to Australia because of the appalling weather, but once we landed at the Gold Coast Airport and chose a rental car, we sang all the way to our apartment half an hour up the coast. "Australia, I love you," my happy brain cried, "with your golden sands and rollicking waves and suntanned people ambling about." My niece's daughter was quite savvy like her mother, and my sister and I were decorative, ageing passengers, although important to the funeral side of things.

It had been a long tiring day motoring for seven hours before we got on the flight. Add to that a three-hour time difference and the task of choosing a rental car. "Oh shoot," gasped my niece. She'd left her bag back at the airport car park some distance away. I spied a cop car outside our plush waterside apartment and, because I'd seen Police Rescue on TV, I said, "Follow me, ladies. We'll get this sorted out."

"We've just arrived in your beautiful country," I gasped. "Left a bag unattended at the airport. Can you radio and see if the airport's closed down? No bomb in our luggage. Just undies."

The cop got on his cell phone, rang the police station, then the airport. We four huddled like helpless immigrants, eyeing the hunk, while the surf pounded behind us. He was cute, affable and gingery. "Yeah," he guffawed down the cell phone. "Got them here. Handcuffed. Kiwis. No worries."

And he winked.

I love Aussies, I mused, and when the chubby cop said we could return to fetch the bag, I gave him a quick squeeze of grateful thanks. My sister and her daughter and the daughter's daughter were astonished.

"He's a lovely man," I said. "Never hugged a cop before. He deserved a full frontal."

And we laughed all the way back to the airport in Coolangatta.

The funeral was a jolly affair. My brother's surfing mates travelled far and wide to attend. They were funny, brash, standing in groups sinking down a few schooners, a collection of thirsty surfie cavemen. My brother was a rebellious, charismatic legend and some of his antics are written in surfing books. Despite being a paraplegic, he wheeled and dealed from his bed, expecting to make a fortune. The sunburnt paddocks of his 100-acre property in the bush were full of sleek cars with fins, Cadillacs, vintage cars, the odd Rolls Royce and boats. He didn't leave a will, so his offspring were in a pickle, and in the following days his farm was a jumble of upset rellies, laid-back sons-in-law drinking beer, neighbours, kids and dogs underfoot. There were teens cooking noodles despite oodles of leftover funeral food. My sister was telling a niece to shut up; she was on the phone and going to sort this mess out. One kid did fake bellowing because a cousin bumped into her.

"Right," I said to the uninjured child. "This is a very serious situation. Might need the Flying Doctor Service," and I began videotaping it.

"Maaa," wailed the kid. "Tell Auntie to take away the camera."

"No," I insisted. "We need evidence. The doctor will be fascinated."

The kid stopped crying, splayed fingers over her face and emitted little shrieks.

I laughed so hard that everyone else began laughing. "You have to scream louder," I said. "There's so much noise in here. Auntie's a bit deaf."

I told the kid I'd raised heaps of kids. I know their tricks and she was a terrific actor. How about another demo? She looked at me warily, while her mother said, "Ta. Good-on-ya."

"Dad loved to surf at Yamba Beach," said my nephew. We'd barely arrived, travelling in convoy after collecting prawns from the wharf, when he said, "Struth! Bushfire! Looks like the farm will go up." We all wondered if my brother was having his own fireworks display, arranged from the grave. Smoke billowed on the horizon, spewing embers 50 kilometres away onto our seaside resort. It was a hot, scary sight but not worthy of mention in New Zealand.

"Darls," I said to hubby when we arrived home. "I could have been incinerated, become a little gingerbread girl, so be happy I've come back intact, well almost."

And I left it at that. After all, it keeps a marriage alive if you have your man guessing.

Chapter Twenty-Two

Tragedy

In February 2009, a television crew came to our house. They were doing a documentary on homeless teens in Nelson and interviewed our Romanian twins. The girls had presented themselves outside a shopping mall and intrigued with the activities, engaged with the film crew. The twins said they loved talking to people, and no, they did not sleep on the street but stayed with friends.

Barely nineteen, the immature twins were doing courses on and off, and looked out for each other. We worried they were being thrown to the wolves, so to speak, but Nelson is a small enough city that word would get back to us if they were in any difficulty. They flitted back and forth from home, with tales of their adventures, sometimes bringing solo mothers and their kids to stay for a night. We didn't condone their lifestyle but were not going to disconnect from their lives either. They were taking longer to grow up compared to their contemporaries.

The film crew were puzzled. The girls were articulate and had a zest for life but seemed directionless. "My mum has written a book about us," said a twin proudly, and that was when TV3 phoned us to get our side of the story. Rod Vaughan, a journalist, arrived at our home with Chris Wilkes (the producer of TV3's current affairs programme *60 Minutes*), the sweet Belinda (camerawoman) and the sound guy, Shane. They then spent six hours interviewing us and our sons. We urgently tried to locate the girls while the crew in Nelson were filming 'real' homeless teens who were on drugs. Natasha had just returned from a trip to the Bay of Islands in a van full of Māori who were her supporters in her role as a trainee Māori warden. They had been away north celebrating Waitangi Day – an important New Zealand public holiday. She had met the Māori King and, we were told, she had charmed visitors and stopped brawls – feelings run high at this annual event.

It was tricky finding the other twin, but the harassed TV crew eventually brought both girls home. I provided a feast, and it was a happy day with them and our daughters at home. After the crew flew back to Auckland, they decided to return for more footage because the twins were engaging, and it was a good story. Why would twins who were 'rescued' from a bleak life in a Romanian orphanage, then choose a transient lifestyle that they could have had in their own country?

Billboards were put up of the twins' profile, and the documentary *Double Trouble* aired on TV3's *60 Minutes* in 2009 The response was immediate. The switchboard was jammed with people either supporting us for caring for our twins or being critical and judgmental about the girls' choice of lifestyle. The girls didn't care, as it gave them temporary stardom, and we ignored abrasive comments.

Three weeks later tragedy struck.

It's every parent's worst nightmare: A call from the police in the middle of the night to tell you your child has been hit by a car and is in hospital with severe head injuries. By dawn, when we arrived in Nelson, we were surprised to see Nelson Hospital's car park full of youngsters sitting in vans, smoking, weeping, stunned. The hospital entrance and stairs were manned by Māori wardens – quite unusual. I wondered if some royalty from the Pacific Islands had been flown in for treatment. "What's going on?" I asked a guard. "Why the security?" He said they were filtering visitors because of an accident during the night involving a teenager. "Oh my God," I gasped. "Is her name Natasha?"

The warden nodded. "We are her parents; we have to see her now." And he escorted us to the Intensive Care Unit.

Our poor wee girl was on life support with tubes coming out of her mouth, and a monitor was flashing and beeping. Doctors said her brain injury was so severe there was no hope of recovery. Visitors were allowed in, several at a time, in addition to our family and Archdeacon Harvey Ruru, who was a calming influence.

Natasha's twin, Joanna, was completely distraught, crying, "It should have been me, not Tash." She paced the floor like a caged tiger, wiggling her sister's toes, waving her hand in front of her sister's unresponsive face, and clicking her fingers as a signal to wake up. Some twins are so bonded they can feel the other's pain. "I knew something was wrong," she said. Joanna was staying with a Māori woman and her whānau, and she had awoken the household during the night, sobbing, clutching the right side of her head. Natasha had sustained fatal injuries to the same side of her head. Joanna's agitation was disruptive for the nurses, and a 'minder' was appointed to be with the twin who was behaving irrationally, but understandably so in the circumstances.

"I need a smoke, Tash, and you better wake up by the time I return," Joanna told her sister.

She was gently led out of the ICU and, in frustration, kicked an ATM on the ground floor. "Did you hear me, Tash! I need a smoke!" Lo and behold, a twenty-dollar note fluttered onto the floor. This was the beginning of a series of inexplicable things that happened to us, too!

As to the incident, the media reported that intoxicated teenagers had been playing, at night, on a suburban street shaded by large trees, darting among traffic and kicking rubbish bins. Cars were blasting their horns to warn the young idiots about being on the road. A driver in a boxy-type car with sharp edges was distracted, and he swerved to avoid the group of youngsters and ploughed into Natasha who, we were told, was riding a bike on the gutter strip. She was tossed up into the air and landed on the road. Incredibly, and unthinkingly, a teen picked her up and dropped her, and then ran off. It was hard to know the exact sequence of events for the police said the teens were being 'economical' with the truth. Everyone agreed Natasha was a good kid and wouldn't go around causing mayhem. Also, she was older, and the police said her blood had a low alcohol reading.

On the first Sunday after her accident, every church in Nelson was packed with her supporters offering morning and evening prayers. Māori wardens comforted the street kids who were in delayed shock, inviting them to the hospital chapel where Natasha's bed was wheeled in. The air was electric with prayers and singing.

More poignant was a bedside ceremony to celebrate Natasha's status. The New Zealand Māori Council made her a Māori warden; it was her dream, as she wanted to help homeless kids and people down on their luck. An honorary badge was rushed from Wellington by Sir Pita Sharples and pinned to her hospital gown. A new iwi (tribe) was created in her honour – Ngati Romanian – the first in the world! Several high-profile Māori wardens from around New Zealand flew to Nelson in a show of support. Others travelled there in vans. We began to see our daughter in a new light. This was not the street kid portrayed in *Double Trouble*. She was a bubbly girl with a big heart, who loved people from all walks of life, even living with some of them. At the time of the accident, she was a student and getting her life back on track after becoming weary of her brief experiment with nomadic life.

We thought Natasha would probably die, so we devoted our time to gazing at her, brushing her hair, talking with her, but all the while silently begging God to work a miracle. Sometimes she'd flutter her eyes, and I'd excitedly call a nurse who checked her reflexes and shone a torch into her pupils. But they remained fixed and dilated.

Our family was devastated. *No!* Not Natasha. She was the kid who didn't make waves. One of our sons quit his job and made a long journey to be with her, sleeping in an uncomfortable, upright hospital chair, monitoring any small changes day after day. It cost him his marriage. Son Tristan, who lived next door to us with his partner, worked for Fulton Hogan, who gave him time off to spend with his sister. His partner's parents generously offered us accommodation, and the Māori wardens fed us 'boil-ups' at the hospital. "You're family," they explained.

I could see why Natasha was attracted to her Māori friends. They were family-oriented and gave one a sense of belonging, more so than in the Pākehā (white) world. They embraced us, hugged us, laughed with us. And even if their kids were ratbags, they never gave up on them.

While Natasha was comatose, we greeted people at her bedside. People we'd normally never have met – all colours, all denominations, all walks of life – from corporate lawyers to ex-convicts. The people came in droves – solo parents with toddlers who wanted to touch Natasha for she had babysat them, elderly people wheezing with asthma, a shrunken oriental man clutching a straw bag, people of all shapes and ages, some on the fringe of society and others affluent, all of whom had stories to tell about our daughter.

There were beefy, heavily tattooed bikers in leather and rough looking dudes from the men's shelter, youngsters from youth groups, teachers and their families, those she randomly met, and parishioners from various churches. It was extraordinary. I hugged every person who came into Natasha's room once she was transferred to a private ward, and I thanked them for being involved in our daughter's life. And miraculously, as they left, they hugged other visitors. Natasha would have loved that. We were bonded in grief but also in hope that Natasha would just wake up and say, "Hi bro!"

A couple of visitors touched me up for a few dollars. While inappropriate, a voice in my head said, *Maybe Natasha stayed with them*, and since this was a highly unusual, emotional time, I opened my purse and thanked them for caring about her.

Once I had to seek a nurse. A guy desperate to save Natasha put a small greenstone pebble into her mouth, chanting, and said that it would cure her. I was alarmed. "No! She will choke," I said. He was angry and insistent, and I had him hauled away by the Māori wardens who hovered in the corridors.

On the third day, Bryan and I returned home for a night to get clothing, collect mail and email people about the accident. One hundred replied in the first couple of hours. In the melee, I mislaid my bunch of keys, which sent me spiralling into a panic. I practically tipped the house upside down searching for them, looking under beds and crying with frustration. A dozen times I emptied my handbag, pulling at the lining, and called Bryan to check once again. Nope. No keys. Gone. In the end we fell into bed, me weepy and weary.

In the morning, as we were getting ready to drive back to the hospital, I opened my handbag. There were my keys lying neatly coiled up at the top! How was this possible? "Thank you, Natasha," I whispered. "And thank you, God" – although I wasn't entirely happy with Him.

Soon after the accident, it was decided it was kinder to let Natasha fade from life naturally, since she was considered brain dead. Some people who loved her did not accept that despite verdicts from several doctors, some even in America where brain scans were sent to specialists for second opinions. What to do? We'd do anything to restore our little girl, but the prognosis was so bad. And now some people were telling us it was cruel to keep her going, while others were saying we had no faith and were giving up, and that they'd look after her even if she remained in a persistent vegetative state.

To appease everyone, Natasha was put on a tube feeding programme and taken off her life support system. Natasha breathed easily unaided but choked when food was introduced through a tube. It was so terrifying having nurses trying to resuscitate her that we agreed to her having a saline drip attached instead, and she'd then exist on water and prayers. When more brain scans were taken, we included anyone who wanted to be there to listen to what the doctors were saying so that we all had the same information. Some people remarked, "You're the parents, stop being bossed around by other people." I replied that this was a major decision; they were commenting out of love and concern, and we were all in this together. Meanwhile, Natasha lay serenely in her white gown while visitors adorned her with rings and bracelets, put flowers in her hair and surrounded her with soft toys, mostly teddy bears. Small children drew cards and others sent beautiful bunches of expensive flowers.

On the twelfth day, we followed the ambulance in convoy as Natasha was transferred to our local Takaka community hospital. There was nothing more the Nelson Hospital could do. It was a relief to have her closer to home, and generously, the staff allowed family and friends to sit by her bed throughout the night, maintaining a twenty-four-hour vigil. We offered food and invited them home to shower. After sitting with her all day, I knew she'd be in good hands at night. Bryan drove me to the hospital every day and spent time with Natasha before returning to work in the orchard. When he collected me, I'd update him on her progress and who had visited her bedside.

Some days were fraught with visitors who argued about religion, or who challenged me when I felt helpless, or who didn't like the other person visiting Natasha. Two unprepossessing men arrived at the same time, both saying they were going to marry Natasha. *Not on your nelly*, I thought. They weren't son-in-law material. It was hard being the peacemaker. I bottled it all up until I came home, but Bryan kindly said he would do dinner and poured me a vino. "You go on the computer, darls, and email your friends. I can see you've had a big day."

"What's wrong with Mum?" asked a teen at home when I was weeping about Natasha whose hands were clawing in, not out. The resident doctor said this was a bad sign and that nothing more could be done unless her body posture changed. "Why is Mum in a bad mood?" the teen added.

I cried, "I'm not in a bad mood. I am sad. I am frustrated, and I don't know what to do." I still fervently pleaded for a miracle. *Please God, she's the only kid in the family who truly loves me*, I prayed. I'd had this instant bond with her in Romania. *And now, God, you are taking her away from me. You have so many people in heaven, just return her back to us, even if she is half the person she was before, and I will do anything. Absolutely anything. Hey God! Do you want me to evangelise in Russia? If so, send the word. I will do it. Promise you God, but please save my baby.*

I didn't rage at the teen's remark. You can't be annoyed about attachment issues, a condition where feelings are misinterpreted. I wept for the stupidity of the accident and the loss of potential of a green-eyed, deliciously chubby, throaty-laughing girl who'd now never marry under our walnut tree. And how do I tell her family in Romania? How do I say, "I am the lady who adopted your daughter. Sorry, but she's dead."?

Three weeks later we were shocked to learn the guy involved in Natasha's demise was in hospital in a Burns Care Unit. We never wished him harm, and when a journalist rang suggesting they do a story on both patients, I said no. Both were victims of a tragedy that was never meant to happen. I was worried that Natasha's friends would become vigilantes, since they were young and impulsive and would make the situation worse.

The days got busier as we were being interviewed by the *Nelson Mail* and the *NZ Woman's Weekly*. Rod Vaughan of TV3 and his TV crew also flew down to update their documentary *Double Trouble*, which caused another burst of comments on their Facebook site and filled our letterbox with get-well cards. Feelings were running high. A couple of Māori people were angry with us – "Youse have got no faith, youse are giving up." At the same time, Natasha's twin, Joanna, pushed people out of the way to sit with her sister, begged people for smokes, a couple of bucks, or a ride back over the hill. I was past being embarrassed.

All my waking thoughts were about pleading with God until a pastor said I didn't need to do that. "God knows what's in your heart. You don't have to keep begging." I gave him a hug. It gave me quality time to spend with Natasha.

A friend, who had also adopted from Romania, put me in touch with her friend, a psychic who lived in another part of New Zealand, and whom I contacted. The psychic said, "Your daughter is telling me she is tired, and her body is *munted*, and she is waiting for someone to receive her, but she doesn't know who. She wants things to be like they were when she was a baby – a favourite blanket and classical music, but not rap music. She wants you to keep stroking and kissing her forehead and to stop crying. She keeps saying sorry, sorry, sorry, and for people to stop trying to make her wake up. She's past it. She just wants her mum and dad, violin music, her Holden blanket and her bracelet." The psychic added that a young boy, who Natasha would know about, was on his way, and that someone would bring in a little fox terrier dog to visit her.

The next day, the events happened as predicted. A visitor brought in a foxy puppy, someone had made a bracelet in the Romanian national colours and slipped it on her thin wrist, and a blonde-headed boy turned up. The seventeen-year-old, with film-star looks, had hitchhiked from the West Coast and was sitting by her bed, stroking her hand, his head bowed in sorrow. Initially, his boss refused to give him time off to see Natasha, so he quit his job. Happily, the boss changed his mind when he heard about the circumstances.

So many people were arriving in groups at the hospital that it was hard to remember how they were involved in Natasha's life. Visitors brought in food, a woman came in regularly to play a harp, and a Māori youth group travelled from Nelson in a van bursting with cheerful teens, guitars and great singing voices. It jollied up the hospital.

When Natasha needed washing, we moved out into the sunny hospital gardens where stories were shared about her antics. One of the Māori women, who called herself 'Nan', chuckled over the time she had a North American Indian chief grace her home. She sent Natasha off to the shops to buy food for the important guest. Natasha came back with bread, cheese and margarine, made the chief a sandwich, and slapped it down in front of him. "Here's your kai (food), bro. Enjoy."

Nan was shocked, but the prestigious guest threw back his head and roared with laughter. "I like that little girl," he cackled. "I really do." Natasha treated everyone the same.

Another woman said she was in the street once, feeling depressed, when Natasha plucked a flower from a nearby garden and snuck up on her. "You're as pretty as this flower," she said, presenting it to the surprised woman.

Apparently, Natasha spent a lot of time at court supporting youngsters who'd fallen foul of the law. Once she ran into a local who was heavily pregnant, and after hugging her goodbye, she then raced back to her. "Oh my God," she cried excitedly. "I've just hugged your baby." When the baby was born, the bemused mother brought her to the hospital and laid her by Natasha's head.

Miss Eighteen rang up, as did other family members, to see how their sister was doing. "Mum, I had a dream about Tasha last night, and she talked to me."

"Really?" I hoped this daughter had a psychic insight. "What did she say?"

"What do you think she said?"

"I've no idea," I sighed.

"She said, 'I'm fucken hungry.'"

It was a shocking remark, but funny too. "Thank you for telling me, little darling," I said. "That sounds like Natasha. Let me know when she comes to you again."

"And by the way, Mum. Stop stressing. Whatever you do is fine by us. Go and smoke some drugs."

Daughters are priceless. I laughed again and hoped there'd be more laughter in the future after this ordeal was over.

Natasha

Chapter Twenty-Three

Natasha

The biblical forty days and forty nights had passed, and Natasha's little heart was still pumping, although she was becoming gaunt. A pattern had set in at the hospital whereby people who had slept by her bedside overnight went off for a few hours, and a fresh lot of visitors arrived. The Fleming family were the most constant, visiting daily, for hours on end. Natasha had gone to school with Ricky and Krystle, and when I arrived, they were holding her hand. David Thorpe, pastor of Church of Christ, called in daily, sometimes with his wife and children, and he was a serene presence. He was gentle and hopeful, bringing parishioners who surrounded Natasha's bed and prayed earnestly. I was humbled by their dedication and devoutness. Everyone wanted a miracle. Trish Martin turned up one day with pumpkin soup, and since we got on so well, she came most days with more of her specialty. In times like this you know who your friends are.

One thing that upset some people, but which Bryan and I considered important, was talking about Natasha's inevitable funeral. We wanted to be prepared to lessen the stress on all of us. Some people don't get that opportunity with a sudden death of a loved one. I was attracted to the Māori way of taking leave of those who have passed, where they hold your hand, hug you and let you rave. I thought Natasha would want a young person's celebration of her life, not a stiff, formal funeral with an expensive walnut coffin. At the same time, we didn't want to lose her to a marae (a fenced-in complex of buildings and grounds that are the focal point of a Māori community comprising a particular iwi, hapū {subtribe}, or whānau), and that upset the Māori wardens who had been so generous and caring. We wanted her to be buried, not cremated, in a place that felt familiar.

"You're the parents, she's your child. Do it your way," said people when I voiced concerns, but I still fretted. Natasha had a foot in many worlds. We wanted to do right by her, but there were so many options.

Still surprised that Natasha was alive by Day 40, we approached a woman we'd talked to earlier, who had a 'green' approach to funerals and provided wooden, eco-friendly coffins and caskets. We thought that ideal for Natasha and for the youngsters who would be involved by writing messages in felt pen on the exterior. It just wasn't Natasha's style, being put into an expensive coffin or casket, and just to please a few funeral-goers who would never care or remember our daughter as much as we did. We talked about what she would want. It was generous of churches to offer beautiful recycled coffins, and we thought about that as well as about what Natasha's siblings might want.

Bryan was insistent. He wanted to cart his daughter around in our hearse when the time came. He wanted to be involved with his little girl and no funeral director would tell him otherwise. We told our kids how we felt, and they never said boo. It felt sad having to pre-empt what we hoped wouldn't happen. When the wooden coffin was trolleyed out into the yard, I said to Bryan, "If Natasha recovers and we don't use this, then you have a gardening box for your brassicas (cauliflowers, cabbages, broccoli, etc.). Or, it might make a little boat for the grandies when they come along."

A very strange thing happened once the coffin arrived. Tristan rang that night, arranging to collect me from the hospital the next day, after he spent time with Natasha. I put the receiver down and was hopping back into bed when *Greensleeves* started up on the phone. I never liked that song from my schooldays, but how does a tune suddenly start playing after you put the phone back on the cradle? It was so odd, and it bothered me that weird stuff was happening. Then I had a thought. "Bryan, I think our daughter is saying she is okay with a 'green' funeral. You know, Green …" And neither of us knew what to say.

At this stage, I was wondering whether I should still share pictures of Natasha with others online. She wasn't dead, just in a coma. I thought them poignant and it might help people understand some of the decisions we were making; they kept asking about her. Every few days the *Nelson Mail* rang for an update, and TV and magazine journalists were also keeping in touch. I emailed that, although deeply unconscious, Natasha appeared to respond to some people; sometimes her eyes half-open and her arm thrust back. The doctors said it was simply muscle-reflex motions.

Late one day, Natasha seemed to screw up her face and cry before resorting to snoring and blobbing out again. That day had been a biggie with so many people filling the room in a prayer group, that it left visitors queuing in the foyer. While some of them were non-believers, all of them were singing and waving their arms. Collectively it was powerful. When the pastor said he could feel her spirit, I bent over Natasha and said, "Move your arms, baby" and one thin little arm shot up. "Blink," I commanded, and she did it, weakly. If anyone could resurrect her, it was this dedicated group. A doctor examined her, but her eyes remained fixed and blank. We discussed inserting feeding tubes into her again, but it was decided to let Natasha dictate our course of action. At the first sign of her hands unclenching and a glimpse of life in her eyes, we'd swing into action.

After the prayer group left, people I didn't know entered the room. They were a mixed bunch, from a burly farming couple to a bigwig in the city council. Her visitors also included a woman with several problematic kids, Natasha's youth group, the public health nurse, a Buddhist monk with two devotees, people from down the road (she sporting a love bite and he a smile), more Māori wardens, hairdressers, itinerants and solo mums. A pretty redhead whose boyfriend had given her a gorgeous bunch of flowers arrived as well, but since she wanted to ditch him, she thought Natasha might enjoy the flowers more. And there was a surprise visit, at the same time, from two lots of relatives who had travelled vast distances from opposite ends of New Zealand. It was like a party. I rang Bryan. "Put extra grub on the table, love. Your rellies and mine have turned up."

We left Natasha in the good hands of a devout Christian from Zimbabwe who, with his Scottish friend, came to visit her every morning and every night, and they read to the sleeping princess, mostly Bible stories.

One of my relatives, Tina, arrived with her daughter and young half-Samoan granddaughter, Renee. While Natasha lay like Sleeping Beauty, the little girl brushed Natasha's hair and sang to her, unlike an older girl who came to visit with her mum. The teen sobbed so much it was alarming, and she was encouraged to go out into the gardens. That evening, as Tina and her daughter were sharing a meal that they'd bought for us, I said, "Where's Renee?" We stopped talking, and a pure, sweet voice emanated from the laundry. "I'm singing a song about Natasha," Renee said. She seemed to be in a trance.

"She's an old soul," explained her grandmother. I was fighting back tears. What a sweet tribute from that angelic child.

Only two of the many visitors were bothersome. One of whom had hitchhiked from Auckland and quit his job to be with Natasha. The teenager, with long matted hair and smelly clothes, was homeless. He monopolised the chair next to Natasha and existed on tea provided by the hospital and snacks brought in by visitors. The second was a daily, older visitor who reeked of alcohol. Both had a dark, brooding presence, and I felt a chill in the air when I arrived at the hospital and found them at Natasha's bedside. They were such a contrast to the perfumed ladies bringing in fresh flowers and little trinkets, or to Natasha's headmaster and teachers, and the ladies from the bank who visited in their lunch hour. When a nurse said I couldn't stop people coming to see Natasha, I went to speak to the head nurse, accompanied by a friend. She sorted it out. These two guys could visit but their visiting hours were limited to early morning or late afternoon after I had gone home. I hoped the Zimbabwean chap and his Scottish mate might even pray for those lost souls.

Later, the dishevelled, unwashed teen wrote me a long letter thanking me for getting Natasha from Romania, and the chap with the alcohol problem went to rehab. He said that while gazing at Natasha in the hospital, she had inspired him to turn his life around. Our little girl was working her magic it seemed.

It amazed me the effort people made to visit Natasha. A friend, who'd tragically lost two of her adopted children, caught an early flight from Christchurch to Nelson, borrowed a car and, after a couple of hours visiting Natasha, travelled back over the hill to catch the plane home. Another travelled four hours, stayed for an hour, and left to go home again. She said, "That girl is special. I met her a few times. My kids and I love her. I didn't want to drive so far, but the spirit kept telling me. It was annoying, but I had to do it." Natasha rewarded her with a flapping arm and by grinding her teeth. The woman said she felt Natasha had made her decision and was at peace. I replied that other people had said that as well, and perhaps she was the person meant to give Natasha permission to go. Others spent long hours on the road bringing food, hugs and comfort to us. Every day was a surprise because I didn't know who would turn up. I bought a book for visitors to sign and write their comments, perhaps adding a drawing, or their thoughts. Then when I wasn't at the hospital, I could see who had come to visit and had kept Natasha company.

Nurses were keeping a closer eye on visitors after someone had squirted Natasha's mouth with mouthwash due to her foul-smelling breath, causing her to splutter, and it required two nurses to resuscitate her. A big sign was put up: 'Nil by Mouth'. Somewhat annoying were those who felt 'closest' to Natasha, who would barge in when gentle visitors were gazing at her, and bossily push them aside and croon over her. Exceptions were made for her twin, but it was plain rude behaviour on the part of the others. Tristan never did that. He'd say, "Goodaye, how's it going?" to visitors as he entered in his work boots, wearing Fulton Hogan high-vis gear, and sit with his head bowed over Natasha before he drove me home. He was such a he-man, but his grief was obvious, and it was silent. I didn't know how to help him and his siblings because I was struggling myself.

Tristan was not happy when we discussed burial plots for Natasha. He wanted the one near the high school he and his siblings attended, so he could drive by in his ute and toot the horn. We felt connected to East Takaka, where the historic church we married in overlooks the peaceful cemetery. Since the plots were much cheaper there, we bought four so we could join Natasha eventually. We chose the front row overlooking the towering hills and the road where she may have hitchhiked. She would like that, having a ringside seat.

I hadn't realised Natasha was connected to so many religious groups. She was mostly bubbly and giggly but confused about religion. When she stayed with us, she went to several denominations to worship, depending on whether she liked the person giving her a lift to the service. She really liked some people from the Jehovah Witnesses and diligently wrote verses on how to be a better person, but when she came home, she morphed into being a confused teen. She was influenced by older people and sought their guidance. A few days before the accident, she went to the Spiritualist church in Nelson with a friend who wanted a reading. The 'guide' dismissed the friend, saying she was more interested in Natasha as she was receiving a message for her from the spiritual world. "Watch out for the car on the road," she warned our unsuspecting daughter. Apparently, Natasha said, "What car?" and was bothered about the message.

When religious groups visited her bedside, they pinned cards and prayer messages on the hospital wall behind Natasha's head. Mother Teresa sat next to Jesus, Indian gurus and the Dalai Lama. I had no problem with that. I thought it was generous of them to spend their time praying for our daughter. Others objected. "Don't worry. We've got her covered," said one group. "We don't believe in Eastern religions." I thanked them but thought it disrespectful to take the items off the wall.

Apart from the Hare Krishnas, and visitors from the Destiny Church, the Open Brethren, the Buddhists community, and the Quakers, plus all the traditional denominations, two devout ladies, one young and one not so, also turned up. They had no religious affiliation but were a small core that travelled around New Zealand caring for people in need. It sounded precarious but they smiled serenely. Yes, it could be hard and frustrating work they admitted, but the Good Lord looked after them and guided them.

I always hoped nice people like that would turn up when some of our kids visited. Miss Eighteen made me laugh; she was so sassy. When I asked if she had found a job yet, she tossed back a mane of bleached hair, fluttered her dark eyes surrounded by a halo of mid-blue eye shadow, and said "Nuh." And that I should know the reason why.

I didn't.

"Think about it, Mother. I might get depressed if I get a job." She said she wanted to be free to visit Natasha whenever she felt like it. Then she rolled up a ciggie, and said to her dormant sister, "Wake up, sis. Got a smoke for you. Mum'll give it to you when I'm not here.

Okay?" I opened my mouth to protest, when she said, "Gotta go, Mum. Can I have a few bucks for petrol to give to my mates?"

I said, "What about your benefit? Haven't you got anything left over?"

She said, "Nuh, too many emos (emotions) going on," and added, "I need to chill out on things, Mother. Nothing you need to know about." Which left me more confused, but it didn't hurt to dip into my purse because none of us knew how long we had left with Natasha.

On Day 57, we had a mighty frost that would have wiped out our kiwifruit if we hadn't got up before dawn and turned on the overhead sprinklers. In the North Island hailstones battered and bruised orchards; a devastating wipe-out for some unlucky orchardists. But they got a second chance. Our little girl was shrinking by the day, like our economy. A large contingent of Māori wardens turned up in a van, including the Archdeacon of the Anglican Church. Natasha used to wave to this jolly guy whose religious cross flapped across his portly belly, and say, "Hello, God." He always chuckled. I expect they were marvelling she was still alive almost eight weeks after the accident.

Dr Russell, our lovely local doctor who'd attended our kids since they were tots and who often popped in, said a fit, healthy girl like Natasha could last a bit longer. If she survived to the sixtieth day, then he would make arrangements for her to go back to the major hospital in Nelson for another brain scan. It felt so sad. Natasha was stunningly pretty with her long, dark ringlets spread over the pillow, a nose that Michael Jackson had paid thousands for, and looking angelic in a white gown. When she sighed and her arms lurched upward, you wondered if it was a reach towards heaven or just a brain-injury reflex.

Harvest time was upon us. I couldn't let Bryan carry the workload alone. It was our annual income that was at stake. I had dedicated supporters who faithfully wrote in the book and who visited and commented on Natasha's movements. I felt guilty spending time away from the hospital, but it would only be for a few days, and we'd rush to the hospital if Natasha's condition deteriorated. We hired several people to help with harvesting, some from the backpackers' hostel. I warned them, "I have to tell you my daughter is dying. So if we ring and say don't turn up, you will know why." And then I bawled my eyes out. It sounded so matter of fact.

Just as we were leaving for the hospital one day, a teenager knocked on the door. Her grandparents' car had broken down and was spilling oil on the road. Bryan collected the trio, and I popped the kettle on. The grandmother knew of Natasha, having seen her in *Double Trouble*, and had formed a negative opinion about the whole matter. I felt tense and upset, but said I understood how disappointing it was to have a vehicle breakdown when they'd planned an outing. You feel helpless. On the way to the hospital I chatted with the youngster in the car about girly things, but they declined to see Natasha. They said they were scared. They began walking away, when the grandmother trotted back offering petrol vouchers. I said no, no, no; we were happy to help, and that it was no big deal. She trotted away again, then turned around and marched back. She opened her arms and gave me a long silent hug that spoke volumes. It made my day – unlike the visit from two prim teachers. Thanking them for coming, I gave each teacher a quick squeeze. Their faces expressed utter shock – possibly the same reaction as mine to the grandmother who'd hugged me. I hoped more jolly, brown-skinned people would turn up with guitars and sing Natasha back to life.

Now that the magic sixty days had passed, and we were halfway through picking kiwifruit, employing some of those who'd come to the hospital to visit Natasha, Dr Russell kept his word. He made arrangements for Natasha to be taken to Nelson by ambulance for another brain scan, and to confer with several specialists. When her twin, Joanna, turned up, we gave her a massive embrace, half for her and half for her sister. "Come on, Tash. I know you can make it," she begged, wiping her eyes. Natasha seemed to half-open an eye, and then sighed. Joanna gave me instructions for making Natasha aware: "You pat her nicely on the head and click your fingers twice."

On Day 64, she developed a wheezy cough and was getting a chest infection. A friend offered to go to the hospital early every day to make sure she had enough blankets. A Buddhist monk sent 'powerful prayers' from 'His Holiness' and beaded blessing bracelets for Natasha and me, which were to be left on our wrists until they dropped off. Four hundred people in a retreat in Toulouse were also meditating and directing the best outcome for the little girl in New Zealand.

Someone in Canada heard about Natasha and sent healing oil. It was associated with a girl called Audrey Santo who spent a couple of decades in a coma, and the oil was supposed to have healing powers, but there's a lot of controversy over that claim. The believers at the hospital were happy to anoint Natasha and gave the hospital entrance a splattering for good measure. Another devout person rang from the other side of the world and said he and his followers were meditating and praying for Natasha. He said I was the link to her healing, and he prayed fervently. He could see her as a bride. Looking at my almost lifeless little girl, it didn't seem possible. "Perhaps she will be a bride of Christ," I murmured. That didn't go down well. I hoped I hadn't ruined Natasha's chances.

After that protracted phone call, the hospital room was lively with mothers bringing in their kids from kindergarten. "Lilly begged to see Natasha," said one busy mum. "She threw a big wobbly when I said we had to go home and get Daddy's tea. I had to turn the car around. She drew Natasha a card." Even the local cops popped in. The crowded hospital room at times felt like one big united family.

"Natasha, baby," I cried. "You are so protected, so prayed over, now show Mumma a sign. We need you at home to drive the tractors. You love that. Blink if you hear me. Say 'Mumma'. You can swear if you like. Say anything, baby."

But Natasha did her own thing. Curled her lip, eyes vacant, and her scrawny arms turned inwards.

Still no miracle.

Chapter Twenty-Four

Losing Natasha

On Day 69, a nurse accompanied Natasha in an ambulance from our local Takaka community hospital to be scanned at the major Nelson Hospital. We would know once and for all what her brain was doing, and we hoped it would stop the malicious gossip going around the courthouse that we were starving her.

Bryan and I went to Nelson Hospital independently, accompanied by some of the family in our hearse, stopping off in Riwaka to see our fruit being packed. We were disappointed as the pack-out was much less than we'd anticipated; the fruit seemed smaller and had staining and softening problems. But that was the least of our worries.

Natasha looked pitiful in her hospital bed, surrounded mostly by her teenage Māori friends and a handful of wardens. She was tiny, bony and the coughing spasms were so bad she was on a morphine drip. They all wanted more time with her, but we only included Nan, who'd spent weeks sitting by her side, to hear the specialist's verdict with us. She could tell the whānau.

Not unexpectedly, the news was bad.

Natasha's brain was so damaged it had atrophied, and there was no likelihood of her waking from the coma. We asked lots of questions, about her feeding, for example, but it was a definite no. She now had the onset of pneumonia as well. The ambulance took her back over the Takaka Hill to the cottage hospital. We'd seen Natasha's twin in the street, and she refused to come with us. "Too sad," she said.

There was nothing to celebrate, but we invited our kids to lunch at a Nelson café anyway. A devout man, Pat Sale, from the Seventh Day Adventist Church, an author and adviser on growing kiwifruit, had sent us a treat: a voucher to eat out, plus extra for a movie ticket. He'd read my book and put two and two together – these parents never have time for a date as a couple. He was right about that. He had an adult daughter who had suffered a brain trauma, and he said his congregation was praying for us as a family. The generosity of people you've never met is uplifting.

Now the end was in sight, anyone who knew Natasha came to plant a kiss on her sunken cheeks and add more rings to her skeletal fingers. She looked gaunt and waxy; her pulse rate fast then slow. People were bringing in cauldrons of soup and baked goods. Sometimes she cried, "Mumm, Mumm, Mumm," and visitors looked at me. "I'm here, darling," I'd say. "Look at all the people here who love you."

I emailed friends who wanted to know how Bryan was bearing up. They knew how I felt but what about hubby? Although extremely upset, he was pragmatic and held in his grief. He'd lost his own dad when he was a teenager and an older sister drowned as a fifteen-year-old. His mother had to cope with these tragedies, and I expect he became private and resilient. I never saw him weep – unlike me. I cried enough for both of us.

On Days 70 and 71, the ward was overflowing with visitors. The head nurse made a chocolate cake and little Lilly, whose mother had already visited twice that day, refused to go home unless she saw Natasha. She'd done another drawing and said it was of Natasha, who had 'many eyes' and could see things. Her mother and I just smiled at each other. We didn't know how Lilly felt, but I thanked her and bought her a fancy doll. My sister's grandsons would beg her, "I want to see Tasha, that little girl in the hospital." I didn't understand the attraction. Neither did my sister but, happily, she obliged them.

Although just a shadow of herself, Natasha remained serene, while I was exhausted answering calls from overseas family and other enquirers. We rang our children and warned them, including our son and family who lived in Australia. No, we're not giving up, but we have to be realistic, we told them. I cried myself to sleep. I will soon never again see this beautiful little girl I fetched from Romania, while a voice said, "Be happy, you have her sister." But it was a false voice. You can't exchange people.

I remember that when I was at the Romanian orphanage, a young carer suggested I choose only one of the twins to take home. I said, "You don't separate twins," but she shrugged. It was practical, in her opinion. Our worlds were so different.

Day 72 was the day Bryan and I had planned to fly out to Cairns, but I'd cancelled that flight weeks ago.

There seemed nothing especially different about that day – just a miracle Natasha was still alive. She'd had Reiki healing and talk of a miraculous 'wake-up pill' to revive her from the coma was out of the question. Bryan drove me to the hospital, kissed his little girl, and went back to work in the orchard. I called him an hour later. "The nurses say her breathing has slowed down. I think she's dying. Come quickly." He rushed back. The usual visitors turned up, not knowing this was Natasha's last day on earth. You never quite know when death calls. We contacted Tristan, who was on a digger, and his partner, and said that they better come quickly. He strode in wearing work boots and stroked Natasha's arm. More than a dozen of us surrounded her bed with a nurse hovering and monitoring. We were silent and held hands. She took a tiny sigh, her last, at 3:50 pm on 30 May 2009. It was peaceful, but oh, so final.

"She's gone," someone said. In delayed shock and unable to weep, we were ushered into an annexe while a nurse attended to Natasha. The Fleming family, who'd visited daily the entire ten weeks, had snuck back home and whipped up food to share. It was a lovely gesture, even if we didn't feel like eating. When we trooped in for a final look, Natasha's eyes were closed, and she had a tiny upturned smile on her face. Luckily her twin wasn't there. She would have gone berserk and shaken her, "Wake us, sis". Dying seemed tranquil. I'd never seen anyone die before, except a badly injured dog, and that was heartbreaking. Perhaps the miracle was what had happened in the hospital over those long weeks. People from all walks of life had come to visit, and they ended up embracing each other and had filled the ward with chirpy chatter.

While Natasha's spirit was soaring to heaven, Bryan and I had a liquid spirit to dull the pain. There was so much to do. We rang our children scattered around New Zealand and in Australia. They all chose to come except for one son who had heavily invested in Natasha surviving, and he couldn't face the bitter disappointment.

The next day Bryan and I collected Natasha, and with the help of friends, we put her in a body bag, collected a death certificate and placed her in our hearse. Then we took her to a funeral home over the hill. We agreed to her being embalmed since family needed time to travel to the funeral. It was all matter-of-fact at the funeral home with prices and other details being attended to. I gave them clothing Joanna said Natasha would want to be buried in – jeans, her favourite cap, a shirt – not very girly. We visited the Men's Shelter and the Holy Trinity Church, which she had frequented, and talked to parishioners. I needed to still feel connected to Natasha and hung onto every word they said about her.

When a family member said I was selfish not having her lie at a wake (for viewing) at the home of a son's partner, I wept buckets. It was the Māori way, but I wanted my little girl with me when she was released from the funeral home – just one final glance. Those who wanted her, of course, were sad, but they'd never invested as hugely in her life as we had. They hadn't been to Romania and hadn't seen this helpless baby in a cot, undernourished and neglected. They hadn't put in the hours of rearing this beautiful teen they now mourned. No. She belonged to us, and her siblings. We were happy to share her but not to let anyone take over her final time with us. Hadn't she said, "Mumm, Mumm, Mumm," once when I'd returned to collect a coat I'd left by her bedside? It was a wounded, primeval cry. Heartbroken, I'd kissed her little face and had run my fingers through her dark, long ringlets. She wanted her mummy despite being brain dead.

When all the family turned up, it was full on with our kids, their kids, meals and funeral arrangements. We chose the local Presbyterian celebrant who agreed not to ramble on in a religious monotone, since it wasn't about converting those that attended and reminding them about their sins. It was about celebrating a teenage girl's short life. The funeral director rang, saying a Māori group wanted to take her for a night, but instead, the tactful Archdeacon Harvey Ruru conducted a touching memorial ceremony at the funeral home in Nelson for those who couldn't attend her funeral in Takaka. Word had gotten around, and it was a full house in Nelson, with a beautiful candlelit service. We also heard over a hundred Māori wardens, including the bigwigs, from all around New Zealand planned to attend the funeral in Takaka, which amazed us.

After Natasha was embalmed, Bryan and the boys brought her home in a coffin which they placed in the study. She looked like a lifeless, cold doll. I wanted to warm her up, to be part of the conversation at the dinner table two rooms away, which was the opposite – full of life and bustling with youthful likes and dislikes of the food I'd prepared. It's the small things that set you off, and I had to leave the table.

"Why did you choose to leave us? I can't bear life without you. I don't want to live anymore," I sobbed to my inert daughter. I heard an anguished wail and didn't realise it was my voice until a concerned daughter-in-law nudged me away from the coffin.

We took her to the Church of Christ, for Pastor Thorpe generously opened the doors for locals and friends to view Natasha in her wooden box. We bought felt pens and told kids big and small to write messages on it. Many of their messages were sweet and sentimental we observed as we read the nicknames that they had given Natasha. Graciously, the Pastor allowed the out-of-town teens to sleep around the coffin for the night. We didn't know whether they were homeless, but food was provided for them. We said we'd be happy for the pastor to say a few words at the funeral, since he was unwaveringly supportive and gentle.

At night, while Natasha's fans dossed down, we attended to our big family, preparing for the funeral the next day. The Golden Bay High School was hosting a sports event on the day, but the headmaster agreed to our holding a service in the large hall and offered us the use of the school projector. Two large portraits of Natasha were blown up for display and two hundred funeral service sheets were printed, which was woefully inadequate in hindsight. A son helped me choose photographs of Natasha's life for the slide show set to the music of Shaggy's 'You're my Angel', Natasha's favourite: 'Lonely' by Akon, and other family favourites such as 'Ave Maria', and appropriately, Andrea Bocelli's 'Time to say Goodbye'.

After dinner, Natasha's brothers spent hours, consuming lots of beer and almost coming to blows, working on a short speech to deliver at the funeral service. They were dealing with grief in different ways – crying, being angry, or placid, or stoic. I wandered out in my dressing gown and told them off. They may have lost a sister, but Dad and I are suffering too, I explained. So go to bed and be thankful you have someone in your life that might need you now. They all hugged me, said "Sorry, Ma," and had a few hours of well-needed kip.

Thursday, 4 June, was the day of the funeral. Natasha had been dead five days. Red-eyed teens had to be pulled away from the coffin, which was full of jewellery, messages, cards, a jar of her favourite tomato sauce, a huge fluffy teddy, a can of beer, neckerchiefs from gangs, a new black, silky blanket from Tristan, photographs, and Romanian momentos. Her twin placed a cigarette in her hand and tilted her cap sideways. We loaded Natasha's coffin into our hearse and slowly drove down Commercial Street with a cortege of cars and crowds following us. It seemed half the town had turned out. A Māori warden, wearing a yellow jacket and white gloves, strutted out in front and marched down the street directing traffic while we inched along behind him.

The school hall was packed, with standing room only. During the service children toddled up to the coffin and talked to Natasha while the pastor said lovely things about our international family and the impact Natasha had on many lives. My cousin, Liza, gave a heartfelt speech, as did a builder, fighting back tears.

"When I first arrived in Takaka I didn't know anyone, but in the street, Natasha was the first person to greet me. She was like a sparkly little Christmas tree," he said.

Natasha used to do bone carving, and the headmaster and teachers at the service all wore the necklaces she'd made for them.

It was hard to tell how many Māori wardens attended, but there were dozens of them. The chief warden flew in from the North Island, as did other representatives from around New Zealand. She spoke of the impact Natasha made on her and reiterated how impressed she was with her at the ceremonies on Waitangi Day in the Bay of Islands, where she greeted hundreds of people, including the Māori King. United, the wardens marched up the aisle as a powerful and single-minded group and placed a new warden uniform in her coffin. Every one of them bent over and kissed her tiny, frozen face. Natasha's twin was on another planet. She walked in and out during the service, and in front of over four hundred mourners, grabbed the blown-up photo of Natasha off the stand and headed out through the school hall's heavy glass-doors.

A devout Christian, who'd adopted three children from Sierra Leone, strummed his guitar while we sang hymns. He and his family had spent many hours praying over Natasha. I had stopped being angry with God. The inevitable had happened, and now I had to count my blessings, even if Bryan didn't feel that way. It was hard to know what he thought, for he remained calm and non-judgmental. He didn't get angry but went through the practical routine of doing what needed doing.

"I don't want you to get a heart attack by not having a blowout," I said. "We're in this together, and we will deal with it and keep loving each other – and be there for the kids." We all had a private journey ahead, one where Natasha memories might ignite unexpectedly.

Once the coffin was closed, we moved out onto the school grounds and loaded it onto Tristan's silver ute for burial at East Takaka, a few kilometres from the high school. Volunteers stayed behind and put food onto trestle tables for those who chose not to go to the cemetery. Tristan's brothers and Natasha's Māori friends jumped onto the tray of the ute, smoking their heads off, sounding the horn and waving to town folk on both sides of the main street. Bryan and I followed in our hearse, and probably for the first time ever, there was a traffic jam in our little township.

A touching service was held with Māori singing at the East Takaka graveside. I'd never seen so many people and didn't know half of them. It felt tragic watching our sons and foster son place our little girl into the dirt vault. My brain asked, "Should she have been cremated?" I imagined worms crawling over her in the dark and eating her beautiful, but dead, face. Should I have donated her organs? The police said, however, that Natasha had not signed her organ donor consent, possibly being influenced by other people for she was young.

A band of Nelson teens performed a haka, after which mourners in a long single-file procession grabbed petals and sprinkled them onto the coffin. We gasped when someone swore at Natasha for leaving this world. My poor little girl was lying face upwards in the grave, and she couldn't defend herself. Our sons and friends grabbed shovels and heaped soil over the deep hole, wiping tears on their sleeves.

As I write, a sparrow has flown in my room and is now circling outside the window in joyful swoops. I like to think it's Natasha flying free.

Back at the school hall, after the service, a Romanian girl introduced herself, saying she had flown from Auckland to represent I-CANZ (Inter-Country Adoption New Zealand) and presented a card from the organisation, with loving wishes. Those of us who adopted through I-CANZ became a large extended family and networked.

After the funeral, the trestle tables were groaning with home-baking but, for some reason, the Māori wardens went to the local marae for their meal. Bryan and I were on autopilot. I would have liked to have personally thanked each and every warden who either flew or came in busloads to the service.

At home the evening began with a fireworks display, and our family and friends gathered around a burning drum in our large garden, reminiscing, eating and drinking until the small hours of the morning. Natasha would have loved her send-off.

Then a few odd things began happening. It was all very strange.

Chapter Twenty-Five

A hovering spirit

A week after the funeral I'd turned the lounge into a celebration of Natasha's life. Over one hundred and fifty sympathy cards fluttered from the ceiling, and a large portrait of Natasha beamed from the wall. "Take the cards down," someone said weeks later, and when I asked why, she said, "It's too sad. A reminder." I said I wanted to remember our daughter being real, and I would do it in my own time. Meanwhile, her twin was a mess. Joanna didn't want to stay at home but rather with friends who'd prop her up. She walked around the streets of Nelson clutching a huge glass-framed photo of Natasha that she took off our wall.

"Don't take her away," I'd begged.

"She's more mine than yours," she said as she hitched over the hill with the framed photograph. "You don't know how I feel."

"I want to know. Stay here and let's talk."

But her head was in another space. And it was hard to talk when other family members were here, or jetting back to Australia or, in one case, going walk-about. The police were actively looking for a missing person. "What has my family come to?" I cried to hubby. "We're all going in different directions. We should be united and supporting each other."

Far more disappointing were the reactions of some people we vaguely knew. They crossed the street when they saw us in town. "There goes that sad couple," I bet they muttered. It felt cowardly but most people don't know what to say. Just "Hi, how are you doing?" would have been preferable.

A local I bumped into asked me how I was a few days after the funeral, and I truthfully replied, "Sorrowful." She suggested I follow her granddaughter's advice. "What's that?" I wondered.

"Get over it," she replied.

It was so brutal. I asked in a small voice, "Have you ever lost a child?"

She said, "No."

I choked back a strangled sob. Logically, this person was trying to be helpful, but I was raw, unhappy and I didn't want to be told how to behave.

Florists were kept busy delivering beautiful bouquets to our home, including one from TV3. The TV channel ran a segment on Natasha's demise, causing an avalanche of letters. Some folk called in with rose plants, which gave us an idea: we'd make a Natasha garden. Well-meaning people sent books on religion and grief. I cried. I didn't want those instructional books telling me how to cope. It felt like a slap in the face and I never read them. Others sent candles and fancy picture frames – much nicer. My American friend, Sharon, from California, posted the perfect present: wind chimes. They sometimes ring when the weather is still. Friend Megan sent a photo album. She had followed our journey from pre-adoption days, and the album was useful for inserting random photos Natasha's friends gave us.

"When are you putting up a headstone?" people asked. It felt invasive to be pressured. On our way to town, we'd take the East Takaka road to say "hello" to Natasha, spilling tears on the heaped-up soil. Tristan lugged a slab of marble from the Takaka Hill as a temporary headstone, while Natasha's teenage friends left coins, jewellery and beer bottles. They also attached photos to the makeshift cross. Some visitors were upset that the cross was at Natasha's head and repositioned it at the foot end of her grave. Māori wardens asked for a portrait of Natasha to hang in a gallery in Rotorua that displayed images of wardens who had passed on, which was an honour. They said they could feel Natasha's spirit, and I told them I felt she was 'helping me up there'. Lost articles inexplicably turned up when I asked Natasha to find them, not ever thinking that was even possible. I hadn't believed in that sort of thing.

Years before, when Bryan was a maths, physics and science teacher in Auckland, I went to the kitchen cupboard to fetch a packet of tea. My mother had recently died, and I was thinking about her. Bryan was marking student papers and needed some oomph. Frantically, I hauled out everything in the cupboard, but no tea. I was upset. "Sorry love, I'll buy some tomorrow," I assured him. I returned for a final look and lo and behold! A packet of tea presented itself on opening the cupboard. I nearly passed out and could only think my mother in heaven was helping me. I've never shared this with anyone. Who'd believe you? Religious people call it paranormal, but when Natasha died, I felt she tuned into us in unexpected ways.

Meanwhile we worried about two of our children who'd become severely depressed over their sister's death. People reported that Natasha's twin had spent two days sitting on her sister's grave. It was our job as parents to hold our flock together. If that meant helping out a bit financially to stop them doing anything silly, then we did what we had to do. It was not the time to give them a lecture and make them more miserable. Bryan keeps a record of what has been loaned or given to each kid money-wise, so other family members don't feel they are unfairly left out. Of course, we should be allowed to do what we want with our hard-earned savings, but in reality, adult kids bring up grievances, justified or otherwise. It happens in all families. Keeping a diary is essential because it's easy to misremember.

Having to work in the orchard gave structure and a sense of purpose to all of us. Sometimes the police visited or rang with updates on the investigation. Later Bryan spent days at the kitchen table poring over the coroner's report, nitpicking its content, piecing information together, and motoring to Nelson to view the accident scene. Tristan helped his dad go over the possible scenario of what happened that fateful night. He was deeply affected, being nearer Natasha's age and a mentor to his five younger siblings. It was months before we collected Natasha's bloodstained clothes, and years before I got rid of them. It didn't feel like an appropriate legacy to leave to her twin. Instead, I assembled all her certificates, school reports, childish drawings, newspaper and magazine clippings, and other mementos into a large plastic container. It would have been easier to accept the coroner's verdict, but Bryan and some of the family disagreed with the findings. A two-day hearing was held to conclude the matter. It wasn't satisfactory, but it did give us closure when it was all over.

Working in the orchard, the pain and loss would unexpectedly hit me and send me into spasms of grief. I howled when no one could see me. It was something I had to work through. Often a fantail swooped and looped so close I'd say, "I'm okay, Natasha," and then I could continue pruning. That year Michael Jackson died as well, leaving millions of fans mourning, none more so than his children.

A friend who'd tragically lost her Russian daughter a few months before Natasha died, said she took up running, but that the heartbreak never goes away, it just gets pushed into the background when you are forced to think of other things. I told her a doctor friend of mine, who'd adopted two Russian boys, sent me a book called *The Shack* (by William Paul Young) that helped me enormously. She said it helped her too.

After the funeral, a woman stopped by asking for directions and we got chatting. She gazed at the sympathy cards dangling in the next room, and I told her about Natasha. Her face remained stony until her cell phone turned on and a bunch of weird signs came onto her screen. She was bewildered. I mentioned Natasha loved cell phones and that odd things were happening to mine. Others reported random numbers turning up on their cell phones, too. A relative said her phone was playing up, so she took the battery out, but Natasha's image remained on the screen. "She's not quite ready to go yet," she said.

I didn't expect to see the woman again, but she rang a few days later and apologised for her demeanour. I sensed there was some sadness about her when she visited. Over a cup of tea, I boldly asked, "Did you ever feel loved as a child?"

Her face crumpled and she revealed an abusive childhood. "I haven't told anyone about this, but I can talk to you." It felt good helping someone else instead of focussing inward on my pain, internalising my own loss. She bought two copies of my book and bear hugged me when I said the profits go to a Romanian orphanage.

"I'm so glad we met. I have made a new friend," I gushed, and after that happily went out to work in the orchard.

The first year after losing a child you are especially vulnerable and comments people make take on exaggerated proportions. When I told a friend that I was wearing sunglasses because I'd been crying, she said, "Oh, I thought you would have gotten over that by now!" I clearly needed to talk to my brain – *Stop being so sensitive!*

One night I got a call from a professional who saw an article about us in the paper, and she talked to me about 'tapping' and a helpful book called *The Brain that Changes Itself* (by Norman Doidge). She wanted to help my brain become happy and offered free counselling. However, we were off to outback Queensland for a short holiday, so I passed up this opportunity. I love the harshness of the Aussie landscape and talking to people in campgrounds, usually in the ladies' toilet blocks! One family invited us back to their makeshift camp complete with cages of cockatiels and pet snakes that slithered over us. As long as they are well fed with mice, they aren't dangerous, they assured us.

I didn't want to return home and face reality, but we had an orchard to attend to. Once back in New Zealand, we drove over the Lewis Pass to Murchison to drop off books we'd borrowed from their library. We put the books into the return slot when suddenly, the song 'Lonely' filled the air. It was blasting from a house next door. That was Natasha's song, one we'd played at her funeral. I'd been happy in Australia but when that poignant song rang out in the stillness, I collapsed on the steps and wept. Then I talked to my brain. *Stop being a sook! It's your little girl welcoming you back home. She is following you and glad you had a good holiday.* Even if it wasn't so, how surprising that *that* particular song blasted itself out of the blue!

The first Christmas without Natasha was difficult because of the sweetness we received from other people. Tristan and his partner left a box of chocolates on Natasha's grave and planted a small fir tree trimmed with baubles. The twin turned up, which made me cry again because she was looking more identical to her sister than ever. She brought along a gay guy who needed mothering, and I was happy to have them both stay with us. They were both crazy and funny. Distraction meant not thinking too much, and it opened our world.

When the first anniversary passed, I was less raw than I thought I would be, largely because of a Buddhist monk who visited us on her way to start a two-year retreat on Kangaroo Island. She was most approachable in her robe and such a sweetheart; someone who gave us another perspective on life. I started thanking Natasha in heaven for making it all possible – we were meeting people who instantly felt like close, wonderful friends. It was pointless being angry with God.

We had an odd experience once when hubby and I slept in the lounge on a fold-out bed. We'd employed trades people for a few tasks and couldn't use the front of the house. It was winter, so we kept the log fire going. No one else was at home. What was strange was waking up at night and finding the hall lights on. Our kids will tell you we never leave lights on. They call us 'tight' and we reply, "LOL. Learn from us and you might one day own your own home!"

"Bryan," I said to my slumbering hubby. "The lights in the hallway won't turn off."

He snorted his way back to life and checked them out. We both jiggled the switches, but they stubbornly stayed on. Creatively, I said, "Natasha, Mumma and Daddy are here. Is that you, baby girl?" We tried again, and the light flicked off.

Once back in bed, there was a rustle in the chimney, followed by a long sigh. Religious people told me it was the work of the devil and to get the house exorcised. Others, including a most sane South African woman, said of course it was Natasha. "She's hovering because it's not yet settled with the coroner." We did call in an electrician and there was no evidence of rodents and the switches were all working perfectly.

As the months rolled by, we carried on as normal, although odd things still happened, but it was more comforting than 'the work of the devil'. Things I lost and fretted about turned up without fail. When Romania lost in a World Cup final, my collection of Romanian language tapes crashed to the floor. My sister played a game of online scrabble and was amazed to find her letters spelt out my name. A bird flapped against the window and then the telephone rang. It was a woman from the Salvation Army in Dunedin who was helping a prisoner. The convict knew Natasha and had gone berserk when another inmate tore down cuttings of our family, in which Natasha featured, that he'd pinned to a wall. He spent his time writing poetry about her and wanted her as his wife. (I don't think so!) I sent a copy of my first book to the kindly woman who had called us, to pass on to the guy. I didn't know his life story, but when people are born, they don't expect to spend years in jail. People need hope and kindness.

One night I was chatting on Messenger with my daughters and the conversation was punctuated with a terse, "Yes" or "No". We all swore that none of us had contributed those words to the conversation.

My diary was my friend because it never spat back or made me justify how I felt. I found it helpful writing about my feelings because our adult sons didn't want to talk about Natasha. I stopped engaging in evening computer chatter when one of our adult sons mentioned their sister should be wearing a wedding frock instead of smiling from her headstone. Suddenly the computer mouse exploded, puffed and smoked. Was Natasha agreeing with them? Or saying, "I'm still here, Mumma. Stop going on about it." I didn't think it was sinister.

Nearly three years later, a friend in the North Island rang with sad, yet astonishing news. There'd been a bad car smash where three elderly women were ambulanced to Nelson Hospital, one in a critical condition. The daughter of the most badly injured of the women – who was now on life support – was flying up from Gore to see her mother and was bringing along a psychic friend for support. It was in our vicinity, over the hill. "Jonquil, go to the hospital," said my friend from up north. "They have something to tell you."

"My mother is muttering; she'll be alright," said the daughter when we arrived at the hospital. We were curious. I'd never met these women before, but when we walked up the hospital steps, they sensed we were the parents my friend had referred to. "My mother said there is a girl called Natasha who is 'with her'."

At the hospital cafeteria we chatted over coffee. I had never met anyone before who could communicate with the spirit world. Birgy was the genuine article. She said that Natasha is 'appearing' and is excited we are here, but that she's busy helping lots of people. She's more in touch with her feminine side now (that was interesting), although she wears jeans, and looks wholesome and well. Birgy felt the smack that Natasha has sustained on the right side of her head, and said Natasha was saying that we did the right thing by not prolonging her life, and that she was happy 'up there' and was 'with us'. Birgy correctly described things about Natasha she could not possibly have known. The previous evening, Birgy said, she'd been dining out and mislaid her sunglasses. She'd frantically tipped her bag upside down in front of diners – no sunglasses – then placed the bag by her feet. Later she reached for her handbag and there they were – her sunglasses folded up on top of it.

Two years after Natasha died, we decided to dismantle the kiwifruit orchard. Like us, the vines were weary, and while it provided an income, it was marginal at best because we live in a valley, and it was difficult growing huge fruit with high dry-matter content in such a location. So, what to do with the 10 acres? We vetoed ideas of it being used for motorbikes, horses and other suggestions the kids made. Their ideas weren't profitable. We toyed with tree planting and growing a commercial crop. In the end we leased the paddocks to a local farmer to grow maize and to use as pasture for bobby calves.

My sister had an interesting suggestion. "You should grow tomatoes," she said. She'd been to Greece at the invitation of a handsome Aussie-Greek man she'd met playing scrabble online. My sister, a vegan, is one of the healthiest people I know, and she was impressed by the delicious, mouth-watering, juicy Greek tomatoes. I told her we had a bird problem here. Our garden tomatoes get pecked to death, especially by wekas. "Get some cats," she replied.

"No," we disagreed. "We live on the main road, and the cats end up looking like fried pancakes after semi-trailers run them over in the night. We don't want any more deaths in the family."

Sis shrugged. She knew the secret to growing those Super Toms. No bird problem once you have cats. She was conducting a trial in her backyard, some 100 metres or so from the salty sea on her large lifestyle property. She was deadly serious. Not only did she order $100 worth of tomato seeds but also two calico cats that reminded her of the ones in Greece. She even chose Greek names for them. When they didn't arrive as expected, she was annoyed and found two suitable ginger kittens with a Greek-look about them, ones that would chase away pesky birds. Within days two lots of cats were being shipped to her. She only wanted two, but since she'd ordered them, she decided to take them on. Now dealing with four cats with tricky Greek names, and the process of bonding with each one of them, another cat turned up. It was her original cat that had gone walkabout a year before and had been living in a church. So now she had five cats. Meanwhile, Sis had diligently built hay bale enclosures, and the now small tomato-seedlings had turned into healthy, transplantable plants. They had all the compost, love and nutrition a plant could want, and the cats looked after those Super Toms like watchful bodyguards.

"What is your secret?" visitors asked.

"Not telling," she replied, as we gazed at five cats and flourishing tomatoes. We didn't know if Sis could make a killing from her project but admired her commitment.

But with every success there can be downsides. One of her cats swallowed a chicken bone that set her back two grand at the vet's, and the original cat escaped back to its ecclesiastical home.

"You're looking seedy," I said to Sis when we visited again. Perhaps she had cat flu or needed a large juicy steak to enrich her blood's iron levels.

"It's the tomatoes."

"What do you mean?"

"I'm allergic to them," she wailed, sporting an unsightly rash.

We left it to her scrabble partner 'across the ditch' (Australia) to console her on her Greek tragedy.

Chapter Twenty-Six

Return to Romania

As the teens were maturing, we discussed visiting their birth countries and tracing their families. Surprisingly, they weren't very keen. I would have jumped at the chance and would have started learning the language! Occasionally, the girls showed interest about their birth parents and siblings and pored over the photographs I had collected, but they found it hard to identify with them. The Romanian birth mothers looked weary, with old-fashioned clothing, posing unsmilingly against grim Soviet-style concrete apartment blocks or a humble mud-floored cottage. I tried to be upbeat and positive. "Look! You girls have green eyes like your sisters," or "Isn't your birth daddy handsome. That's why you're such a good-looking chick." And they'd yawn and change the subject.

Of course, it would be a mission to take the Russian twins back to their land of birth as their mother had died and their father was unknown. They weren't inquisitive either but liked the video footage I'd taken of them in the orphanage, which I showed them in an effort to see if they remembered anyone. "Gee, I look a dick," laughed our Russian daughter, Masha. "Mum, was I mental?"

"Of course not, little darling. You were excited to be out of the orphanage, so you went a bit crazy walking on tables and tickling that bald man's head with a feather on the plane. Now who remembers the Russian word for pancakes? Let's make some." These were gentle, bonding times. When the teens left home, I gave them souvenirs I'd collected as a reminder of where they came from because they were sure to reflect on this now and then.

When TV3 filmed the documentary *Double Trouble* about our Romanian twins, we had discussions with the crew about taking the three girls back to their birth country. I'd started learning useful phrases in anticipation of that event. It was definitely on the cards that we'd go, although travelling with Natasha's twin would be tricky, and we'd need an aide. She was a bit feral.

Then when Natasha died, I didn't want to return to Romania, so I put away the language tapes and hundreds of Romanian words I'd jotted down and diligently memorised under the kiwifruit vines. I'd spent over six months in that country in 1990 and 1991, adopting the three girls, leaving Bryan to mind eight children at home and run the orchard. I had a love-hate relationship with that country. I loved the people I met but hated the judicial system. I'd been accused of wanting children for nefarious reasons because I had several at home. The uncertainty and stress I experienced so far from home was worse than any teen antics collectively.

It was soon after the execution of Ceaușescu (December 1989), the tyrannical leader of Romania, when it was revealed that thousands of children languished in orphanages. For New Zealanders, there was a nine-month window of opportunity to adopt a needy child in Romania, and I squeezed in two visits during that time frame. First the twins, then Cristina, our youngest adopted daughter. The story is too complicated to tell here, but I've written about it in my earlier book *How Many Planes to Get Me?*

"Mum," gasped a familiar voice down the phone. "You won't believe this, but David Lomas of *Lost and Found* (TV3) is interested in helping me find my birth family in Romania."

"Go for it," I urged. "What a wonderful opportunity. This will be closure for you. Wow!"

"But, Mum, I'm scared."

"Do it, Cristina. We'll support you."

The *Lost and Found* TV production crew visited our home after we brought Cristina, her boyfriend and her best friend, Haley, up from Christchurch. They couldn't guarantee they'd find Cristina's birth family but were keen to try. Cristina was cheerful and co-operative. She spoke sensibly about the matter, and since she had her own young daughter by now, she saw this was a big opportunity for her because living in a small flat as a solo mother was limiting.

"I don't want to go without you guys," she admitted. I said of course we'd go as well, and I found cheap promo flights, going via India, on a new Dreamliner aircraft. "This is a big trip for Daddy and me, too," I texted. "Suggest we have one extra day in India. Only one day out of your life and you will see things you never imagined. I love that country."

Since we were paying our own fares, I thought that was a happy compromise as well as culturally enriching. Otherwise, she could fly by herself and meet the crew in Romania, which was a challenge for a young mum who hadn't travelled much. When my English cousin, Joanna, who'd helped me years ago in Romania, said she wanted to be involved in this with her god-daughter, it was full steam ahead. She lived in London and could squeeze in a trip flying out to Romania, before doing a walk in Kathmandu to raise money for charity.

"It's meant to be, cuz," she emailed. She'd been instrumental in me choosing five-month-old Cristina in an orphanage in Romania's Iași County, although we'd originally flown out to adopt Bogdan, who'd been promised to me on the previous trip when I'd adopted the twins.

The rules had changed since then, and Romania was clamping down on adoptions after news that some children were being returned because American families were unprepared for the 'orphanage behaviour' displayed by their newly adopted Romanian children. On the day we chose Cristina, I found another baby girl, Catalina, whose seventeen-year-old mother lived in a damp cellar with a dozen or more relatives. "Such is the level of misery in this country," said the elderly man I stayed with. "You must take this child (Catalina) back to New Zealand for her to thrive." Sadly, I lost two court cases in my attempt to do exactly that, and appealed in the Supreme Court in Bucharest, the first Kiwi to do so. Although victorious in bringing Cristina home, I wondered what happened to Bogdan and Catalina. It had taken four stressful months to get as far as I did, and I swore I'd never adopt again. Like rearing teens, the pain subsides over time, and eight-year-old Russian twins (a boy and a girl) joined our family four years later!

Once our trip to Romania to meet-up with the TV3 crew was confirmed, we fast-tracked a passport for Cristina before flying from New Zealand, via Sydney, to Delhi for an overnight stay. We oldies travelled light with a backpack, while Cristina had a suitcase filled with new clothes lent to her by her 'bestie', Haley, for the filming.

"This will be the third country you've visited in two days," I reminded Cristina when we landed at the airport in Milan.

She was distracted. "Where is my fricken bag?'

It was panic stations when we were left gazing at the empty luggage carousel. "They've stolen my suitcase," she wailed. "It's your fault for going to India. Shit food, shit country." How ironic, heading to the Lost and Found department to report a missing suitcase when Cristina was starring in TV3's *Lost and Found* documentary! Somehow, we survived the night at a hotel near the airport while the daughter skyped her woes back to New Zealand and received assurance that the airline would send her suitcase on to Bucharest.

Arriving at the airport at Otopeni in Bucharest, the daughter had another melt down. Another mum I'd been in contact with, who'd also taken her adopted daughter back to Romania, said they'd come to blows on the trip and were barely talking when they arrived back home. This was the biggest event in our daughter's life, apart from giving birth to her own daughter at a young age. She'd glimpsed Australia, India, Italy, and now the country of her birth, all within a few days. Cristina looked Romanian, but she couldn't speak the language. Outwardly, she was attractive, stylish and self-assured. Inwardly, she was one big stress-ball, and we bore the brunt of her frustration.

Travelling with another generation is interesting because while they are up on the technology side of things, their tolerance level is low. At Cristina's age, I'd hitchhiked around the world and visited fifty countries.

"Perhaps your suitcase will turn up tomorrow," I soothed, once we'd found our hostel. "Tomorrow we are exploring Bucharest. And then at night, we're going to meet your godmother who is flying out from London."

Bucharest had changed so much in the last twenty-odd years – crazy traffic and colourful hoardings. I didn't recognise some streets I'd spent months walking up and down to fill in time between court cases. I had flashbacks of being ripped off, accosted and having my handbag slashed by thugs. Then, I was a lonely mother of eight, filling in time, never sure the courts would allow me to adopt Cristina. I was so miserable at the time that I cried every day for four months about the uncertainty I was facing, while now my daughter was clearly upset because of a mess-up with an Indian airline! It was important to her. Also, I was dealing with Natasha's death. We'd come to her birth country, too. I had to face my demons, and Cristina was facing her heritage and being reunited with family. I kept my mouth shut and focussed on why we were back in Romania. Families promenading at night with woollen-capped toddlers on their dad's shoulders, children playing in public gardens beneath city lights, and lovers on park benches smooching, impressed Cristina. In New Zealand most families would be glued to their TV sets instead.

Cousin Joanna saved us. She was upbeat and fun. When the lost suitcase turned up, we climbed aboard a day train to Iași, Cristina's birth city. I wondered what she was thinking when glimpsing seedy railways stations, peasants working in the fields, quaint villages and remote churches. While interested, she relied on her cell phone a great deal – wondering what was happening at home and skyping her small daughter who had little understanding of her mother being so far away, possibly trying to 'find herself'. "I'm beginning to feel Romanian," she admitted.

In Iași, the night before we were to meet the film crew, we booked an affordable hotel. When the taxi swung into the street, I gasped, "That's the same street in which I met your birth parents, Cristina! Hey, cuz, remember us going there to ask if we could adopt her?" Joanna remembered.

The couple we had spoken to about the adoption had been living in squalor in a concrete jungle, but they no longer lived there. "Amazing, cuz," she replied. "It's as if we're being guided here." More buildings had sprung up, and so, like Cristina, I was seeing things through new eyes too. At the hotel we befriended the young receptionist and her dad, who dined with us. My cousin and I were keen to know if things had improved in the last two decades. Sadly, it had not for some kids who still lived in sewers. The dad added that he ran a charity providing free food for the homeless, and that some of them were choosy! He said his parents thought life was better in Ceaușescu's time, but he thought not. He took us to an Aids home for young people and to several monasteries.

At the flash Ramada Inn, we met the TV3 crew, David Lomas and Graham, the cameraman. David had news. We were to travel about 60 kilometres the next day, but he didn't reveal the destination. Cristina was nervous and highly excited. My cousin came out in spots. Cristina's mother had been located, and so had her half-sister, Magda, and we were off to meet them both.

"Crikey," I gasped when the hired taxi drew into a village that looked familiar. It was Bivolari. "The twins' family lived here, too. Or they used to. What an amazing coincidence!"

Horses clip-clopped down the main street, towing carts laden with haystacks or school children, tethered goats bleated, and ducks and geese flapped down lanes. Dumpy women in headscarves and aprons cranked water from the well. It was a picturesque time warp. Cristina had no inkling people lived in such primitive conditions, let alone her birth mother.

David pointed to two figures huddling down the end of a long, leafy dirt-lane. It was to be the longest walk of Cristina's life. "I don't know what to say to her. Can you walk with me, Mum?"

Several curious villagers sat on a wooden seat, watching the drama unfold. Cristina headed straight for Magda before embracing her mother, who'd been wringing her hands. To them, Cristina had stepped out of a fashion magazine, outwardly confident and attractive. Cristina didn't shed a tear, but the mother wept. We group hugged when I joined the circle. I'd kept in touch with the mother for some years, sending photos, and when friends visited Romania, they took snaps of both birth families and handed them American dollars we'd saved.

Mihai, our interpreter, was middle-aged, ponderous and reliable. He'd been used by other TV production teams locating lost relatives in Romania. Cristina's birth mum and sister couldn't speak English, so his services were invaluable. He said Cristina's father didn't want children and was happy for his children to be put either in the orphanage or up for adoption. He was twenty years older than Cristina's mum, and after Cristina was born, they had another daughter, also put up for adoption, who the film crew were trying to locate. I knew about this daughter but had been unable to adopt her as well because the laws had changed in Romania.

Magda, the half-sister, two years older than Cristina, had questions. She'd sent a letter and photos to Cristina when she was fifteen. It was in Romanian, but Cristina was going through her own teenage journey and 'finding herself' at the time. Becoming involved with her half-sister was too foreign for her then; she hadn't finished school yet and was living for the moment. She told me to let it rest until she was ready.

But when TV3's *Lost and Found* came knocking, Cristina was more than ready.

Having a daughter gave Cristina focus. For adopted kids who have lost their families and heritage while being brought up in loving families in different parts of the world, there is one question that irks them – Why didn't my birth mother try harder to keep me? They feel hollow and have a fantasy about what living with their 'real' parents would have been like if they hadn't been adopted.

Cristina was in for a shock. Her small, toothless mother looked older beyond her years and damaged by her choices in life. I felt an overwhelming sense of sympathy and sadness for her, but Cristina seemed unmoved.

"At first I felt Romanian," she said. "Now I'm glad my parents gave me a life in New Zealand. I couldn't live here." A man on crutches with a wooden leg limped out of their home and was introduced as the new husband. We were all invited into the rented dwelling surrounded by overhanging grapevines, and we met the landlord who lived next door. He pressed a flagon of home brew in our arms, which we gave to our interpreter. It felt intrusive looking around the dark shabby abode, with its outside toilet and a tin bath for washing out by the woodpile. "Where do you get water?" Cristina asked, and she and her sister were filmed walking down to the well.

I was the only one not shocked by these conditions. I'd witnessed families living in makeshift dwellings of plastic and cardboard on side streets in cities. In fact, I thought Cristina's birth mother's circumstances had improved by her living in the country.

Mihai said an onlooker had approached him and, pointing to me, said, "When is that lady bringing my twins to see me?" It was our twins' birth mother who'd been watching the filming! He told her to go home and wait, and he'd bring me to her.

We all trooped down to her small blue cottage at the end of a rutted lane, where she stood flanked by several grandchildren and daughters who'd remembered me even though they were school age in 1991. The

Three Romanian sisters reunited

mum and I flung our arms around each other and sobbed and sobbed. She had to know the truth about why I couldn't bring the twins – one was dead and the other, impaired by grief, couldn't travel. I gave both mothers a photograph album of their daughters growing up, so they'd know the girls had had a good life with our family.

Back in Iași, there was more exciting news. "See that couple in the distance, Cristina? It's your other sister with her boyfriend. Go and say 'hello'."

"Oh my God," she cried excitedly. "You've found Geanina!" She clutched Magda's arm and while a chilly wind bit the air, the two sisters walked across the cobbled square to meet their youngest sister. The three girls hugged, making little squeaks for they could not understand one another. Cristina could speak only English, Magda only Romanian, and Geanina only Italian. Cousin Joanna was invaluable for she spoke fluent French and Italian. After much persuasion, Geanina's dad had allowed her to fly to Romania, but only if her boyfriend accompanied her. Her father was not keen on her meeting her birth mother, although she chose to do so. It was touching watching the three sisters trying to converse using Google Translate. *These three could have been my daughters,* I thought, *if adoption laws hadn't changed.* Geanina had been in foster care for several years before being adopted. "I love them all," my happy heart cried. It was life-changing for Cristina. She now had an inkling of what life could have been like if we had not adopted her, and she'd bonded with her sisters, more so with Magda. "I feel I want to protect her," she admitted. Her older sister, Magda, a shepherdess and mother of a little girl, revealed she was pregnant but reluctant to tell her birth mother.

David Lomas said it was the easiest and most co-operative filming he'd done. "You are a star," said cousin Joanna, beaming at her god-daughter.

We were delighted when the film crew drove us back to the village where the birth mother got to hug her three daughters. Magda had had some contact with her birth mother, but the connection with Cristina and her Italian sister was fleeting. The sisters had been brought up in affluent societies and were astonished this was their 'real' mother. It's common for adopted children to fantasise about their biological mother, constantly questioning, *Who am I?*

We were thwarted in our attempt to visit Cristina's orphanage, and once filming was over, we took Cristina to Moldova, once part of Romania. "Romania was like this when you were a baby," I said, gazing at streets full of beggars and visiting jaw-dropping churches and monasteries.

Returning to Iași, we hugged cousin Joanna goodbye, took a train back to Bucharest and celebrated Cristina's twenty-fifth birthday. She was keen to fly home now, but first we had to catch a flight to Milan, where we wandered around the city of culture licking gelatos, before catching a night flight to Delhi.

Locals in Delhi thought Cristina exotic, wondering if she was Syrian, Italian or Indian. "Can I take your photo?" asked a bold lad in a group of young men. "Yeah, but don't touch me. My boyfriend wouldn't like it," she warned. Even Muslim groups wanted to photograph us all.

"Where do you want to go, ladies?" asked the Delhi taxi driver.

"Anywhere – but not the shops," I said.

And since I got on so well with him, he said, "You like to come to my daughter's for lunch?"

It was a humbling experience witnessing how this poor, shabby driver lived. Since it was the annual Delhi Bird Festival at the time, the daughter had been preparing a variety of dishes, squatting on the floor of the one-room concrete block. Her husband was nursing a broken leg, and their two sons sat on the bed wide-eyed. We ate from small bowls and pored over faded wedding photos of their arranged marriage. It was another experience of extreme poverty and kindness, unknown in Cristina's small world.

Back in New Zealand it felt flat, safe and normal after our whirlwind action-packed trip. When the *Lost and Found* documentary aired on New Zealand TV in 2016, Cristina's status was elevated again. The programme was so popular the newspapers ran a story about three sisters living in different countries being reunited. Many said they wept watching the documentary.

We've had contact with all the birth families of our adopted children, bar two: one had died (the Russian twins' mother) and the other chose to protect her privacy. Maybe she will have a rethink about it one day. We hope so.

Our extended family is vast if you include the birth families and their offspring. We never imagined our life as a couple would turn out like this, being blessed many times over. We do feel we have led the richest of lives. And how did it start?

It began with a kiss!

Epilogue

My! What a roller coaster it's been.

The kids are all grown up now and some are procreating, but none of them plan to have as many children as we did. They can't afford it in today's climate.

It's been several years since Natasha died. Most of our adult children have included her name in those of their offspring. A friend called her son Nash, and one of our sons, who had a boy, remembered a nickname he had given Natasha, and his son now bears it. So she is always there in our thoughts. Natasha's twin, Joanna, is still struggling, but we never give up on our kids.

It's fun being grandparents because now that we've done all the hard work, we can revert to being light-hearted, somewhat zany, and enjoy the grandies. The most important thing kids want is your time. Even big kids. It's always been like that, but parents seem even more stressed nowadays, at a time when owning your own home is almost out of reach.

All our kids stay in touch, two still live with us, and when they gather for family events, hubby and I look at each other in surprise and smile. "Where's your glass, Mumma Bear?" asks a daughter-in-law. "Come and join the barbecue." I gaze at the partly burnt chops and our laughing family getting on so well together and, like raising teens, it's softly, softly. Don't be too correcting. In the end it doesn't matter.

I still like my mother's motto: 'Be happy even if it kills you.'

That will never be a problem for us. We are happy that so many kids were gifted to us, and we love each and every one of them in their own way.

Other books by the author

Available from www.jonquilgraham.com
or email jonquil@callsouth.net.nz

www.ingramcontent.com/pod-product-compliance
Lightning Source LLC
Chambersburg PA
CBHW021939290426
44108CB00012B/890